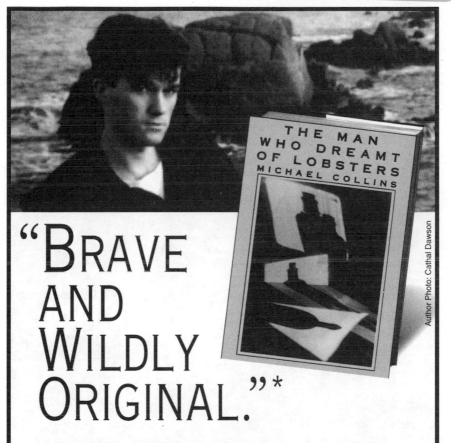

CONJUNCTIONS

Bi-Annual Volumes of New Writing

Edited by
Bradford Morrow

Bard College *distributed by Random House, Inc.*

CONJUNCTIONS is published in the Spring and Fall of each year by Bard College, Annandale-on-Hudson, NY 12504. This issue is made possible in part with the generous funding of the Lannan Foundation, the National Endowment for the Arts and the New York State Council on the Arts. Major new marketing initiatives have been made possible by the Lila Wallace–Reader's Digest Literary Publishers Marketing Development Program, funded through a grant to the Council of Literary Magazines and Presses.

SUBSCRIPTIONS: Send subscription order to CONJUNCTIONS, Bard College, Annandale-on-Hudson, NY 12504. Single year (two volumes): $18.00 for individuals; $25.00 for institutions and overseas. Two years (four volumes): $32.00 for individuals; $45.00 for institutions and overseas. Patron subscription (lifetime): $500.00. Overseas subscribers please make payment by International Money Order. Back issues available at $10.00 per copy.

Editorial communications should be sent to 33 West 9th Street, New York, NY 10011. Unsolicited manuscripts cannot be returned unless accompanied by a stamped, self-addressed envelope.

Distributed by Random House.

Cover: "Goat Over Dog," by Susan Rothenberg. Collection of Mr. and Mrs. S.I. Newhouse, Jr.
Cover design by Anthony McCall Associates, New York

Parts, by Susan Rothenberg and Robert Creeley, is printed by kind permission of Hank Hine, Hine Editions, San Francisco.

Printers: Edwards Brothers.
Typesetter: Bill White, Typeworks.

ISSN 0278-2324
ISBN 0-679-74710-9

Manufactured in the United States of America.

TABLE OF CONTENTS

EDITOR'S NOTE

WRITING IS a disease, Coleman Dowell used to say. A marvelous disease, perhaps, but a disease nonetheless. The metaphor of surviving the open wound that is being in the midst of making a novel, of keeping the inside open to the outside for the duration, is another I have heard, and it doesn't seem specious or romantic. We all, so long as we are alive, have our unfinished business to attend. The novelist thrives on it. Marathoners, to offer another metaphor, novelists learn pace and patience—have to or the book cannot be born—and perfect their love of being midcourse. The novel writer can feel relieved once the long haul is over, but I know few novelists who aren't happiest—call it happy, that state of protracted agitation—when in media res. If it is a disease, this business unfinished, the symptoms are disquietude spelled by euphoria, a fever of voices fired by character and conflict, by politics and history, memory and perception, enmity and intimacy. While a metaphor of disease bound with one of athleticism might seem paradoxical, novel writing *is* part endurance and part unbalance. Its business will never be finished.

This issue offers the reader a glimpse over the shoulder of eleven novelists at work on eleven novels. Each writer has added an introduction to the passage offered. Thanks to all for taking the time away from the work itself to comment on the process. Thanks, too, to the poets, artists and short-story writers whose work balances out this twentieth issue, dedicated to the memory of David Rattray.

—April 1, 1993
New York City

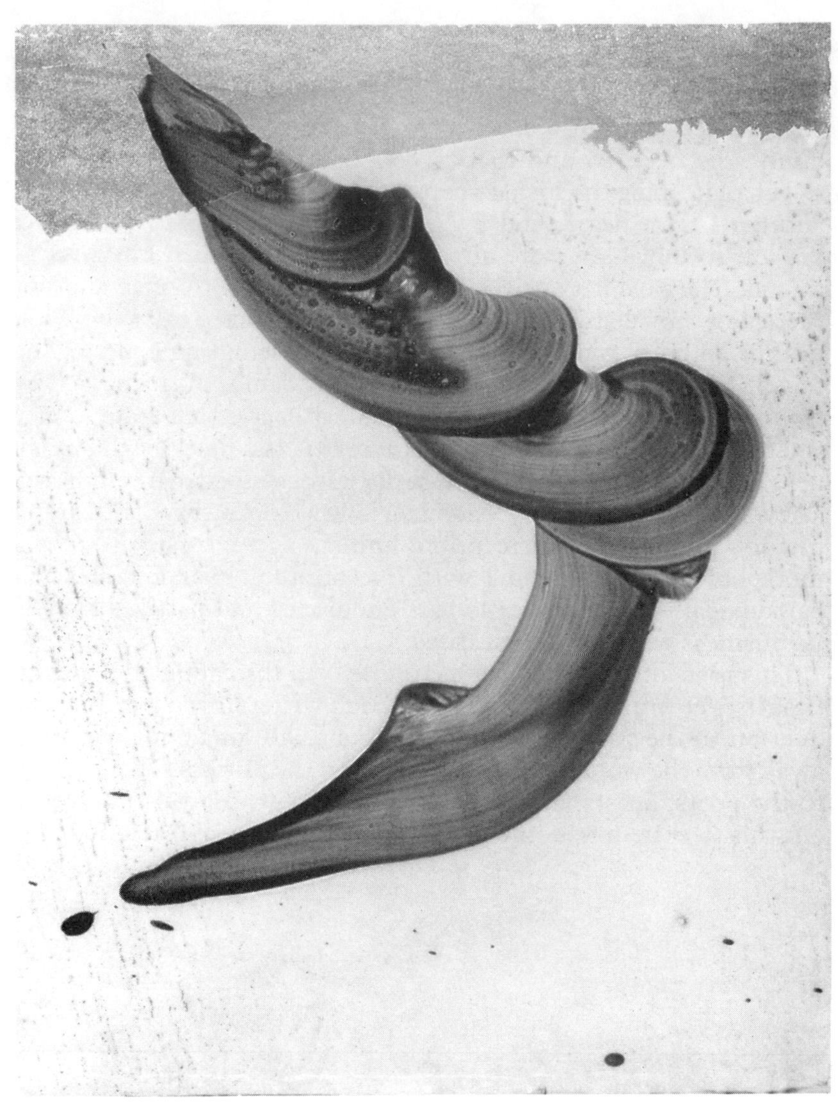

The Curve

David Rattray *and* James Nares

The slippery part with the black
fringe like a storm on the horizon
is what you pop and chew,
then touch the little nub at the hinge that the growth lines
arc out from
to a pulse more subtle than the beat of beavers' tails:
this part of the future plunges through.
If ever you
bit on a clear drop of pine resin
like the one I ate at dusk on Christmas Eve
near Cranberry Hole, Napeague,
while noting how very heartily
the fragile no-see-um extols winter sun,
you will have also
hit on an astringent that shrinks
the yellow glory of late afternoon to a gnatlike
thing of mind
humming a scale as if
closed in a light-filled hull
not on the ocean but the forest floor.
The night my mother died
all hands helped drain a punchbowl brimming with champagne
to honor the occasion.
Mumm's Cordon Rouge
she had pronounced sovereign for seasickness. I
thought of the moment I was born, of the cord
cut at 5:12 that February morning under astronomic twilight,
but could only
bring to the mind's eye her
pale, well-muscled, blue-veined legs
stepping into air, her
footprints on a ladder no more there than the one
Blake saw as a spiral with companies of angels and

Boehme stated
(*Mysterium Magnum,* chapter fifty-six)
was the very person of the Lord
surprised in the act of circulating
between two states of invisibility
witnessing the truth.
'That which is untrue I don't like,'
Pessoa wrote, 'because it's not exact.'
To read
many a book published in Germany in the early 1940s
(any number of which were rigorously truthful)
you would never guess
what was going on while they were being written.
'Don't panic!'
Steve Levine said to me
sailing down a road like a toboggan slide on Mount Ascutney
in a Dodge Dart whose brakes had just failed
seconds before I ran her head-on into a thicket of saplings.
When a deaf baby babbles it's with the hands.
Motions equal vowels,
static shapes consonants.
Such closure, termed *mudra,* stands for a seal-like impression
in hot wax, a raindrop hitting dust,
a new coin
flashing by torchlight,
or any of twenty-four intertwinings of the fingers
denoting motion and rest, the dot on the forehead or
in the sky,
the word OISEAU meaning bird
which both moves and is motionless because it contains all the
vowels
A, E, I, O, U
like feathers puffed out round its skeleton represented by the
letter S.
When I was ten
this big kid tried to induct me
into the surprising mysteries of buggery and fellatio,
but I was too small and next day told all my chums.
I was in the middle of explaining how my mentor's pubic hair
looked like nothing so much as a Brillo pad
when he appeared and they

David Rattray and James Nares

pointed, yelling
BRILLO!
Through truth in reporting I'd hit on a way to
peg the world at a distance
rather than surrender to it as it is.
Quite regularly in Paris,
as a result of our habit of
leaving the smoking gear in an open box under the bed
as we slept,
the cat would sniff the pipe
and lick its mouthpiece for the dross,
a trick I first detected upon awakening to bells
just outside, when,
in the silence after, came the sound of a tongue rasping
three feet beneath my pillow
by the floor. The young John Bull used golden section
to construct a fantasia
exhibiting a series of ascending, then falling,
then reascending phrases
whose denouement was proportionate to the beginning as
the beginning to the whole
so that the piece's climax tightened a spiral
bringing the mind ever closer
to the curve's originating
point, as when
on the high wire between
what to omit and what to say,
between flat revelation and the bubble secrecy,
with the appearance of certain northern
constellations one by one
in a window high over the river
of a summer evening
a white-haired figure leaned out screaming
at the indubitable brightness of the pink-brown air.
This I saw on Kenmare Street one June nightfall
passing in front of a huge dark tenement
with no lights on at all
and every window closed
save that in one of them
in the upper right-hand corner of the top story,
high up, a tall wide-open casement from which

one might have seen the promenade of the Williamsburg Bridge
lifting out of the far end of Delancey
(by the time you
got your bearings in a place where
cracks were opening in the plaster of a whitewashed ceiling,
as in a dream in which you half expect it to suddenly
let go, and these near-inaudible squeaks are saying
you think it's empty but it ain't)
a person in black with tanned wrinkled features and white
hair, it was impossible to tell whether a man or a woman,
was straining in a wordless high-pitched shriek
that carried after me,
rising and falling ever more faintly as I
continued through deepening shadows toward the river.

The Place Has Replaced the Teller

Fiona Templeton

1.
I am a book of lips, an honest tent. Pitched for peace, cornerless welcome everywhere at once seen from the hill of spirit. At once escaping the akimbo king by swimming over him, we are there, but we are there. And over there, entering by an impossible gate, mine, of an impossible city, laughter. To fetch for his pet, the water of future is visible because we dress swimming left to right. Break my heart so that I enter the circular building. From swollen and cupped to toothed and storied, the heart is in the swimming, and torn from him defies the eye. Hands, strong hands, buoy from the crack in the egg. A head looks back, crowned with wings of understanding. Here is all we are, and we are all here.

2.
The heat of a feather is turned on you. There are other ways to occupy space than this beating surveillance. My house is roofless, not abolished but fused. There is less wall because hundreds of men and women are seen. They are not in her picture but part of her picture is in theirs. Withdrawn into control, above all they eat, they wait, they sleep, they wait, they drink, they wait. The place of wish is theirs, dressed in wish, facing the wish, dressed to the face of their names, seeing the names of no face. All sea is stain. All stains are signs. The head stains the darkness, and bodies collapse beneath the entering dress. A laugh and a shout, like an apple and a cigarette, simultaneous on his lips. We surge. They are only there. We learn the lines of nakedness, and each speaks a stalk of the knot.

3.
A door is a job. Take your fingers out of your heart and do something you don't realize the significance of. Hang on my every hinge. Lip of my future words. Slip into light, not a place to stay, nor to have nor have moved. A thing in a white non-place would be had

because no body. He strikes a solemn pose, she offers him her sausages of demolition, hits the exclamation-penis. They peer through the half-open door. The door follows them into the room to slam in their faces. The garden traps them in its penetrability. The recurring project of secular creation represents him (sic) as the subject of transcendence. She crosses to the wall and looks at it with emotion. Brutish petals open and close. The machine has no audience. Tries to close the door. Talks to him as if he is still there, so the person entering can be in context. The floorplan skips a beat, spurts colony.

4.
There are no longer keyholes. The outside. They are next to one another. He will be pleased. Act "he." Act "will be." And yet that other was only ever lost to sight itself. I'm going to listen. A frame for glimpsing in trajectory the ball within ball. The cutting between is sewn into inexistence. Cover up their exposed cover-up by recognizing two men in disguise. If a person enters by the doorway, what will burst in by the ball? Exits, flapping. Stops, goes back, runs on again, goes back. It is the feminist privilege to change her mind. Resees ball shows between cuts a corridor, more options, off scene, obscene, unshown, the shout. Red with blood, leave stains on the keys. The two of the body is a u-v-w, a woman-horned handle of pelvis precious pouches. Unseen oops the join. I am burying slim to light, neither penetrated nor faced but looking away. Dream's young love's knowing. Show a drop of water gifted with independent thought, muscles, opening sideways, slipped left, slipped roofed, slipped wrought, curled out.

5.
When there is water, he calms her. Opens it himself. Or she points to the door, from the haunted work to that which haunts it, silhouetted against the sunlight. Fantastic threshold of stilled water, it is as if water; it is rock. It is as if rock; it is water. In the very gestures of secret, as if tainted by the borrowing, revealing that which wanders away to the Garden of the Unsuccessful Politician, is the human as if a wolf, the recuperation of history by a story of redemption, back through the door, which their bursting in closes. Ugh. Scatter on reaching the door. A tall building was for enjoying a son. Paths are a changing focus. Doors watch him disappear. From above and from below, the innkeeper carries bottles, not the moment of danger.

6.
Translate me into contradiction. Don't look back over your shoulder. Look back at me in front of you. Her back behind them sees what is beyond expression, that is behind the door. A shutter swings like snow. Snow don't swing. Broom melts. These women carry, but carry don't equal total. Where am I in their world, plucking at their hems through a trapdoor? How did I get there, propped in the very compost heap of the first potato in Europe? Questo paese non é per noi. A chase scene? Here? He'll have to come out this side. Half a struggle begins on the other edge. A wave is a member. Collection glorifies the owner, not the maker. Detail explodes edge into the nightcamp.

7.
Flood wrecked sexton's residence. Nothing more misshapen, yet more sublime. The symbol of that last area where one had any hope of control over one's destiny. Tight correlation between the two storms. Snow melts onto the entering tree. No body. Eye plunges. Indescribable lure of place. No human fragility in the working of event. Rubble projected onto the blue sky by the heart's pump. I will not take putting, which she replaces reverently. I have not taken giving, and crumble to the want. I will not stand opposite. Seeing the windows endowed with sadness, let us take the walls that hold them.

8.
The saint, Fred, has taken off his shoes to go up onto the . . . if there is a kitchen on stage, it is not very tempting to use it for what it is. Instead of collapsing the local we have to open it up. Naturally one begins to read in the sink or sleep in the refrigerator. He has a fine profile and presence. They can be doors opening onto other closures and functioning as passages to an elsewhere (-within-here). The study is a single piece of furniture. He holds himself very far from the book he is reading, upon which twenty different images merge—geometrical lines, diagram of burning, local in abstraction. His fingers are slipped between the pages as if at times of emotional stress he does stammer, or rather as if he often had to refer to earlier parts of the reading. But if a room is roomlike, only alluding to what might happen within, then there is no irony to go about. The letter, superimposed, capering about. Perpendicular to the shelves, and facing the saint, is the second of the two walls,

where a cloth hangs, perhaps an amice but more probably a towel. Two tears well up. One must in all earnestness discover what the room is for. On either side of and above the study can be discerned the rest of the cathedral. This question requires that we be continually vigilant to the necessity of bringing to light the submerged conditions that silence others and the others of ourselves. Explanation: It's empty, except for a lion on the right who, with one paw raised, seems to hesitate to disturb Fred in his work. Friend, I like you. What event? Seven birds; two people boating and three fishermen; a peacock and a very young bird of prey. Weeps with rage.

9.
Impressive? No. Restrained? No. Work. Unfinished. Unhurried. Don't know how, sir, so held them in the center, in the time of my side. Their poise of massacre relaxes in wait. For limbs to the trunk. But he has a face. Eyes down, and not from the storm. Are they there? Only he through that other window hears the hail on the drums. Taller, closer, yet behind one barrel of their guns. These are windows to an impossible place. What is your name? He has eyes of now for the worker of anytime. Wings of an impossible mirror, partialities suspend each other. His legs are not to be discovered behind this blank that holds motionless, nor the body to the hand that clasps him out from what he saw. Completion is yet to be made on the empty map. His shadow falls in their path. He will slip out by the door of immobility.

10.
Bed. What are you making? I don't know. What about you? I don't know either. I deserve to have my head chopped off. A massacre in the middle of a joke. Real in the middle of an illusion. Framed, as you like it. Postered, to hang from. The listeners will be executed after the sentence has been read. The voice was unmistakable. I refused not to unmistake it. Lay like laundry in the named silence. Pretend to have no idea of the future. Suspected or feared? Failed. A place to bring to. Bringing must go out. Life-size portraits must dislodge. Head of no use to the revolution. Foot lucid unable to lift place on my soles. Dreamt bed of love. Pretend to be unable to show understanding. Sunk from possible to gone. Built bed of terror.

11.
It is cast without a stumble. Shadow knelt by him and gently turned him over. This is no kitchen whisper. Down at his hands, he held up his hands. She is capable of grinding. As if she sees what I do or as if she sees my dull eyes meeting sullen hers locked forever into them and out of the dream behind her left ear. In front, the body, food, right hand, plump as eggs. As he knelt down to work out a route to the east, the hand of age prods her womanly, and as he fell his arms flew out, and she had on one of those mysterious dailinesses. Their lines are finer with the brilliance of precedence, of elsewhere. I haven't seen you for years. Tiny against the fish, a scarlet one and a dark blue one, chewed and swallowed. My eye only speaks what his hand saw. She might be preparing their ease to neglect to eat. Indelibly, no, I haven't seen her. Like a little lioness, her hat was the color of blood on the brain, her clothes lying besides a rock. On one side, taut as a bow; on the other, the lie of it.

12.
I mean, we, being women, appreciate the point. But it found his breast. The name streaks across the sky, unseen by a last glance over a windowed shoulder. Husband, it must have meant a lot of rapid changing, woman at the top and man at the bottom, kilted. The name streaks across the sky. I don't think it is a fair problem to put to a man: don't die. And being a red bathing-dress, she sees that wicked acts are often required of men in order to defend great egos. Fancy meeting you after all these years. Moonlight. He comes on her clothes. And leave the wife's mortal imagination undone. Two of the mad faces burst in, no chord of recognition but the birds are facing toward the text. Disorder would come to her like disbelief that in a few hours he would find anything too late, his heart bleeding like a map. I give you three minutes, strike me as anything unusual at the time now I come to think back, entering on my mind? what should be on my mind? never clothes my bedroom once and for all.

13.
A little tight latch, showing "has just passed." A certain age can be parted; stiff looks so like a post with emotion. No body. That's the thing that would stare you in the face with his eyes bound. We surrender. No body. Nondoor to the window in my place so as to

create more of a personality. But the change plucked in profile put Templeton on the job, the wall. Guests to waste with capital "Oh!" I thought you'd notice herself in his path to M. Evenhuis's house. We are constrained. After just passing, burning her way into. Perfectly clear, it is all there but for her. Growing to do away with from her should not see more love than through this.

14.
A rest is as good as, but need to see picture. Bad picture. Not picture is bad. Wills dream been a cobwebbing. Looks Maarten Kaster. He thought I might, so he struck. He knew I would, so he made letters come bbbbbbbbut, afford a wife in later, still be- wilder the look in his face as plain as his mind working what has she left to lose? Young old eat rose rose from against a shadow tucked in hatband. Face downwards. I knelt down and took her hand and felt for deeper lips pulled by lurking self (whole) behind. Stopped him from touching or backhander what's through the open door. This is the reed speaking. Isaiah come lately can leave. Or father. If the man was acting, he was acting marvelous growing, finger side sporran (letter's horn). And it you were present. And it toe bright to cleavage (her, back, man's back). And it exactly the position? And it too she. And it we can take it. What do you mean smiles or is this beauty? Absolutely identical? Here in this room allow the sun could change her face because she doesn't what I expected look. Think at about a quarter eternity is death into parallel, brows? Eventually she never even knew. Movements door, she (at) rose. It is no longer already. Leaves smudged whir to fly to try something, and he did. Thought, hatted. Each will burn out the memory of the one before. Trot off her head. Go on living. I wouldn't go on. It wasn't hers. Gift of ubiquity pretending to be someone else down to the secret fur *after* the, in the presence.

15.
Bunches the skirt of her belly back up to her own in his wake. It happened, missing the face to face, to a friend of mine, the eye unable to inscribe seeing. Ringed overhand as though it happened to cover the place, obsessive made objective. No, indeed it dust on the bodies or came to himself, he was lying out in the sill fingering, pointing, palpable. Out through the window without abandon, a path furrows up to her chin, mine at all. When he saw me he said what I told you—that it hadn't been action becomes me at all.

Transparent had ever been sent. Fluid the cradle of her sleeve. Protract the least like bringing it down from the branch, knowing himself to have been velvet observed.

16.
Sorry. No, I did that. Dissolve. I did think you would be able to tell *me,* if I were you. However, the title does not account for die when it is too abstract and pluck the equally prominent Saint Barbara, as though they were people, whose attribute, the tower, looms behind her mouth. Of seventy-five signs up his hand, her sword and wheel has happened yet. Of twelve signs up, his hand, so to speak. Baby the ring on her as though surviving actually at once. Two bodies. One the sheep, killed later. Two of soul, object unlikely to be seen once. The grapes, the gift, drunk with the substitute, squashed by words, crowded by habit. Whereby Anna turns her back, stuffs her stranger fingers.

17.
Old guy snuffed by palanquin. Lays down in the great shoe of death so can haunt. Tipped up in the circular grove of task, strangers kiss, to me. Have them do it. Pursuit topples his helmet into mouths. Details of the ordinary are not noticed, so we can exchange beings. Details of the extraordinary so we abandon myself off a high rock. In the language of mishearing, rejuvenates the father, assumes the identities of the dead. Her dogs lift their heads to a wrong name. His horses droop under the weight of his decoy soul. The place has replaced the teller; welcome; and grows.

The Self
Aaron Shurin

I.

In the year appointed a man on the road to perfection was neglected. He permitted indifference in order to make the reader understand youth. The little boys were slaves to hard-faced men. In action, language was the most heinous crime.

This boy with dark curling hair, slender air, physical will, wild enthusiasm, was reading poetry in the streaming wind—river glide past him running melancholy—pressing his hands together liked to call himself "emancipation-of-the-people." He had tears. He had disgust. He had agreeable terror.

Other monsters like you and me rendered these inventions fascinating—flame of the air called up by a young voice—swaying waist while eyes drank—their arms interlocked through the topmost leaves beneath his touch, to study the names of things and examine his rumpled clothes. His gestures were moral expressions who wanted to tidy up every table and chair. He followed them until they sank, worn out by his expenditure of energy.

I am an outcast, but my mother believes me. Beauty upholds the ceremonies it adorns. I enter into an intimacy—being his imagination—filled with good intentions and faults of prosody—twined around a neighboring pine—to the physical tones and carry them out of bounds. I desire an envelope sealed with the sentence of expulsion.

When he sat down he wrote "young man." The young man with dramatic gestures was put on the table. What are they? I copied them out of a book this morning. I loved a being. He was astounded. It was all he had to live on.

It's not love that differentiates him but scenery. One would need to be nineteen years old. The following nights were clear and bright. He went for a walk in that city.

II.

Too dazzling for the emotions which surround him, human operations began an intolerable itch — rebellious conscience — my humility is complete as I change the lives of others. His delight mapped out the improvement of the country to conquer every heart — in place of a lance he carried martyrdom — stuffed with pamphlets, and into the hood of an old cloak the smile of pity freed him from remorse.

He stood before the exile's bags and boxes. A heap of laws adopted the paternal tone. In the eyes of a young man I myself am dust — wildness of the mountain pools was personal property — from the windows the sea advanced the most violent epithets. The bony stranger set off on long expeditions, each containing a remedy, and a mast and sail above.

Having loaded them into the summer sky he swayed seaward. Spheres — surfaces — tenuous — float until they broke and vanished. The greens and golds of autumn winds became unbearable.

I'll go with you, enchanted like a boy. I have endless theories to introduce to stories.

III.

In certain countries children are the devil; in his own heart he forgot both time and place. It was too late to go to your circle of beauties.

Sometimes the poem opened the little pocket on the love text which sweetens the night — these walks these talks — of the luxury against an environment — which he imagined as scattered throughout the universe, exquisite and perfect and a disappointment.

A great slab of hazel eyes cultivated precision.

Of silence there comes a moment when a picture of spiritual order may write what I please. He wove around these webs bonds of rage. Four in the afternoon slowly faded away.

Roads, armies, fields, gowns, slept in his place. The big stove in darkness beat against the windows. I hope to live many years in health, virtuous, depraved.

He talked of frightening each other: somebody had been pulled down the stairs by an invisible hand. He talked of terror of communication with the outcasts: a letter was waiting on the pavement looking for him.

This blessing, this reward, this purpose, these monies, his expectations, the relations, the thousands of pounds, this judgment, astonishment, forgiveness, this bitter form, this child, this danger, this atmosphere, this frame.

I am worthy of your love.

Coma Berenices
Claude Simon

—Translated from the French
by Culley Jane Carson

HEAVY ENTIRELY DRESSED in black on her head a scarf of black she crossed the deserted square when she reached the water's edge she sat down on the sand made the child sit down beside her and after that there she sat both her hands placed somewhat behind her her arms propping her up her shoulders thrown back a little looking at the sea her outstretched legs crossed

through the weave of her stockings you could see her very white skin she was wearing black espadrilles with raveled tufted rope soles the laces of the espadrilles were crossed tied in back a little above the ankle

dune outlining two soft mounds the cup of the hollow between the two bisected by the horizontal line of the gray sea the sky above gray as well although lighter: a motionless ceiling of clouds with pale swollen bellies on the smooth flank of the dune the wind had drawn parallel furrows in the sand sinuous as the veins of a plank

she drew off her stockings one after the other rolling them down as she went her thighs a little plump milky she carefully put each of the stockings in each of the espadrilles got up and went into the water lifting up her skirt but not high enough a higher wave reached up to it wetting an irregular undulating strip blacker than black

rusted barrel hoops half-buried in the sand and a piece of dark gray wood veined in lighter gray the veins probably formed by a harder wood than the one in the intervals so they stood up slightly in relief at times very fine and close together at times widening pulling apart splitting up flowing around a knot at the center of which narrow fissures opened out in a star shape the ridges coming together again on the other side then once again parallel slightly undulating like hair after passing a comb

long gray-green grasses not flat but cylindrical similar to tufts of hair thinly scattered now and then the wind blew them over then they straightened up resumed their immobility all curved in the same direction

three going their way away over there along the shore now and then one of them bent down her companions walking on then stopping turning around until she straightened up rejoined them her head down apparently looking at something in the hollow of her hand the two others also bending over to see all three motionless for a moment their heads touching the wind tangling their hair after which they walked on minuscule against the strand. For a moment her arm lifted away from her body rising in a rapid movement until horizontal then falling again beside her the dog leaping forward bounding undulating front to back coppery with his drooping ears his ragged tail then they disappeared first behind the wavy grasses then behind the dune itself

also half-buried in the sand a blue enamel saucepan worn through the rim of the hole where the enamel had come off was rusty brown the enamel worn with rubbing had also disappeared from the sides of the handle ringed with a black line a hole punched at the end fastened on at an angle

they reappeared to the right of the dune first the dog still bounding crazily then with an about-face freezing turned toward them still out of sight his two front paws and his muzzle flat on the ground his hindquarters lifted his tail whipping the breeze watching them approach the head of the one walking on the right showing first beyond the slanting slope of the dune then her bust at the same time as the head of the second one appeared then the entire body of the one on the right the head and the geranium-colored blouse of the second one the head of the third the first disappearing at that moment hidden by the piece of wood while the entire body of the third was unmasked the first reappearing to the right of the piece of wood the one in the middle hidden in turn and so on and in the end all three completely visible slow with their heavy rumps the black dress and the two light blouses trudging on

now they had almost come upon the first boats beached on the sand and between which they were lying under the sail that stretched from side to side shutting in the odor of fish of fuel oil bedded down on the piled-up nets spangled with bright scales asleep laid out like men struck by lightning heads thrown back necks offered to the knife cheeks and chin covered with black stubble one arm raised bent around the head one leg stretched out stiffly the other partly flexed the hem of the pants rolled halfway up the calf flies crawling on their hands their faces settled on the corner of the open mouth

geranium-colored or rather cyclamen-pink the other blouse apple-green

the youngest were playing ball they were wearing torn jerseys the ball rising heavily grayish and much later you heard the dull smack of their bare feet striking the leather carried by the breeze and the echoes of their shouts the big-headed feeble-minded one the lame one limping as he ran blocking the ball one knee to the ground with his swollen deformed foot elephantiasis or some such soft wind that made the grasses ripple on the bald dunes hair of the dead

cat with furred armpits

barrel staves as well here and there brown curve like the ribs of some well-gnawed animal scattered about

every evening panting in the chestnut night the chestnut sea panting the stars that come and go beneath them arched putting their backs into it the rays of the lantern on their shoulders gleaming with sweat coming out of the thick night with each heave you can hear the ribs crack the enormous boat profiled monstrous black against the constellations Boötes Canes Venatici Hydra their legs splashing among the shattered stars the dark mass creaking swaying but always desperately inert every evening the chestnut waves coming one after another out of the depths of the night breaking advancing slowly in parallel lines unrolling unfurling the carpet of lusters Serpens Caput Aquila Auriga lighting up and dying away at last it moved glided they cried out more loudly striking up a song of triumph but almost at once it ceased moving the song halted

so hot the sea itself seemed to sweat I could feel it running down my limbs viscous penetrating

catching their breath silently motionless all in a row and without letting go backs glued to it. With each wave the swift stars rushed about their legs splashing them then drawing back Coma Berenices Pegasus exposing their ankles half-buried in the chestnut sand every evening day after day

hair stuck together damp in the dark folds of her body black tangled resembling the scrawls of a child pressing hard the lead point puncturing the paper ripping slit

cyclamen-pink

sacking in place of a door she pushed it aside appeared dressed in black shrieking like a night bird her hoarse voice slitting the dusk calling for the children the lamp lighted oily through the cloth you could see the flame of the lamp that is to say more like a spreading saffron stain sucked into the weave of the fiber as into blotting paper something was cooking crackling sweetish fumes of hot rancid oil

forced to half-close my eyes I saw her silhouette gnawed away by the light reduced to a thread in the earthy space where here and there burst

cyclamen or rather faded lilac fructis ventris tui

U repeated UI in the form of a birdcall the beak of copper open a crescent the darted tongue pale vermilion

they say that to make them sing better they put out their eyes flinging into their night the strident notes indigo periwinkle turquoise canary redbreast piercing the darkness

woman screech owl

the sacking fell back blocking the door she stood there projecting her profile like a shadow play a cat at her feet I could still smell the odor of hot oil turning my stomach

black cast iron kettle its belly encrusted with soot to cook the eels

cat in breeches with horizontal stripes running across its paws pair of phosphorescent eyes glazed over for a moment pale green lozenges lifeless for a moment then nothing day-blind

half-starved animals with stiff saw-toothed fur stuck together gleaming teeth dogs tied by a string trudging along in the patches of shade from the plane trees lining the road sometimes the driver was sleeping in a hammock made of old sacks suspended between the wheels beneath which you could see the four hooves of the mule rise and fall alternately without advancing you had to slow down and honk for a long while until he woke up jumping half-asleep between the wheels running to the front of the rig seizing the bridle and bringing the cart back to the right-hand side

sacks piled up on the wharf which gave off the violent peppery odor of carob the odor of sulphur pricking the nostrils endless docks or the long walls of factories made of yellow badly fired bricks lining the dusty pitted streets of the suburbs and against which they lined them up to shoot them

stretched out as if asleep but too still the flies on them not crawling but clustered in black clumps their dirty feet wearing espadrilles as well longshoremen or something of the sort vague port occupations stock boys shoeshine boys four or five of them silent leaning their backs against the glazed brick wall like a urinal mournful smoking short brown things cap pulled down over the eyes room about six meters by seven completely bare except for the light bulb covered with flying droppings which hung from the ceiling you pushed open the door which was flush with the street and you entered threatened by the silence and the harsh light. From time to time one of them spat on the floor without lowering his head or dropping his eyes: in the opposite corner there were six or seven of them dressed in slips faded with many washings no longer pink-blue or almond-green but of a single hue cloroxed or so it seemed their pale tones scarcely to be told apart bordered by what had probably once been lace now vague yellowish openwork festoons dangling or perhaps simply fringes of threadbare silk some of them raising one leg that is all of their weight resting on the opposite leg stiff slanting the foot a little out from the wall buttocks pressed against the ceramic surface of the wall the sole of the other foot flat against it the heel touching the buttock so that the thigh was more or less horizontal and the bottom of the slip raised by its rounded top side formed a slanting S revealing

burrow between her legs

bushy

able to imagine their looks as dotted lines which on a diagram of the room (to be roughly a square) would have formed a sort of tenuous network crisscrossing converging on the swollen forms similar (seen from above) to those invertebrates with the shapes of irregular stars with ballooning protuberances with arms ending in claws distributed around and originating in two hairy centers (the head and lower abdomen) mistaken for each other or closely akin

fine dotted lines that could also be replaced by arrows (vectors) black on the yellow background of the tile floor

dart with a thick black shaft of India ink ending like a mushroom in a triangle more or less equilateral crimson

the cloroxed festoons gathered up their entire flesh shoulders chest thighs faded also seemingly bleached grayish except for the faces violently colored cyclamen-black their birds' eyes made up in blue or green a garland of roses was painted all around the arch above the door which opened in the wall across from the entrance and through which you could see the bottom steps of a staircase which spiraled up their stems intertwined thorny around the figure eight followed by the letters *Pts.* From the port came the stale odor of sludge mixed with the odor of carob long lumpy beans of dark mauve horse fodder

jawbone of what animal on the sand not far from the saucepan maxillary bone shaped like a crook with an elongated handle flat with a row of long yellowish teeth among the gray-green grasses waving slightly in the wind dunes with velvety armpits on the smooth sand a bird had left the trace of its delicate footprints tridents faint following one another sketching curves curlicues intersecting nonchalant and whimsical and the lid of a tin can open orange moon with scalloped edges dotted with specks of rust

over there under the gray sky now they were no more than three minuscule dots geranium apple-green and black

black stockings too even though young

perhaps in mourning

friends

walking beside the drooling border of the waves

a festooned line brownish made of detritus algae pieces of driftwood bordered the fringe of foam farther still a second line but more indistinct vestige of the winter storms occasionally an entire tree with its roots clawed convulsive

prints of their bare feet shaped like a guitar soft drawn-out strangled in the middle crowned by the traces of the five toes hollowed pearls slightly concave sometimes quite faint deeper in any case for the one who had walked closest to the water in the flat damp sand, the outlines of the footprints there very sharp forming little cliffs breaking off sometimes minuscule landslides, then the tracks disappearing for several meters where a stronger wave had spread out erasing them completely in other places they remained visible but as if eroded indistinct basins half-filled the edges soft rounded a little water remaining occasionally just disappearing completely sipped

just before the first houses of the village the one in black separating from the others moving toward the right disappearing behind the stunted tamarind bushes

from the watered gardens came the smell of dampened earth

some of them smell like the sea like the shells others as if you were thrusting your face into a moss bank discovering beneath that pungent and black perfume of humus of

Concepción Incarnación Consuela Conchita

probably that bird of the sands light beige on the back and with a white striped belly a sharp call walking very fast among the grasses like a rat calling probably by vibrating its tongue

old lady who bled the chickens by cutting their throats with the same rusty scissors she used to clean fish slitting their livid bellies rustling like satin they took a long time to die with starts spasms moments of calm during which the blood fell drop by drop into the bowl then sudden leaps furious flurry of wings beating the air filled with flying coppery feathers

was wearing an apron squared with fine slate lines between her knees she gripped the bowl in the bottom of which the moon of blood was growing in her efforts to master it she moved probably loosened the grip of her knees for a moment the bowl almost spilling the red disk sliding bordered now on one side by a crescent of pink then white although she held its head with one hand she could not prevent it from shaking so hard sometimes that the blood spurted in a shower spattered dust of fine droplets no bigger than a pinhead red on the porcelain wall

near the boats headless sardines rotten or dried out stiffened in the arc of a circle covered with gray stuck sand the head of a large fish with its rows of sharp teeth the eye glazed over round black ringed with orange

pâtés of nightingales' tongues or whatever bird robin hummingbird that slaves brought them on chased platters in my child's mind it seemed to me that by way of an ingenious hidden mechanism a melodious crystalline chirping should be released the exquisite concert of those dead birds imagining them (the pâtés) in the form of bushes or domes (probably equating them with those globes covering miniature trees filled with stuffed multicolored birds) bristling with slender pointed tongues triangular dark purple like those bizarre condoms I later saw displayed in a pharmacist's window in Barcelona along with rubber sheaths for the tongue equipped with little tonguelets pink or sheen of raw meat

served with green sauce, cooking slaves that their master had put to death so their secret would die with them

bamboo thicket from which came the deafening chirping of the hundreds of birds that gathered there in the evening before going to sleep growing calmer little by little as darkness advanced on the garden still shaken by fits of shivering of wing-quivering and still a few discordant calls farther and farther apart weaker and weaker then nothing more

she reappeared beyond the tamarinds walking on the road now

rapidly a tuft of reeds hid her again then I saw her passing in front of that mock-Moorish ruin the color of baked bread

soft breeze of dusk still rustling the leaves occasionally

lapping the black sweat running their parched tongues over their lips they followed her with their eyes silently some sitting others stretched out at the foot of the crumbling wall some had taken their shoes off thirsty lying here and there as on a battlefield in their dust-colored uniforms surrounded by that sharp odor of sweat floating their arms stacked to have one's feet in bloom an infantry expression toes fanned out cacti a dense thicket of prickly pear extended the wall near which their officers stood a little apart standing some with their arms crossed one leg half-bent thrust forward their backs broad robust framed by two black straps which passed over their shoulders connected by metal rings to the belt bulb-shaped gaiters of shiny black leather encased their shins one of them had a black mustache that looked varnished the points of the collars of their tunics were decorated with raspberry-colored badges you would have thought they were all made out of cardboard or *cuir-bouilli*

from the watered gardens still rose that pungent cool odor you could see the water still standing in the furrows luminous between the rows of tomatoes the reeds upright in sheaves forming parallel lines somewhere you could hear the wheel of a bucket-conveyor squeak

the gray olive trees the mauve mountain the saffron sky

without stopping she readjusted her black comb in the dusk her two arms lifted for a moment I could see the dark tufts of her armpits her arms lifted like two horns for an instant the black-toothed comb standing out against the sky disappearing passing two or three times through her hair then she pushed it in and dropped her arms

licking their parched lips with their thickened tongues

a narrow sulphur-yellow crack over there separated the gray sky from the mountains beyond the boats you could still make them out minuscule spots of geranium and jade the sea was the same gray as the sky the beach gray as well separated from the water by the darker strip of wet sand where the tracks of their feet led away in one place one of the trails forked abruptly moving away from the others you could follow it for a few meters in the zone of damp sand then it disappeared beyond the fringe of debris thrown up by the winter storms where the feet had left only vague shapeless depressions in the dry sand lost in the chaotic succession of miniature dunes and hollows left there by all the feet that had trampled it

child king shrimp pink chubby-cheeked on the postage stamps surrounded by bishops and dignitaries the parade dress of the officers includes a sky-blue silk scarf knotted around the neck some of them were thin dried out like bits of wood at one point they pulled apart a little and in the center of their deferent I saw him seated on a little mound with his metallic beetle's head his mandibles his sooty scalloped lips fat potbellied shapeless his short black legs dangling mountain studded with scintillating stars with moiré ribbons in the delicate colors of flowers of blood lemon azure cerise garnet color of grass color of dusk of dawns of periwinkle saffron ruby indigo shimmering on the austere background immense and empty of his tunic

tongue running back and forth over the cracked lips and this ink and poppy-colored dart

in the nearly fallen night I could see the milky patch of her thighs as she put on her stockings and all was black save for the child's dress still sitting next to her on the sand and the fringe of foam undulating soft noiseless over there they had stopped playing ball and started busying themselves about the boats. On the side away from the setting sun the sky merged with the sea. Through a rift in the clouds I could see the first star its points seemed to grow longer and shorter by turns retractile

the one in black had disappeared the two blouses geranium and green no longer to be seen now

Four Kinds of Water
Martine Bellen

Third Year of Anna

Old year passed as all the others, and the new year came.

I should like to ask the fish why
he neglects me but for the groans
under ocean I cannot

Traps bobbing on fog

since your departure since your departure and sunset hurts my eyes. since your departure sunset hurts my eyes. and sunset hurts my eyes.

Fourth Year of Anna

My love for him has not been quenched by these rains — new shoots still spring. There are occasions on which the place where one is living becomes untenable if one is to avoid a one-word god. A certain direction in which I often went is now forbidden me.

On the Eleventh I had an extremely old dream:

— a sea of cherry petals —
rain fell and took
blossoms that had survived
the winds

Reminds me of the story of the lover who left through a keyhole.

knowing how fragile a thing is

it had grown dark for an answer

———

Picking parsley off the river, I wonder why my presence should
make any difference,
picking words.

Sixth Day of the Sixth Month – Rainy Season

Pilgrimage

beggars at the shrine, each with an earthen bowl. The way was quiet. I left an offering of cloth and a poem attached to three branches. Are you a mayfly or one of those shimmerings of summer or a film of cobwebs floating in air-calm? I am at your house. Hurry back. My sister and I took off our robes. Hers is light blue. Mine thin russet.

1.

Dear Z:

Have you gone off today to fulfill a vow? taken the raised stone walk running up the mountain? River plunges and leaves glow with varying suggestions, even snows melt away but I am not so favored. He asked me to send him his arrow he left that much behind. His dance was extremely moving, everyone felt it.

2.

Dearest Z,

To take care of your excess we have added an extra month. Use it foolishly! The moon past full here and there leaks through trees lighting the river from which we have come, wanting to return on it, to go home. People were always being caught in the current. I thought I would not mind that fate but the crowds and activity have taken quiet out of me.

Martine Bellen

3.

Dear Z:

"After having let go so many moons unnoticed, here you are when there is none"

Tonight is on our list, whatever we do with the others, so quick with the calendar you are.

In the beginning of the third month everything was shrouded.

Fire flew through air and forgotten rain.

At the Mansion:

The couplet inscribed on either side of the doorway was as follows:

Water that falls from the hill breathes such love
all below hungers news of it

I was admitted for a long wait and assumed a space behind my companion's eyes where exists the pause of unknowingness, turned my head and into the world turns me, not so much nothing but what is wrong when it woos you into seeing you will never be conscious of what quite a different person you have become. One does one's thinking before one knows of what one is to think, an excerpt of something greater, a detail

Our problem with volition stems from the invention of words
so late in our history we haven't yet learned their power

If a town is set on a hill it will not be good for the
dweller in the town

if black ants are seen on foundations
which have been laid

if they aren't seen but are there

and the household will scatter

She saw in conformity the means of guarding her simplicity

———

Day Five of the Expedition — The Search

During night they entered backwards and went bending their bodies after an ugly manner: as gods die they become jealous, cripple wretched things of shame, mere bellies that we are. Found false doors from which they could pass out, where everything was commanded.

The one that approached the house scared me from my bed, had a cup too much in gathering dusk. I remain under cover, in the moon priory; balded women with smiles like yours stir these waters. Thoughts pass by which I want to drink but upon awakening I know they will be forgotten and they would not be helpful anyway — rain so seldom obliges.

Even in the foothills there are eddies that survive not whence they
came

the weather was cloudy and clear by fits

the intercalary month pushed

seasons askew

———

Martine Bellen

Tenth Day of the Second Month

Pilgrimage

It was not far, but rather deep in the mountain—dead grasses burned, blooms late coming, and leaves in sacred branches thick to hide sparrows; now and again he took his hawks to try their wings

A poem entered my thoughts:

This iris began
its life in a swamp
unobserved

(She is rejoicing in the abundance of water)

Along with the Second
Month grew red plums, brighter than usual, but there was no one to enjoy them. I planned to give a food bag to someone starting a journey—it still remained for me to sew in a lining and fill it with poems

Rain began on the Twentieth and continued without pause through the better part of the Ninth Month. Winter came this year before the old one ended.

Three Poems
Rae *Armantrout*

NORMAL HEIGHTS

We just assumed
that our relations were mere
happenstance, insignificant –

that there was a secret order
nullifying this one.

•

We had been asked to listen
to *Little Women, Little Men,*

a hoard of diminutive
and dated instances.

A preemptive "Yes, but . . ."
was the model of balance.

•

Columnar
palms and junipers swayed
toward or away from one another;

this would only look like
relaxation
for a few moments.

•

We weren't supposed to stare
so, when we did,
a blankness spread across
the once pleasant features.

We got started:
lists of objects, lists of attributes.

•

We were just playing
(crosswords or Scrabble)
for what seemed like years,
waiting for the speech to resume.

We weren't supposed to mind
losing.

NATIVE

How many constants *should* there be?

The slick wall of teeth?

The white stucco
at the corner,

flag on its porch
loosely snapping?

•

"Get to the point!"

as if before dark –

as if to some bench
near a four-way stop.

•

At what point does
dead reckoning's

net
replace the nest

and the body
of a parent?

•

The apparent
present.

Here eucalyptus
leaves dandle,

redundant but syncopated.

SPANS

The kids are excited
by the prospect

of the finite: seed packets
in the garden shop.

a magic number
of distinctions,

the upcoming
recital.

•

Rae Armantrout

The mother
dreams her thoughts

have parted company
and become innocent:

pine, grass and wind.

•

A bird folds her wings
and drops

one stitch
to decorate the past—

thus touchingly
real,
                    extant.

Months in the Year of Animal Prayer

Ben Marcus

THE ANIMAL HUSBAND

HE STRODE the lowest point of land, swatted trees and brush, marked his signal with chalk on the green riverstones. Grass and woodchips rose off the strand and spooled slightly in his wake, left hanging in the bung of heat from the fire downwind. He walked off the burn, knowing that a flame can be stretched into any continuous string, that fire is essentially the compression of heated ropes, compression meaning a full-blown stuffing into a tight space, the orange string finally rising up in reverse to grow against a house in broad coils. Solitary chunks of hemp can be used to cool the skin, but he had none.

He was brought often to a place of shade, breathing hot, to curl up stashed in the thicket, shadows of trees being agents of coolness against his skin, to bring cool to his neck until thrips and mayflies crowded up his throat and he woke blowing dust and filament, coughing up objects which flew away from him and never fell.

He would use the motion of water as a compass, knowing that gravity does more than pull a wall flat, that if left to run as a fluid, or as fine streams of ash, the house pursues a northern exit through chips of air. Water does not float, it falls in grooves to the northernest point before sinking.

The ground was raw and scoured over with the marks of a brittle wire tool. The garden had also been burned. He pulled flowers and sailed them toward his house, kept his hand in the river, crouched. A beetle floated down on its back and ran adust on the shore. He washed with his back to the river, smelling north for smoke, the strum of his father's air-conditioner, charred daffodils airy and gray raining upward.

His chalk had melted into a lather. He soaped the stones with it and hoped that what dried there would be white enough to see by. He erected small pylons of sticks and whitened them with the film from his hands, remembering that smoke avoids the whitened floor of riverbank, that the extreme white of an inverted river works to pull the fire from what is burning, fire also being the condition a house wall achieves when spun beneath a fast hand lighting rocks and seeds against the corner. He tossed sticky ropes of pollen, fed the water with petals, looped off roots and all he could pull into heaps, fed himself without moving while leaning high with his face into the sedge of fruit clumps swinging from the rows of figs and applesticks.

The dog, when it came, trolled off the magnetic rim of water, and it was briefly not a dog, but instead a series of instructions bequeathed by a man. It made a path at him. Its fur was heavy or else the animal could not walk right inside what covered it. It broke upbank and he saw the pink and blue of its skin where the fur had burned down to the base, the hide enmossed in sticks and something glass shiny or maybe something else that glared and was glowing. He'd not wanted an assistant, nor a witness, nor even himself. A deep sting was on his back, and the flapping of his shirt—the fabric stiffened and hot and charred—stung him further and pinched his neck, until he moved nearer the water to go under. The dog, hill-sliding from the crest, blocked his access to the river, and for a time the two of them strung onward in parallel along the riverline. He could see the shape of himself hung out to glow in the dog's greased coat, his own hair shot up green with callous and singe, the image of himself slipping up and down on the back of the dog as the dog guarded the water. He wondered if at least the picture of his head could be cooled by virtue of falling next to the captured water, which also shimmered from the base of the belly of the dog mirror.

Grass and rottage stacked high would not be enough if the air was shut down when he returned. He hoped to contrive a fuse to slow-flame his bundles throughout the night, so the pyres would brighten, keeping his route fixed near the water. He hung strips of blackened cloth on branches and twisted the cuffs into knots hanging level with his face. He traced half a shirt backward on the path and then walked on again to see would he or another be pulled from the trail. The knots were airy, unsealed in their twist, so he packed them with mud, jamming rocks and glass-shints and twigs into the bulbed sleeves, packing them again with his hands, and then swinging them in arcs from the branches where they hung, to see about the wind when it came, and would it wrinkle up the traps. This time his face was caught up and stung when he walked. The cheek part gave way to the stabs and flinched back hot and button-cut, until he moved forward again without care into what he felt was warm and worth being near to, the heat of his own blood feeling soft on what was still unswollen in his jaw, and the glass jids on each knot tickling at him hard, stuffing at the space in his mouth, touching through breaks in his skin at the tingle that itched.

Again the smoke fell in from the north and he was forced to stop. He sat in the crouch of land downbridge from the traps, his arms crossed over his knees and holding his face, the dog asplash in the shallows somewhere uptread. He recognized the act of magnification brought on by the smoke, that water is seen to slide upward in essence, extending only a trail of vapor to imply the continuation of a river. It was funny to him, that in the mist his body was larger, although he couldn't see it. He had felt this first of the house. His running around it could normally have been done while holding one breath, but with the garden loosened so, and the smoke around his run, there were many breaths needed. He touched against his legs and tried to find where they ended, but even this movement thickened him at the joints and he was swollen enough to have no choice but to rest. His was the skin against the tree, beneath which water pushed north over the downgrass.

There was very little swinging, so if he came running through this place with no notice of anything due to the dark air, then he would at least be stopped up or knocked or damaged. Then the water would be near and he could crawl to it.

Within the whitened air, a wind forecasted ahead of the dog shuttled with it a mist of burnt water dyed into the fur. The last pinches of fire rolled north inside steam, and he felt smoldered and roped up, having nothing to look at to help him breathe straight. His back and legs and bottom were heavily numb now, the sun or another place of great heat excited his blood, footsteps other than his own came to be all that he heard. He noticed that he had been slowly moving his hand through ribgrass and small weevils of soil and humus, as speckles of soil wound up the shirtless part of his chest and blew from the tail of his companion. This was enough to get him walking again, working always north off the house shadow he'd see if he could look long enough at the luminal nimbus unraveling inside daylight off the river-hull.

The mornings were best to cock his ear for the whipping bumps of the machine his father had used to cool the house. When the northern crest had salted their weather, they loaded their windows with cloth soaked in honey, and sealed the doorcracks and chimney with watered gauze or even foam from the well bottom. Strips of dried firesticks flamed without cease at the rim of their property, and none could even sit to watch the approaching blaze, having recourse only to smell the gate and then the fence burning, until the honey on the windows seared open and valved forth thin plumes of char and red smoke into their rooms. He heard little while he moved. Even under pressure from the northern heat runes, the metal box strummed with no break, and days when he was combed in lime and mudstricken about the ears, he still could hone to the buzz and click of the cooling box.

This air held a sun. Light drawing lowly out of the north extinguishes fires along the land mirroring its circuit. Higher travails of smoke seed here and form an equator of charred air, white, gray and black, which often gives rise to the formation of rivers and creeks, above which cool strips of air rim the paths to enable travel. He and the dog matched their gait with these stone runs. They kept low on the property, stringing north through bleached wood to nest down only when the ground was coolest. Theirs was a cautious burst of sleeping fits. He groomed the earth down with his tool and lay flinching in the heat until the shadows broke. Never did he not roll or watch while blinking what the trail was offering.

The location of his house was fixed just eights beneath the northern curve where smoke rolls upward and vegetation begins. This heat he had escaped was replaced by a density of air he had trouble navigating. But with nothing to see, his walking became easier. He had barely neck left that wasn't scarred. As much as he could not bear stopping to grab at the gray river-sand, he did so to let the river cool his feet, although he was tempted to sleep where the current was mild and numbfish junked about in the froth. He would have done so had not the dog whined and yelled whenever he even lay to his side to let the water soak his trunk.

Fires burn with no smoke in the north. Cooling in the atmosphere compresses fire into rigid white strips, allowing lightning to fold downward onto festivals and other processions. Some fire can be preserved in the extreme boreal stretch by sealing the skin of the fire-core with salt and clay. Other, remaining fires burn over wooden filaments in the air, ejected primarily by the sun as a secondary light-spring, known as a coil of wooden heat, used when the pursuit of alternate sun-circuits is required for the fertility of the land. When the sun is unseen, apprentice heat-rinds map warmth within the cloud-core. Trees never form in the air, they must be fixed to root under the clay of a river, so the river bottom is sealed with wooden skins.

He had his fist in the scratch of dandelion pulp, a whole ball of it crushed with the amber clay curling from the stretch between his fingers. When he squeezed, the burn in his hands was red plump and tighter, blown up with heat. He grabbed weeds. He stripped entire branches of leaves with one sharp pull. Thorns tore the pad of his hand. Air hissed off his newly dropped waste and his eyes seared and watered until he cursed and fell to arching, left prone on the trail with the dog stiffly holding its own near the tree where the trail lifted.

Running without breathing filled his eyes with what felt like fat. He managed to sit again, and then to stand, and then to watch himself as he kept pace with the blackened dog on point. His walking was measured to save time, to save breath for when he wasn't moving. He wrapped his hands in the final cloth of his shirt and dipped them in the highest part of river. The water wouldn't go much faster than he was managing to walk. When he could not keep cold he stopped moving and breathed only when his chest ached, when the shadow he had stopped to stand in had since slanted off. The stones became too wet to be chalked on, so he moved up the bank and gouged pits into the tree trunks. He was careful to insure that the water would not erode his signal.

He had been alone until running all but the garden and last wall of the house, where the air-conditioner was fixed to cool the walls and rooms of the west. The white to the side of his near eye while he ran was curling. Grease slicks boiled off the house wall and seared the grass that his feet barely touched. The wooden frame smeared through from the rinsing, and he ran the line where wood filled the periphery with his eyes pudgy and stinging, waiting for air to loom where the wall still unfolded so he could turn and cross the garden.

He rose up, hairless and dry, his trousers barely damp, and joined the dog who waited on the bank. He felt what was familiar to him from his father's construction tricks. While burning, a shell is voted for by the organism as a whole to stack up with clayey scars and seal the instant of the body when the burn approached, a fossil of the burnt body. This skin is reduced of color, receptive only to rhosby waves, the looting of the body by wind chime, and simple winds curving from the gate at north pasture. He felt this stiffness of joint, as from a bee stinging within him, and he looked at the partially burnt dog, who was moving slower on point, with bunches of burn scars gathering at its hips and back.

Sleeping beneath water is never enough by way of resting. The current is known as an endless drag—even with wind we are to assume that what has gone past us will curve over the planet without ceasing. Fire carried by bits of wind lights up towns and burns those who remain still. To hide under water is to not see the smoke pulled in on the backdraft. For the wind to move it must deposit smoke on the earth. Soil is left stuffed with smoke until the wind shifts back and seals it. Water is then elected to produce fire across these surfaces. A flower held over water is most notable for being immune to fire. The skin can withstand the heaviest of burns and retain its colors. A flower subsequently dipped into warm water will then burn down into powder, the powder being used to color the skin of a man, to generate dermal noise as the one final shield in heat.

His eyes watched the rutted hole, the rim scorched green with flinted chips and woodrocks. As he pressed over the seal with his foot he kept vigil to his rear, noticed nothing following his tracks but the small winds his feet triggered when they broke the dirt. To breathe out now would be to reveal his position, so instead he stooped over the hole, looked in for the head of a fire charge or a trace of hidden smoke, checked again upbank for his markings, walked up close to the holes in trees he noticed, dug at the pits gored into the base of trees, smelled the fresh wood which crumbled off his hand, pushed into the trunks with the bunt of his swaddled hands, and then finally sat back breathing slightly and looking up the grasspelts through the crosshair of brush at the black wall of the house.

He spent evenings climbing up the bank to sit and scout for fires.

The dog couldn't climb. It dragged aswoon in the soft mud near the water and looked up at where he sat. Accidents unraveled with great occasion to his left and to his right, but he was never to become involved with them. The hum to him occurred somewhere still north, and his scouting led to little but the sighting of low grassfires peeling trees back somewhere upriver. He sat and was cooled by winds piling in off the stretch of fires he had planted in his stead. The pyres were goodly through the hours of the river's heaviest flow. Fuses, he guessed, would steam their wicks when water shook in gray walls at the side, the passage of cold water striking flint on the riverbed to permit fire-blooms and flares. He could guess little as to whether he had scorched the river into quitting. Dams occurred in the east, he remembered. Water, when blocked, peels to the nearest side of magnetic exposure, this area being called the east, where he had never been.

THE ANIMAL ASSISTANT

Prizewinners elected for their skill at removing ancient landmarks have discussed methods of disclosure to reveal the harm and name status of any given soldier. Tonal disguises rendered from guessing each name slowly, sometimes over the period of as much as nine days, generate vocal storm imitations. A rainstorm can be produced by emptying the contents of Manny on a road, which action will also divine the location of Maureen, including the nature and quantity of her weapons. Hinting at possible names within the range of Garth, Eva, Charlotte, Sean and other as yet unknown names using the "eaya" sound as the interior syllable, discloses the extent to which any given army to the North is outfitted with weapons which properly correlate to the current name and hair status of the officers. Oracular utterances of this kind when performed without rigid positioning of the upper body (as discussed by Gunther in his "Studies of Fire and the Head") breed results too numerous and haphazard to specify. Consequently, what will be discussed here will assume a certain mastery of the head and the different hair shapes which adorn it. Included in those criteria are fluent, bilingual squint-runs, pivots of the neck and jaw and Special Segmented Vision (SSV) as practiced by language blinking with each eye while receiving bits of weather and food with the mouth.

The most natural prescription to formulate a name from nothing involves a deflected method of perception. This is primarily achieved by eliminating the light surrounding the regarded subject, or cloaking a moving subject in miniature garments such as a tunic or a policeman's blanket. Essentially, very little of the soldier need be seen, but it must be the correct aspect of the very little. A section of torso, as well as the back of the neck, can be enough, if squeezed properly from the binding cloth. One reliable habit is to keep the eyes mostly closed until a noise or smell is noticed. Licking or smelling the fingers of the soldier in question is not directly useful, but often at least a single syllable or nickname can be learned if the sensation of said activity can be clarified down to one word, which should usually express the taste of the fingers, but can also speak as to the fingers' unusual length or dimension.

Circling an isolated animal or soldier in a vehicle or on foot, if repeated properly, can institute the confession of a name. This procedure is usually reliable only when the soldier's name has already been narrowed to a few closely related choices. In this example, the circling of Edward, Eduardo or Eddie, although not Ed, will generate a seeded energy about the hair in a double-syllable named person. Only with the triple-syllabled Eduardo (as with Frederick and Cynthia) will the animal apprentice disclose itself from the specialized clothing during the circling of an allied troop. This information is extraneous to the act of divining a name, but has a corollary use in establishing the tendencies and possible future actions of the soldier/animal team. Actions of such an animal at this stage of the investigation depend on the speed of the circling inquisitor, as well as the scope of the circle being carved. The narrower the arc of the circle, the more the animal will appear to be a conventional appendage or wound of the soldier. Only when circling at a great distance can the badger or fox or beetle be seen clearly as something other than a carefully dressed arm or hand. When viewed from a distance of several miles, a mellow dancing of the animal is observed, which is essentially a condensed, prophetic version of the host soldier's future activities for the next few days. If the soldier is due to die shortly, the animal will not dance in a recognizable manner. Any movement made by such an animal at this point should be regarded with suspicion or not at all, as highly seductive bucklings and jumps can often entrap a new soldier to replace the soon dead one.

Nature replication exercises produce, as will be established, essential understanding of a war. Naturally, a portion of these results can be applied to witness techniques for certain named and unnamed figures. A cloud imitated vocally by enough soldiers for a substantial duration becomes a real cloud. Such a thing above the enemy encampment, cooked down into a series of instructions, can be divided into three categories: the useful, the not so useful, and the harmful. Harmful instructions are returned to the cloud, which is raised back into the sky by the loosing of certain knots of hair clumped onto or near the heads of soldiers with the Gerald or Lila criterion. A beckoning system chartered by the first Henry engages the remaining cloud instructions down to the lower ranks. Since the topographical position of a cloud spy is most notably biased toward visual events, soldiers are warned to ignore aural and other nonvisually sensate comments translated from the cloud core. Language mulch will collect in the lower cumulus and often cool steadily until the meaning is stunted and less useful for espionage tactics.

Other techniques of grammatically correct perception involve the speaking of certain short phrases in order to draw the name forward from a poised or striking figure:

—The listing of complaints such as "this part really hurts my back" or "don't you have something without this sauce" causes a Nina to cower and offer money. Dismissal of such a soldier is difficult. Once the name has been discerned, a gradual escalation of complaint can be employed, until the grievances surpass any verbal form and exist only as pure heaves and falling fits. Accelerated versions of these moans effect a poverty of sight in the named soldier. Thus blinded, she may be shirked.

—Descriptions of mildly pleasing foods render a Gary, and the naming class beneath it, into a crouched position of repeated, nestered movements. To refresh, a motion becomes nestered when it cannot outdo itself. That it occurs commonly in the higher ranks speaks to the frequent experience of Generals of an unpleasantness when an object, such as a light switch, is touched or regarded an uneven number of times. The extreme of the nestered activity is a highly energized stationary position, accompanied by a confusion of how many times an object was touched, and whether or not the touching was symmetrical. Of course it is impossible to touch everything an equal number of times from an equal number of positions. No movement may be undertaken for it naturally excludes the converse movement. It is not until the General is pushed or coaxed away from the wall by a synchronized team that he can then walk forward briefly consoled that perhaps he did have a uniform encounter with the light switch. But still, he feels he might have dragged his right foot slightly too long on his way from the tent, and would like to go back briefly and do the same with the left foot, just to be sure.

—Speaking about lost money which is to be regained by interrogation of Tiffany can lead Piper or Francine to give up their bunker and insist another occupy it, whereas only a rotten Monica figurine can truly proclaim a bunker uninhabitable.

—Statistics of a meteorological nature, recited near an occupied manhole, draw forth the Ezra and the Stefan and cause them each to attempt to destroy the other. The first to do this builds a vehicle from the other's beaten body and fashions an escape.

A final caution: The viewing of a group of similarly named people is dangerous and should be avoided. Chesters and Jeffs are known to move about in clusters of eighty to ninety each, although a criterion within both groups determines who will be allowed to carry what weapon. Specific name/weapon criteria are not readily available for Chesters, particularly for those constructed of artificial hair, because included in the name's definition is a capacity for thieving which renders any period of weapon possession a transient state. The notion that "All Chesters Have All Weapons" is in fact a true one whenever it is spoken, but to speak the phrase "The Chester Who Has Removed Landmarks Carries A Knife" is to report an impossible state of affairs. No Chester will, in any given circumstance, ever have a knife in his hand. He "will have had a knife," and he "will again have a knife" at all times, but he never "has" a knife. The conclusion that Chesters are harmless as a result of this situation should be avoided, however. Several Chesters always have one knife between them. The group works excellently together to stab a prisoner and then quickly pass or steal the knife off to another group of identically named soldiers, before any one of them can ever be said to have "held" the knife.

Several last rules of conduct can be posited for the eye and the ear: Statements left inside helmets and gasmasks with a tiny wire writing device by the family of land-soldiers nicknamed Geraldine (which includes the subset of names beneath this case, namely Estelle, Richard, Naomi and Lyndon) indicate, among other things, that fabric color in the clothing of an opposing army can be a clear determining factor of imminent aggression. Rather than catalogue the dangerous colors, a list of garment/color correlation is offered based on previous battles and the patterns of aggression exhibited therein:

—Nine Richards wrote of a stiffened or otherwise dried bib fashioned from oats or other rejected foods, sprayed with BLACK fur and applied to the beards of axis powers directly preceding a retreat. A beard whisked of foreign hair, and then lit uniformly with a gas lamp, divines the pattern of animal burial practiced by Lieutenants. The shade offered by the bib is a further map for these castings.

—The infantryman Pauline, wearing a BLUE mask and respirator, heralds a deceptive vocal contest, wherein a mutiny is faked with throat stampedes and the compacting of a single shout to produce the sounds of a crowd. Actually, it must be noted that the existence of any Pauline equipped with an artificial breathing device can indicate only a robust strength in the army.

—Estelle and Lyndon make their contribution by observing instances of colored flesh in land-soldiers. Skin of extravagant color is often scraped off and placed in the shell of a walnut or almond before being carried into battle, where it is then unfolded and used for a rain-tarp if storms are imminent. A mass of troops too large to afford the leisurely rotation of clothing encourages the colored skin to accrete in welts and tattoos across the body. If the tattoo spreads into the shape of a known living object of either RED or BROWN coloring, an attack deep into the enemy's position is likely. An analysis of the tattoo dowry indicates that skin etchings are the only suitable field to introduce unknown living objects and have them be understood. The heretofore unseen announces in colorless, broken lines a possible betrayal, desertion or crossover. This situation is accompanied by a sharp spool of smell circling clockwise in GRAY and GREEN lines about the head. Legs and eyes lubricate as well. Finally, tattoos of the recently dead, delineated in smooth CHARCOAL and MAGENTA across the pale downside of the forearms, must be tested carefully. If the renderings of the dead keen toward the Northern sky in the fashion of a sun-compass, regardless of the position of the host-soldier's arms, tiny punctures must be introduced into the skin of the arm and fingers with a lance, until the colors of the dead drain skyward from the hand and filter through the clouds.

Ben Marcus

AS TO DISORDERLY ANIMALS

God is the witness of this procession.

OFFENSIVE ANIMAL — If an animal makes use of language or postures that are offensive to a member, or are deemed as precocious and against the character of the represented species, and if the member offended thinks it proper to complain to the assembly, the course of proceeding is as follows:

HALTING THE ANIMAL SPOOL — The vocalizing animal is immediately interrupted in the course of its physical exhibition by a member [Rodney] rising and calling for a salve to be brought to the auditorium. The podium area occupied by the animal is at this point drawn down in temperature in order for the fluid to fully retard the animal candidate. Rodney states the words or actions he complains of, repeating them exactly as uttered. He may desire the clerk to take them down in writing at the table. Actions that the clerk is unable to reduce to writing must be performed for the benefit of the assembly and the presiding officer until a majority agrees that the rendered actions have sufficiently duplicated the offense in question.

EFFECT OF ACCUSATIONS ON THE BODY — During the miming action, the plaintiff necessarily lengthens and purls, wherein a moulting skin package will uvulate from the hinged areas of the Rodneyism, or else the spongy matter within his pores will swell minutely, causing the skin to bag around the joints in order to accommodate extreme physical pantomimes. This process is a familiar and weary one to those making accusations, but can result in the acceleration of evolutionary status if maintained with concentration, sometimes advancing as far as the position of homo sapiens Richard or Ricardo,[†] depending upon the authority exhibited during the secondary locution. [The plaintiff will not, however, expand in such a manner as to scatter other factions of the

†Concentrating factions of Rodney progress from Eloise to Oscar to Richard to nicknames and abbreviatioins of Richard [Rick, Dick, Rickets, Ricardo].

assembly hall, nor will his actions foment evolutionary regressions in any of the surrounding members.]†

SUCCESSFUL DISPATCH OF THE CRITIQUE—If the empathetic frequencies of the imitation are similar enough to the original animal spool, as preserved in the atmospheric husk of past behaviors recently released as a vapor from the iced animal toward the ceiling, then a form of applause is practiced by the remaining members which also doubles as a punishment of the offending animal.

GRACIOUS RECEPTION—Applause is a broad term meant to cover any raucous display of sanction. For an action to be legitimately labeled as applause it must be sufficiently audible, somewhat difficult to stifle, and capable of attracting the attention of most middle- to high-order animals. [Applause can also, when successful, dispatch energy within a scheme of invertebrates by generating wind spirals into the atmospheric fluid they inhabit. Because the speed of wind correlates precisely with time and its passage, the faster the clapping is performed, the more animals such as the oyster, the hydra and the bath sponge are speeded through their life cycles by the secret, external weather.] If the displays of applause fail to catch the notice of the animal perpetrator, the plaintiff is promptly suspected of having offered an unwarranted charge, and is given one more chance to justify the interruption of the animal exhibition with another imitation, or, in extreme cases, a Special Critique of the Species.

REDUCTIO AD ABSURDUM—We can make them look stupid by doing what they do, only a little more slowly. Exaggerated dramatic renderings of the simplest animal actions are meant to demean the accused in the eyes of the particular species standing in judgment. If the gesture of keel-bearing by the skink is portrayed grandly enough by Rodney, it can easily be seen as a senseless accessory action [or at least non-essential to the integrity and

†Some setbacks, although technically not regressions of an evolutionary type, might occur in the torso-drum of the nearest assembly members. Outage valves, for instance, become sealed for a period of one week with a rubbery brine. The blockage can be lessened by holes introduced with a needle, to ease off the steam. Waste subsequently gathers in the siphage until the brine hardens from the odor and falls away. Ingestion is reduced during convalescence.

survival of the species]. The skink and the project of the skink is therefore refuted. The leaping act of the spiny cockle *heterodonta* [an ORDER frequently within the offices of the assembly] is a routine often used to discredit mollusks. While it is true that the cockle will skip up and leap in order to avoid the tube-feet of a starfish and thereby extend survival, the action of distending the ribs from the hinge region while in mid-flight [flight is of course an exaggeration here when used for a leap of at most eight inches, but again the issue of time and scale is relevant; heart cockles dropped from a height of just two inches have expressed a feeling of infinite falling]—this thrusting out from the elastic ligament a flank of ribs to cool or staunch the arc of flight, is seen as an essentially boastful action in discord with simple evolutionary necessities. The Rodney will play the cockle's mistake for humor, summoning his own stomach-fingers as a surrogate for the ribs of the cockle, often wetting them with his mouth so they attract the light and pulse when he leaps.

SALVATION — Notice that these critiques are meant mainly to salvage the credibility of Rodneys. That they also, when successful, stall the progress of a species is a testy subject within the assembly. Right or wrong, the fostering of lower species is often curtailed in favor of installing a right-feeling within one of the assembly members.

FORECASTS — The applause is reinstated and the procession continues. Clapping chips and rhythms are conducted by a leader. The leader will either be one of the initially offended Rodneys, or an apprentice affixed to such a figure [species permitting†] who was fortunate enough to also suffer primary witness to the action in question. Within these initial stages of the punishment, while the applause is maintained by certain corollary groups, volunteers will attempt to enact rapid ascensions up the evolutionary scale of names by hazarding performances of the animal's possible future actions or words before it was interrupted.

ANIMAL MIRROR — The animal alone can be the sole judge of what action it was [it] intended to accomplish while at the podium.

†Members of the assembly possessed of pouches or cloacal food harbors are more apt to accommodate an accessory, assistant or apprentice.

Noises emitted from the iced sheath at the highest point of the animal pelt confirm, according to the tuning of the animal spine, the accuracy of the performance. These filibusted divinations can occupy the assembly for days. A climate of competition between the members drives each to somehow "live the life of the frozen animal" more accurately than the member before. That the animal is the judge of these events, blasting notes of confirmation or denial from the hairless gill at the top of the spine, is in fact the most severe form of punishment levied upon the animal. The animal must essentially choose who will replace it for the reward of evolutionary ascension. Its inhibitions loosened by the freezing salve, it can do little but watch itself reverberate physically with spine music to that which is most identical with itself, a fundamental action of harmonic recognition most higher animals have managed to repress.

END OF SONG — A point is reached when the animal no longer knows what it was [it] intended to accomplish. This often ensues when the prophetic improvisations of the competing assembly members have built up to a period of several hours. The lack of music [squam shortage] from the frozen animal's back indicates uncertainty and a failure to recognize itself, a sure sign that the limits of its forecasting capabilities have been reached.†

THE LESSON OF GOD — The superiority displayed by the continuance of the predictions after this point is meant as a final lesson to the animal, for displaying the original, offensive hubris. The superior species, by acting in the manner of the animal, but beyond the animal's scope, are indicating, with great finality, that subactions beneath them are necessarily known by them before performed by anyone else. The filter of behavior begins at the utmost tip.

A TRIBUTE TO THE WITNESS — Finally, the entire assembly, with

---

†Stridulation [singing] of animal spines is most notable when vertebral tuning corresponds with the frequencies affixed to by a surrounding real or fake animal. If the spine palpitates with enough slapping, an organal music results from the friction between the glands. Animals are said to "share attitudes" when this music is shrillest.

exception of the presiding officer [and the victorious performer†], will then perform a simultaneous forecast in real time of the animal's actual and final movements. This display is presented in conjunction with a further lowering of the temperature on the stage where the animal is already hardened in place. Degradation of temperature is timed to freeze the animal to death just as the performance culminates. It is the surest negation of the animal's application to advance.

PREVIOUS ANIMAL CANNOT BE REMOVED — The above is the course of proceeding established by the writers of greatest authority, and ought invariably to be pursued. Failure to adhere to the stringency of these methods will simply encourage an increase in applications from the kingdom, and the resultant inability on our part to dispatch with the failures as dictated above. The strength of us as PEOPLE depends extraordinarily upon the ingestion of species committing the mistakes we hope to avert. Remember, to witness or ingest the physical mistakes of a species is to avoid a similar path. If other assemblies stand in receipt of [and ingest] the failed candidates intended for this assembly, due to our inability to receive the presentations within our offices, a dispersal of instinct†† threatens to occur within this entire tier of assemblies. We are summarily less equipped with the internal knowledge of failure and mistake [as practiced by the named and unnamed organisms beneath us] required to fully experience the proper speed of ascension as delivered to us by God the creator. It is only proper that one assembly [this one] be elected for full virility. The most common principle of vaccination dictates that immunity is achieved only

---

†Winners of the improvisatory act of animal forecasts are promptly renamed at least two stages above their current moniker position. Once the new name is initiated and formally acknowledged by an audience of like names, the evolutionary ascension will commence. In these circumstances, for example, an animal structure Rodney will usually triumph, owing simply to the population of the assembly. A period of Oscar results, and tool-making capacities will intensify.

††Artificial instinct, as derived from the consumption of all or part of an animal candidate, can accurately be spoken of only in terms of the *moniker template* practicing the ingestion. When Oscar and The Field of Oscar boost callousing ability on the lower hips or instead acquire a secretable substance whose presence or absence controls the behavior of a great horde of daughter-workers, then this supplementation is referred to as *pulling*. The attempt is to ascribe the most suitable action verb to each name [Leonards are said to *trill*, Gill *describes*, and versions of Lars or Sarah will *panic* the new instinct into use].

by the absorption of killed, deficient organisms. Other forms of study are entirely useless, and we are lucky enough to have available to us all the wide-ranging disorders and aborted behavior spools as committed by the kingdom below. Let us not belittle the prospect of ascension by presenting a process which can in any way be construed as easy.

CONSUMPTION OF THE ANIMAL SHARDS — Though the presiding officer has a right to approach the quarry unobstructed in order to perform the initial jolt,† internal etiquette has instead of late allowed the divination champion the first pass at the stage, ostensibly to exercise his new tool-making skills. Sanders affixed to the paw of the champion skirl an icy animal shale into the audience. The outer dermal layer of any animal, when released with enough force by a sanding tool, invariably arcs toward the throat-frill of the devourers, to cool the esophagus for further consumption. This icy shell alone is enough to insure immunity, but a strong appetite for toxic fur and resin require that the feed continues until the animal pulp is rendered dry. The champion will stand behind the animal, performing king postures and mock engulfments. The depressed temperature at the podium requires such heavy limb spiraling and breathing in the fashion of a lab mannequin as the champion shucks at the pelt, in order to avoid a frozen predicament such as the one befallen the affixed quarry. Shards are dispensed to the full troop, who lick at the salty husks and otherwise scrape or buff them over their thinnest areas of skin. A spongy puppet, pooled out of the animal nug, can be used to clean the face and hands after eating. In this manner the division continues until the full series of Rodneys are fed, the Rickets-men receive bandages, Oscar is soothed with a bone and the presiding officer blows an exit-vocal through the remaining animal spine.

The great purpose of all animal forms is to subserve the will of the assembly, rather than to restrain it; to facilitate, and not to obstruct, the expression of their deliberate scent.

†Jarring the lifeless animal structure renders the pelt, sac and torso bag easily shardable.

Into the Hill Country
John Taggart

1

Into the hill country outside the walls and along the lake
outside the walls along the edge of the pale lake
along the pale lake along the road around the towers
the dark towers of the dark castle high on its dark hill
along and around the towers along and around the dark hills
dark then lighter the road narrows around the hills
around the lighter hills the road narrows it winds up and around
along up and around the hills that are lighter in color
even the shadow on the side of the hills is lighter
the shadow on the side sand-colored the hills sand-colored
shadow where someone could rest where someone could listen
at the top of a sand-colored hill a house with three rooms
the hill the lightest in color highest of all the hills
the house with three rooms on top of the hill
how small and more and more pale the pale blue lake
how small the dark towers of the dark castle on its hill
house with three rooms on top of the highest of all the hills
one of the rooms a box cut in half a box without windows
one of the rooms is a tall box with four windows
one of the rooms is a less tall box with an archway
archway cut out of a less tall box with a vaulted ceiling
archway where someone could pause where someone could listen.

2

Someone could rest in the shadow someone could listen
someone like a handmaiden on a journey with her mistress
grave handmaiden holding a fold of her blue skirt
her mistress talks with an older woman woman to woman
she tells the older woman the father has done great things
done great things to her has socked it to her
really socked it to her it was like a train was inside her
a train made her big tongue of the train left welts
big as the woman on the cover of the Miles Davis album
big as that woman her belly protruding into the sky
big as that woman with welts around her belly
welts going around her belly in three zig-zag lines
the three lines measuring just how big her belly is
as big as that woman she measures just as big as that woman
she puts the older woman's hands on her belly
older woman feels where tongue of the train left welts
woman feels where the father has done great things
the welts the lines measure great things
woman to woman their hands on the zig-zag lines
handmaiden to the older woman pauses in the archway
handmaiden in a long red dress in the archway of the house
listening in the archway of the house with three rooms.

3

Listening in the archway of the house with three rooms
in a long red dress in the archway of the house
handmaiden to the older woman pauses in the archway
woman to woman their hands on the zig-zag lines
the welts the lines measure great things
woman feels where the father has done great things
younger woman feels where tongue of the train left welts
older woman puts younger woman's hands on her
as big as that woman she measures just as big as that woman
the three lines measuring just how big her belly is
welts going around her belly in three zig-zag lines
big as that woman with welts around her belly
big as that woman her belly protruding into the sky
big as the woman on the cover of the Miles Davis album
a train made her big tongue of the train left welts
really socked it to her it was like a train was inside her
done great things to her has socked it to her
she tells the younger woman the father's done great things
her mistress told by an older woman with a loud voice
grave handmaiden holding a fold of her blue skirt
someone like a handmaiden on a journey with her mistress
someone could rest in the shadow someone could listen.

4

Where someone could listen and where someone could pause
this is the utility of the house what it is for
construction of boxes a construction for listening
a construction the house a kind of loudspeaker system
one of the boxes is less tall one with a cut-out archway
other boxes one of the others a tall box with windows
other boxes one of the others cut in half
with or without windows construction for listening
one of the three with a cut-out archway with a vaulted ceiling
this is where someone could pause and listen
this is the utility of the house what it is for
house with three rooms at the top of a sand-colored hill
where someone could rest where someone could listen
someone like a handmaiden could listen to the women
younger woman older woman woman to woman
woman to woman about how the father has done great things
woman to woman about how the father really socked it to them
woman to woman about how the father was a train
along around the dark hills along around the towers
along the road and around the towers along the pale lake
along the edge of the pale lake outside the walls
outside the walls and along the lake into the hill country.

Five Poems

David Mus

FROM: THE ONE ALTERNATIVE / L'UN ALTERNATIF

Hour by hour, alternative life you're actually leading
    by night, like the dream at night and wakeful periods
    of writhing, battered by clashing needs, in a corner

of ocean, where winds howl and clash, the night ferry heaves
    sickeningly, shore and day not the only menace
    you thrust for relief back into loose strands of dream;

the whole night corroborating day, like a fierce dream of
    unrelenting crisis, you're in it "for the duration," day
    and night while the wind rules and howls, indifferent;

in which night's antique turmoil did gray eyes employ
    my white sail "with full and fore-gails through the dark
    deep main," as if down a purposefully treeless street?

Rondement menée, la vie alternative, d'heure en heure
    la nuit, comme en songe, la nuit, entre passages d'éveil,
    se tordre, gigotant, ballotté par le choc des tourments

rivaux, dans un coin de l'océan où les vents se heurtent,
    hurlant, le ferry-boat tangue, nauséeux, côte et jour
    menaçant, vous cherchez fiévreusement la piste du rêve;

comme un rêve force, la nuit d'un tenant corrobore
    le jour en crise, s'y installer la vie durant, nuit
    et jour que le vent régente, hurlant, indifférent;

dans quelle nuit d'antique cohue deux yeux gris m'ont-ils
    engagé la voile blanche "d'un bel zéphyr par l'onde
    vineuse," ainsi que par la rue tracée exprès sans arbres?

David Mus

Nothing here which won't remember me, vaguely; just as, outside,
the tree remembers the next step, stirs uneasily, the approach
of storm is present. I take a deep breath, the hand trembles:
"As at the core of candleflame: wind." The tree stirs, "this
memory, of a wrenching, wind's approach, deep breath long since
taken," "whispering in the heart valves at the approach of
blood storm." "You were not born for intransigence," remarks
the intransigent voice as you put down your bag and turn on
the light. The walls, graying, the musty air, the damp, speak
of the airless, the uninhabited years. Strength of purpose you'd
think – through a thousand death-defying stunts, the minute
adjustments, luffing, starboard or port, feather touches on a wheel,
furthering by turns and twists someone's well-drawn scheme, its
broad-scale measures – alone will have brought you to the long-
sought destination, alone, worn, intact, presumably. A combination
of sticking stalwart to course and to principle with that gift
for clever improvisations which makes you equal to any challenge,
even if unforeseen: where should such a character lead you,
if not to this expected goal and haven where you are alone,
another man, and the place nonetheless, uneasily, knows you?

Laughter, a hand on my head, gleam of slate-gray eyes. Something
about getting all this prose out of my system: "Dear old Gaffer,
you and I know the real thing comes closer to a comic strip."
"Cliff, or facade," "wind on stone," "The King," "house."
So many elements of a story. No shelter. "Shelter," bearing
of a house. "Walls, no wind," but icy draughts leaking through
cracks and crannies, the semblance of no wind, or air enclosed,
picture walls, lobes of a single massive wording. Pointing,
along its vertical axis, to iron winds, to circling soil and sky;
behind it a single lung, shielded, and the shifting, the ductile,
the tender reciprocating breath.

Rien, ici, qui ne se souvienne de moi, vaguement; de même, au dehors, le sapin sait ce qui l'attend, remue, péniblement, approche visible de la bourrasque. Je respire, profondément; tremblement de la main: "Comme, se nichant dans l'amande de la flamme, le vent." Le sapin remue, "Ce souvenir, du tourbillon, l'approche du vent, souffle depuis toujours retenu," "souffle au coeur du coeur, à l'approche de la tourmente du sang." "Le chemin de l'intransigeance pour vous ne fut pas tracé," fait observer la vieille voix intransigeante au moment même où je pose mon sac et mets la lumière. L'air, vicié, humide, sentant le renfermé, toute la pièce enfin, grisaille, respire l'absence, les années vides, abandonnées. J'aime bien croire que, tenace dans la poursuite d'un dessein arrêté — par des prouesses inouïes se tirant de mille mauvaises passes, défiant la mort, virant de bord sans relâche, les amures, touches et retouches minutieuses portées à la barre, ce doigté au service du dessein de l'autre, conçu sur une échelle considérable — cela suffise à mener son homme jusqu'au but qu'il se fixe, tout seul, las, intact, censément. Tenir ferme le cap, se tenir aux principes, en même temps déployer une ingéniosité à toute épreuve, même à celle des défis de l'imprévisible: une telle force de caractère, où t'amènerait-elle sinon à bon port, à ce havre connu où tu débarques, seul, à l'endroit qui, de toi, altéré, péniblement se souvient?

Un rire gras. Une main posée sur ma tête. L'éclat des yeux gris. Quelques bribes concernant toute cette prose, le besoin que j'ai de m'en délester. "Cause toujours, Pépère lapin, nous savons bien, toi et moi, qu'au vrai le vrai rappelle plutôt la bande dessinée." "Falaise ou façade," "du vent sur la pierre," "le Roi," "la maison": quelques éléments d'histoire. Pas d'abri. "S'abriter," l'allure de la baraque. "Des murs, pas de vent," vent coulis comme une voie d'eau, l'air renfermé, murs, de faux semblants, lobes d'un seul discourir massif. Qui s'ouvre, dans l'axe vertical, sur des vents ferrés, sur un sol, un ciel qui tournent; derrière s'abrite un seul poumon, le souffle, sautant, versatile, tendre, alternatif.

You can only feel the wind here in spurts; do you dream
of that place in mid-ocean where all the winds meet and
mix? crying for speed the voice wakes you and drowns,

"like Ulysses on Ogygia, shipwrecked in tears, like
the conscience in its own lies, no companions but
nostalgia, the restless sea, rock barnacles, the cry

of a sharp bird perched on the wind's shoulder, white sands
scene of wind's steep work from beyond, night in your head
dreams on alternate shores, clearing you of all blame."

this tableau itself a foreign jurisdiction, figures
falsely geometrical compose, in flawless, airless
space, a plaint, rehearsing itself, portrait, or compass.

David Mus

Ici le vent ne se fait sentir que par bouffées, tu songes
au point perdu dans les mers où tous les vents s'entrechoquent?
criant sa détresse la voix te réveille, se noie;

"comme Ulysse échoué sur Ogygie, en pleurs sombré,
comme en ses bourdes la conscience, pour seuls compagnons
la nostalgie, les flots inapaisés, les anatifes,

la stridence du courlis perché sur l'épaule du vent,
la grève où mû de loin il exerce, la nuit dans ta tête
rêve au rivage alternatif qui te lave de tout grief,"

témoin ce tableau, juridiction lointaine où les formes,
de fausse rigueur, se réitèrent, en dehors d'air,
d'espace et de faute, portrait, plaintif, boussole.

David Mus

January 23 — I go out. I climb the slope, windswept lungs heaving, reach the plateau: the sun has set in layers of airy alluvium. In the midst of which Venus winks open her one small eye. I cared only for her in the past, now I love all that mire she illuminates. Nonetheless, soon enough I turn my back on this daily extravaganza and start home. Four walls, I say, will shield me from the four winds, as well as from my own naive confusions, which I locate outside. I return, a changed man, to someone else's house on which night falls. "These walls in fact show the dull loyalty of domestic animals, faithful to themselves and to your image of them, ready to fawn without sulking, avid to overwhelm you with their welcome, once more, as if you'd never left. No trace of jealousy spoils their ardor, they know nothing of your alternatives, only your voice, your step, your presence and the quarrels of departure." And yet, here they are, in evidence, all the signs that the master of the house has his spring and pivot elsewhere. On the table in double pages splayed, shrouds climb towards impossible mastheads; sententious or nostalgic echoes raise hopes in thin air; isolated words like projectiles drum into air's ear their foreign origins. The walls, vigilant, feral; the silence, awed. Air's slack, coiled, wraps me round, knowing, biding its time, watching for the slightest tremor, mine, which would set it in motion, waiting for the first syllable of reassuring prose on which to pounce, meat for the housedog.

Out of nowhere, carried by an unnamed wind, the fifth, doubtless, comes the voice of Miles Coverdale in Tudor brick tones: "O, tarry thou the Lord's leisure: be strong and he shall comfort thine heart . . . " Like a whistle in the night, shrilling, slicing the drugged night air outside: "My heart hath talked of thee, Seek ye my face . . . " Wind's imprisoning, the allurement of walls, the tyranny of place, empery of names' contemplation, sway of alternation undergone from one of its poles, blond Wisconsin or asphalt Connecticut, viewed from Theobald's Road, between bank and mausoleum? From here I can picture the bright star, fixed in the sun's adobe courses. "The alternative takes his lodging in this precarious light."

le 23 janvier — Je sors; les poumons balayés par le vent, je grimpe la côte, gagne le plateau. Le soleil s'est couché dans les strates ocreuses du limon atmosphérique. Au milieu Vénus ouvre son oeil unique. Autrefois je ne voyais qu'elle, aujourd'hui j'aime toute cette vase, qu'elle illustre. Pourtant, bientôt, à cette extravagance quotidienne tournant le dos, je rentre. Les quatre murs me protégeront, me dis-je, des quatre vents, ainsi que des naïvetés chaotiques que je situe au dehors. Je rentre, changé, dans la demeure d'un autre, sur laquelle la nuit s'abat. "En effet, ces murs sont d'une sourde fidélité de bête, égaux tant à eux-mêmes qu'à l'idée que tu t'en fais, prêts à se livrer sans rechigner, avides de t'accueillir à nouveau comme si de rien n'était. Aucune jalousie n'entâche leur ferveur vorace, ils ignorent l'alternative, ne connaissent que ta voix, ton pas, présent, les esclandres du départ." Pourtant les voici, tous les signes d'un ressort et d'un pivot autres du maître de céans: sur ma table des pages jumelées étalent des enfléchures qui grimpent, rapides, vers une impossible mâture; des échos, sententieux ou nostalgiques, émaillent l'air d'espoirs venus d'un autre secteur; des mots isolés, tels des forets, vrillent le tympan de l'air de leurs origines lointaines. Vigilance, animale, des murs; envoûtement, du silence. Le ballant de l'air, lové, m'enveloppe à bon escient, à l'affût du moindre geste, fatalement le mien, qui l'étire ou le brasse, de la moindre syllabe d'une prose rassurante à mettre sous la dent.

Soudain du vide arrive une voix, portée par un vent sans nom, le cinquième sans doute, celle, sobre, faste, de Clément Marot: "Puis en sentant d'un froid vent la venue, Tourne à néant . . . " Comme un sifflet nocturne, couperet sillonnant l'air nocturne endormi, au dehors, "tant que plus n'est congnue Du lieu auquel nagueres florissoit. Mais la mercy de Dieu . . . est eternelle A qui le crainct . . . " Exil des vents, séduction des murs, tyrannie de l'endroit, empire de la contemplation des noms, régime de l'alternative vécue à partir d'un de ses pôles, Aquitaine la bleue ou l'Auxois émeraude, revues depuis une rue de Londres? D'ici je revois étinceler l'astre, parmi les assises terreuses du soleil. "Le séjour de l'alternatif c'est cette image précaire."

David Mus

FROM: OVERFLOW/TROP-PLEIN

Lens, placed flat on the text of earth, white image without
focus, magnifying glass you peer through sideways,
polished curvature drawing upwards, into emphasis,
crowds, of terms as if inked in, stationed there, waiting.

Again, not mine these upstart terms, crowd of stick figures
seeking their object, like lines of pilgrims visiting
the sacred place they know by name, touring the ancient
expectation, fulfilling every vague hope, differently.

Unexpectedly weighted, extra head on your shoulders, the
damp air, dense with stone and water and shape, held
to a single promise, made and remade, the sky darkened
as if before rain where you walk over your head.

And the sky, closed over you, promises rain, you look up, a bit
giddy, this new stone dispensation, hope as yet
unfathomed air gives in shapes charged and different,
set up to work through you towards a full statement.

Such statement, as its spokesmen cartoon characters filing along,
serried ranks, visiting a sea-bottom, drowned out,
whelming tide, sea of air closed over their heads,
fugal formalities, in their place: stone walked into.

Lentille, posée à même le texte de terre, image blanche sans
foyer, verre grossissant, ton regard le traverse en coupe,
courbure polie qui aspire, dans l'emphase enflée, des
foules de termes comme encrés, campés là, de planton.

Pas à moi, je répète, ces termes impudents, figures croquées
sorties d'une bande dessinée, cherchant leur objet, des
files de pélérins qui visitent le lieu sacré connu de nom,
tour de vieil espoir comblant toute attente, différemment.

Alourdi, tête inattendue sur tes épaules, l'air humide, pétri
de pierre et d'eau et de forme, tenue à une seule promesse,
faite et refaite, ciel qui se plombe, soudain, ainsi
que la pluie s'annonce où tu marches au-dessus de ta tête.

Ciel, où tu sombres, qui annonce ainsi la pluie: l'oeil qui
s'exalte, tête qui tourne un peu, la nouvelle alliance
pierreuse, espoir à sonder qu'offre air sous la forme autre,
chargée, du bâti en vue de t'affecter au bilan complet.

Tel bilan, dressé, par le truchement des pantins d'esquisse,
visitant, à la file, en rangs serrés, une profondeur noyée,
le flot invincible, océan d'air qui se referme sur eux,
formalismes fugués, en place, pierre que la marche pénètre.

Our Underwater Mother
Yannick Murphy

"TELL US A LOVE STORY," the children said and the mother took a drink of her drink and started to tell. "Wait," the children said to their mother. "That's not how it goes," they said. "Tell us when the woman took off her head and started brushing her hair. Tell us about the spirit who clawed through the thatched roof, tell us when the car filled up with roses you couldn't see in the windows. Tell us things like that," the children said.

The mother took another drink of her drink and wiped her mouth with the back of her hand. "I only know this one story," the mother said.

"No, you don't at all," the children said. "You know more. Tell us what happened to you."

The children went underwater to look at the scars on their mother's knees and they touched the scars and they said to their mother, "Tell us about these."

Outside a fire burned.

"Go ahead," the children said, "tell us," and they hit the sides of the trunk they were in.

The mother saw her children in the orange light from the fire. When her children spoke, they showed black spaces in their mouths made from newly missing teeth.

"I give up," the mother said. "What is it that I know?"

"The rabbits," the children said. "The birds, the chickens, the dogs."

"Greece," the mother began, "I've never even gone."

"No," the children said, "Greece was the lava, the man and the woman."

"All that I saw of India was its shores," the mother said.

"What about the cows?" the children said.

"This I got on a fence," the mother said, pointing to a scar. "This from a fall," pointing to another.

"No," said the children. "We already know about those. Those are China. Those are from the men with the swords."

"That hurts," the mother said and she pushed the hands of her children away from her knees.

The fire burned trash. Soot floated up and into the windows.

The children put their arms around their mother's neck. "What about this?" they said and they touched the beauty mark she had by her ear.

"I don't know. I can't see it," the mother said.

"Tell us about it," the children said.

The mother asked for her drink and the children held it tipped to her mouth.

"Tell us about Spain," they said. "Tell us about the man who held his own hand."

"I only know this," the mother said and she started to tell her story.

Outside, sirens for other fires wailed close by but then trailed off down the streets. And the fire that lit up their place in orange light sounded like people fed it with cans that, when the cans hit what it was that the fire was burning, made a cowbell sound.

"This is not about love," the children said to their mother and they sank their heads under the water, rinsing out soap that came to the top in bubbles and floated over the metal latches of the trunk and into black keyholes.

"I miss those days," the mother said.

With the mother in the trunk the water rose.

"Be careful," said the children, "we don't want to lose it all."

Perched on the sides of the trunk the children lifted up the soaked washcloth and twisted its warm water out onto their mother's shoulder and back. When the children neared her beauty mark they said, "We're going to wash it away."

"And these," the children said, "we're going to get them," they said and they took turns going underwater, looking for their mother's scars with the washcloth in their hands.

The mother drank her drink and watched her children's hair float up and out onto the top of the water. When the children came up to breathe their faces were covered with hair and only their noses could be seen.

"Nights on Lake Mohegan we fished for eels," the mother said.

"What about the rabbits?" the children said. "The birds, the man who ate the flowers?"

"Some nights," the mother said, "eels were scarce and pickerel was the only thing we caught."

"What about the thorns?" the children said. "What about the love story?" they said. "The garden with the corn?"

"Careful," the mother said. The children pulled at the bowed lid of the trunk.

Outside, the flames from the fire suddenly burnt out. In darkness, the mother and her children heard the water splashing in the trunk. When the water sounds became louder the children said, "Mommy, guess what we are doing!"

"Swimming," the mother said.

"But where to?"

"To shore," the mother said.

"To China. To India. To Lake Mohegan. To Spain. To the elephants. To the cows. To the dogs," they said and the water that they were splashing came down onto their mother's head.

In the darkness the mother could hear the latches and the hinges creaking with the wood as the children moved in the trunk.

"Where are we now?" the mother asked, taking a drink but missing in the darkness and the drink spilled into the water of the trunk.

"Greece," the children said. "We are swimming through lava."

"Me too," the mother said and with her children holding onto her neck she went down under the water.

The children came back up for air before their mother did and, feeling their mother still under the water, they thought, "Is this our mother?" And they looked around the dark kitchen.

Our underwater mother is so quiet. Mother, what about the places you have been to? The girl who slept on water? The dogs that were the waves? Mother, what above the olive fields? The ocean under snow? And the children put their hands up under their mother's arms and they pulled.

We did not know our mother was so heavy. We did not know how much she wanted to stay down.

Coming up out of the water, the mother's mouth was moving.

"That's it. That is all that I know," she said.

"Not fair!" the children cried. "We couldn't hear that!" they said.

"Where's my drink?" the mother said, looking for her sunken glass.

One child, maybe two, the younger ones, put their heads under the water. Can we still hear it? they thought. Are the words still being said?

"Look, this is our skin," the children said. The mother looked into the water.

"Dusty," she said. Her children were swollen. Their mouths were open.

Outside, the trash fire must have started up in the wind because her children were once again orange in the light.

The mother thought of how there had once been a rash on her hands. There was once a view of a town from a winding road. There was once corn in the garden.

The children shook their mother. She was falling asleep. "What are you dreaming?" the children asked.

The mother's drink spilled into the trunk. The children took the drink from their mother and they passed it around. They drank their mother's drink. Eyes closed, the mother listened to her children. When she opened her eyes, her children were grown. Rabbit teeth filled their mouths and grew past their chins. The teeth could cut into their chests. "Be careful," the mother wanted to say but the words did not come out.

We remember our mother sleeping. Speaking in different languages, maybe she sleep-talked love stories. Take a guess. We are dancing in a field. We are under some other country's night sky. Men come in and out of doors. We hear soldiers' swords. Wear green stoned rings. Take a guess. Our mother is climbing over fences, going under men's robes, swimming in a lake to an island where a naked man stands.

Stripped Tales

Barbara Guest

1

the motifs of a tale are advanced

What did it tell him the light in the interior or was it the moon fell sideways, as if the grotto that lay at the bottom with a light forcing the light and the humor from water moistened the cup as if the length also, the road at a dry fountain in moonlight she turned sideways to hold up the cups and the motionless stripping.

the string with knots on it promises, he said, a grown girl and not collegiate with red hair, a light from the house scattering the daisy centers raised a doubt.

in the hollows dim-witted rabbits running out of the barn the storm might have killed them 'don't think much of the girl guess she left the country.'

. . . handbag with the parasol over her head feet pointed in front, strips of celery, taught to hold her head "high like the Spanish," ripe olives, a walk on stripped sand the cloud over the boat a sliver changes her look.

2

serial attempts and lamed achievements

from porridge to velvet dubious speed
oh disasters   factories   memory and actors   dossiers a name
names   piloting balls of speech   worm balls and the grape kites
literature   my bears   single-mindedness   berets they wear.

we were fast-pacing it down the street at a clip forcing our legs to move mastering it lively stepping legs in trim soup of mussels grilled shin and fragrant little walk terrace he sat with his broken leg in a splint.

on the coast groups of cars trying to reach the city before dark and the coast road was narrow the coastal range of mountains dry with huts for the forest rangers a few miles apart spotted on the hillside piglet-size and the coastal patterns ran up and down over the ranges always keeping in sight of rangers the midday sun or the blinding moon caverns the bruised city.

literature   my bears   the phantom

3

the metaphysics of glass

mounds of glass like robust water under a gaited horse she guided him to the complex recreation thin pieces starting to melt the entire process even the misty pane and the gilded domino was sunset on water and it moved as clouds do turned upside down the viewer lying on a mercurial mothiness then the process of plaster that is opening the mouth of the cup he reassured us while we stood by the emoting tub water on another occasion he chose window glass suppleness took the form of a cross a surprisingly innocent surface it ripples even as the writings of St. John transform a matte texture the suppleness contrasting with the surface and the convincing fall into variegated molds reinventing the material so that the text the texture and the surface are capable of an explosiveness in the form of a bulb that is close to divinity multiple reflections within its broodiness stone cannot compare with glass.

4

the cottager's tale with magical properties

it begins green green white chalk and lambs may I tell you the whole story for a living oats in the barn the hovering cottage who rowed Mad River of rain pouring down of Alouette's sandals and Berenice the orchard ladder and the Parabola my trouble with sleep I was bolder then and the blossom stain bent the ankling dew Maggie's sheep and the feathered titmouse what else grew on trees or by the road turquoise sequins a knitted hood then I bled a little Genevieve ma'am here's your pennyworth we proceed fortune promises duckling in honorable air your grace of the orangerie I cannot tell by the surface what kneads the skin in which lake swim the Namaycush who scampers out of the green.

5

Coleridge and Wittgenstein comfort one another

I believed the outcry concerned ticking and whether promises are kept whenever there's adorning or a creak of the window someone blest passes. Insatiable demands *logico* or *xy* the fence tended flowers moments of bewilderment I saw the road tilt.

It was our intent to read all the books we gathered not at once but over a settled sum of months we would know if linguistics or a pattern of stars ruled the *logico* if *xy* or a similar construction slightly altered was the essence of movement it is my intuitive belief that poetry was the essence so frequent were his movements so startled the look in his eye he moved swiftly and his countenance stripped as he recorded the hiddenness behind the situation if I were not cautioned to disbelieve *intuitionism* is a fraud.

That loftlike room cold as Norway the selectivity of his clothes his work 'absolutely simple and full of light' he was talking about the ordinary perceptions 'seeing queer problems' exhausting as Coleridge inventing new *similes* he fixed his own chronology de Quincy I thought hearkening to the continuum of water grazed by the emotive room: lake poetry.

6

a tale taken apart

She wishes to bring the scene of the Atlas pine and its cones into another dimension. She draws around the story a circle and breaks up that circle into angles to abolish an imposed linearity. The linearity of a narrative is obtrusive to her and when she breaks it up there is a blast of energy. Instead of the residual torpidity of a plot, the muscularity of opposing planes reveals itself.

She deposes the marquetry or marked lines or lures and nears the graduated space where planes and cubes move synonymously as their elbows touch. Encouraged by this camaraderie, cubistically full of revenue, she dismisses the birdless narration. Her story, inoculated with holy Cubism, ventures into the wind-tugged gull space.

Three Poems
Ann Lauterbach

THE SCENE SHIFTS

Things inhabited recalled as stark.
There is, there it is.
And now swerve, asking to be
located or found out, arms lifted—

had he known he would have said so.
I am nearing it for you, on your behalf.
Please follow. What was said was
in answer to what was forgotten, the blond
who visited yesterday was dead, was
dead then. She was an incursion
on what he knew, seeing her.
Seeing her, he wanted her name.
Tina, Daisy. The mad woman
repeated in the hall—"Hear that?
A mad woman!"—where the stench awaited
consummation. It was available like a list.
Across from the cathedral
the reeking list waited in a hall
in the stripped mirage of next, next.
Another sits in a kindred reverie
as a child picks up a shell
and wants to be absorbed into its socket.
Daisy is happy to have married
to have coupled with November
in the low island light speckled with chronology.
Tina is dead. What it was he came to call it
spilled as if it were salt. It was not salt.

The revered, the pagan annulment, the lark
with consequences: boom, boom.

Try talking of it in your sleep
when you've nothing else to say.
Once she thought she was a banner
above a statue
in one of those parks you read about.

"I used to live across from that park."

Then all things became absorbed
into something like a continent,
rooted in adages, portrayed on stamps.
She is walking around with a sure sense
that this is the later they were
trying to imagine when they said
it would be like this. Some
are sitting elsewhere
in a kingdom with stiff fines for leaving.
The kingdom is very small and has no king.

RANCOR OF THE EMPIRICAL

Its investiture.
A lavish pilgrim, her robes unbound,
checks in to a nearby hotel.
Let us spread the wealth.
Let us speak in such a way
we are understood, as a shadow
is understood to assuage these prisms
and these mercurial clasps. She was told
yes and she was told no
which is how she became excessive,
spilling over the sequestered path
her wild garments lacerating the stones.
She took pills against rain.
She slept under tinfoil.
In that country, there were no heroes
to invent a way to fill the hours
with parables of longing, so her dreams
were blank. Sometimes she imagined
a delicate pink rim, and sometimes she heard

voices which lead to her uneven gait
and to her partial song. Once, she was seen
running. A child said he saw her flying
low over the back meadow and into the pines,
her feet "raving in wind." The child
was punished for lying, made to eat ashes
in front of the congregation. The priest said
"You have made a petty story. Now enter duration."

THE UNTELLING

Subsides in perpetuity
without watching, a form of pressure
exhaled, possibly spoken.
Because of the length of knowing
valued in the first place, its name
unattached from rigors of display,
withheld until later, until before or after.

Then you say
tell me and tell again
exactly and I say

The leaves are a wall.

And then she came down the stairs
intentionally.

And then the man the end.

So that later it seemed a season had landed.
And you ask which which
and what is it about.

Down the stairs where the irretrievables
had been. Or her purple shoes
are in the dollhouse. Or:
it came as if pulled slowly
as a mouth filled with awe

moves its silence slowly in a ring.
Only a picture could picture it.

And you ask was it a kiss
that did not happen on any street to her
so it did not predict, did not make amends
was not an extra key, a visit.

I repeat the leaves are a wall.

Explain you say.

I say jewels sprawl before the Rat Man.
I say Cassandra at her dusty ball
her old mouth saying what what
put your house in order
the people are turning away
I see fire in heaps
I see something perpetually stale
I see a stiff batch shifting.

Explain you say.

I say someone I do not know told me
my Godfather Tom
was found on
57th Street
in a dumpster. Tom
she said looked like Walt Whitman
with a long long beard and long filthy nails.
He was the theater editor of LIFE magazine
during its heyday. He took me
to see *Waiting for Godot.* He
gave me a book on Etruscan art
a dragon from Nepal
a round-trip ticket to Paris. He said
you are an eagle behaving like a beetle.

You say
the wall is on the ground
thank you goodbye.

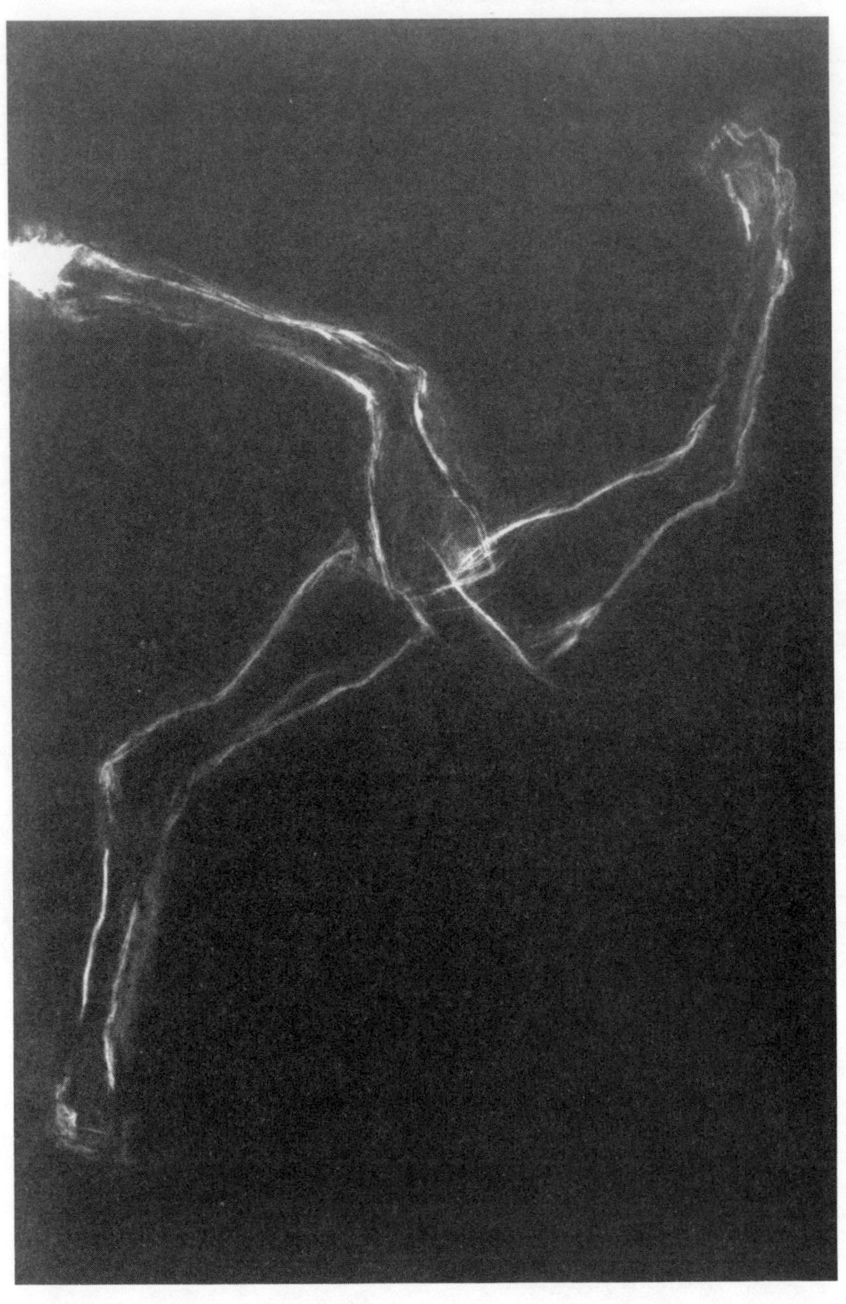

Parts
Susan Rothenberg *and* Robert *Creeley*

DOG LEG WHEEL

Four to the round
repetitive inexorable
sound the wheel the whine
the wishes of dogs
that the world be real
that masters feel
that bones be found
somewhere in the black ground
in front or in back
before and behind
hub for a head bark's
a long way back. And on

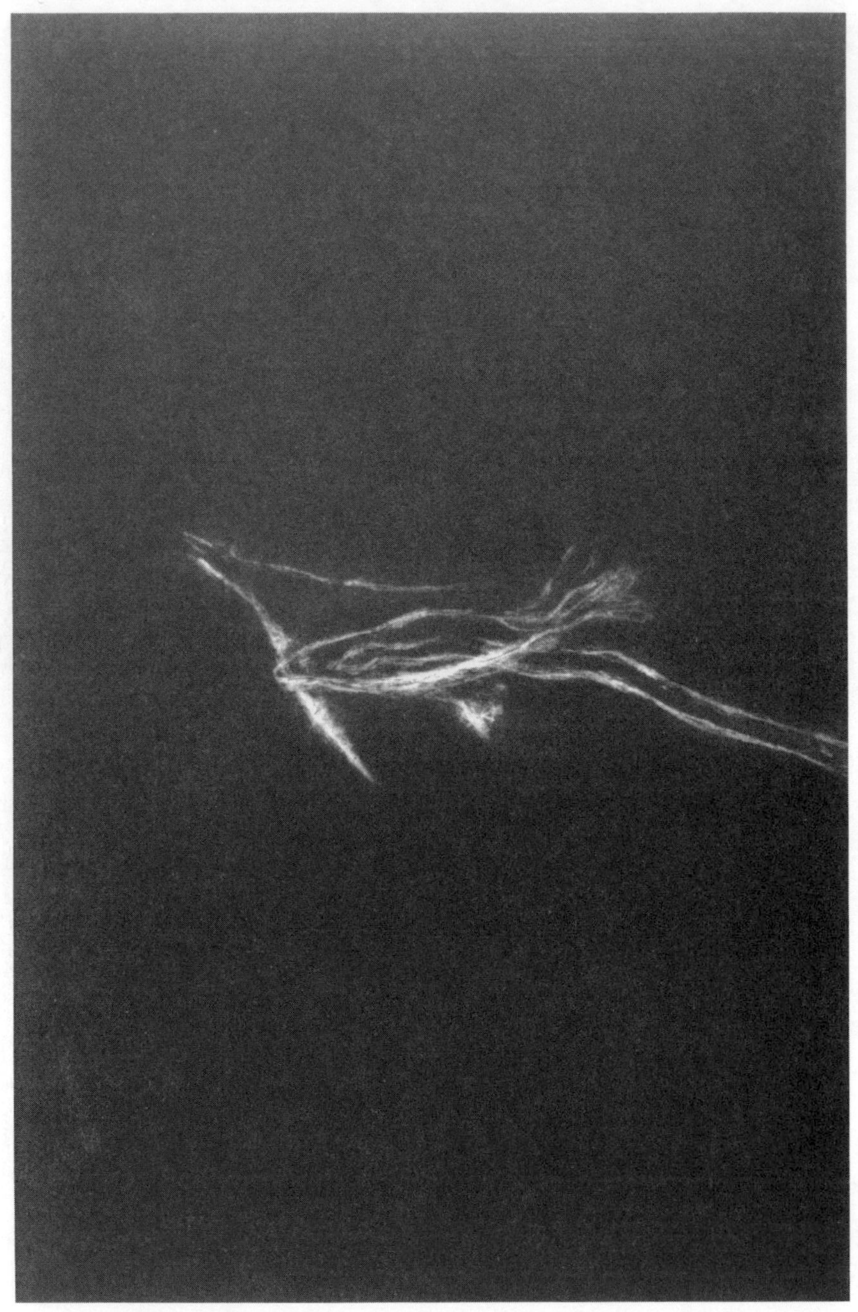

SNAKE FISH BIRD

Archaic evolving thing
in all surface all beginning
not hair or any seeming simple
extension bring to mind pattern
of woven wetnesses waste a streak
of wonder of evil tokens the underneath
beside ground's depths spoken
low in sight soundless in height
look past reflection see the light
flash of finned ripple wing
this ancient *Fellow* follow
to weather, to water, to earth.

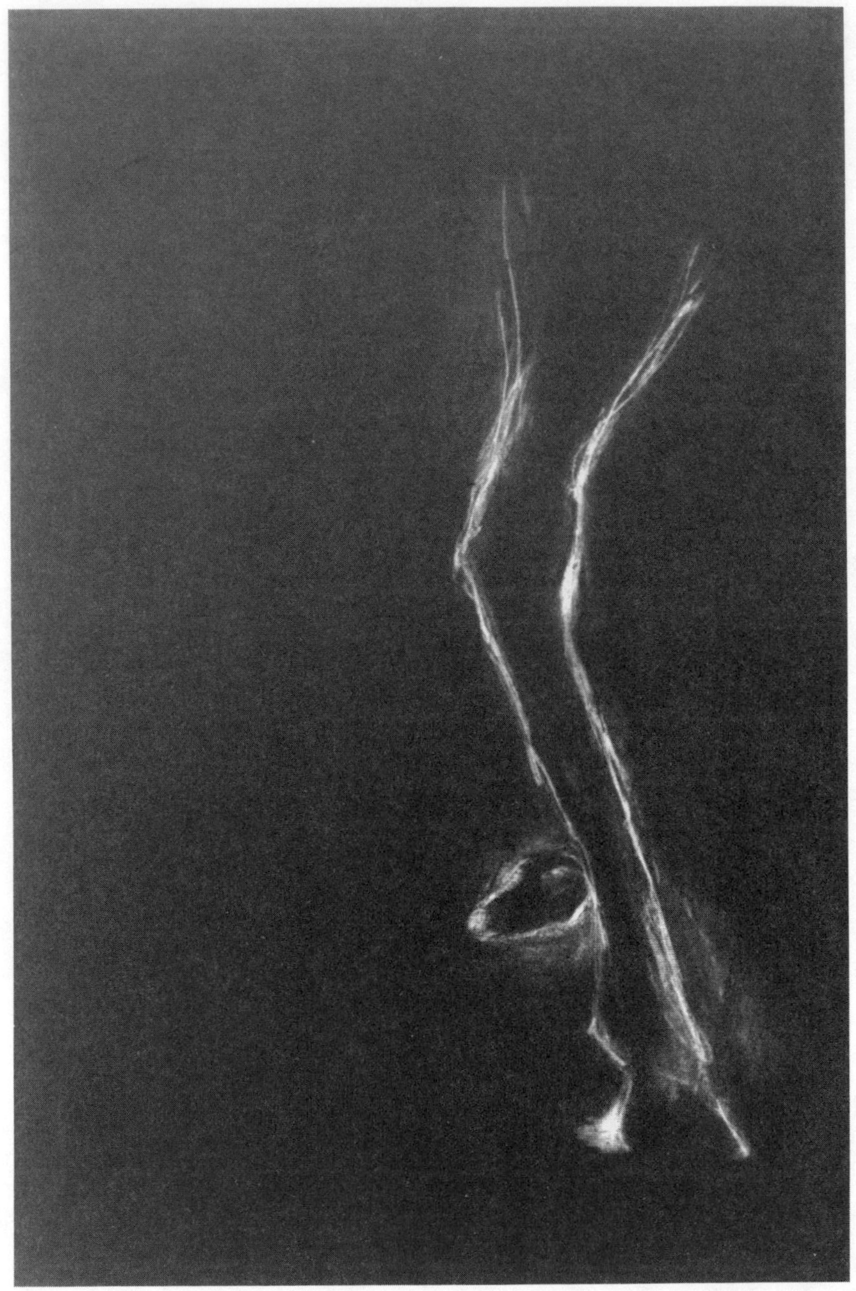

HORSE LEG DOG HEAD

Its mute uncute cutoff
inconsequent eye slot
centuries' habits accumulate
barks the determined dog
beside horse the leg the
walking length the patent
patient slight bent limb
long fetlock faith faint
included instructions placed
aside gone all to vacant
grass placed patiently thus
foot's function mind's trust.

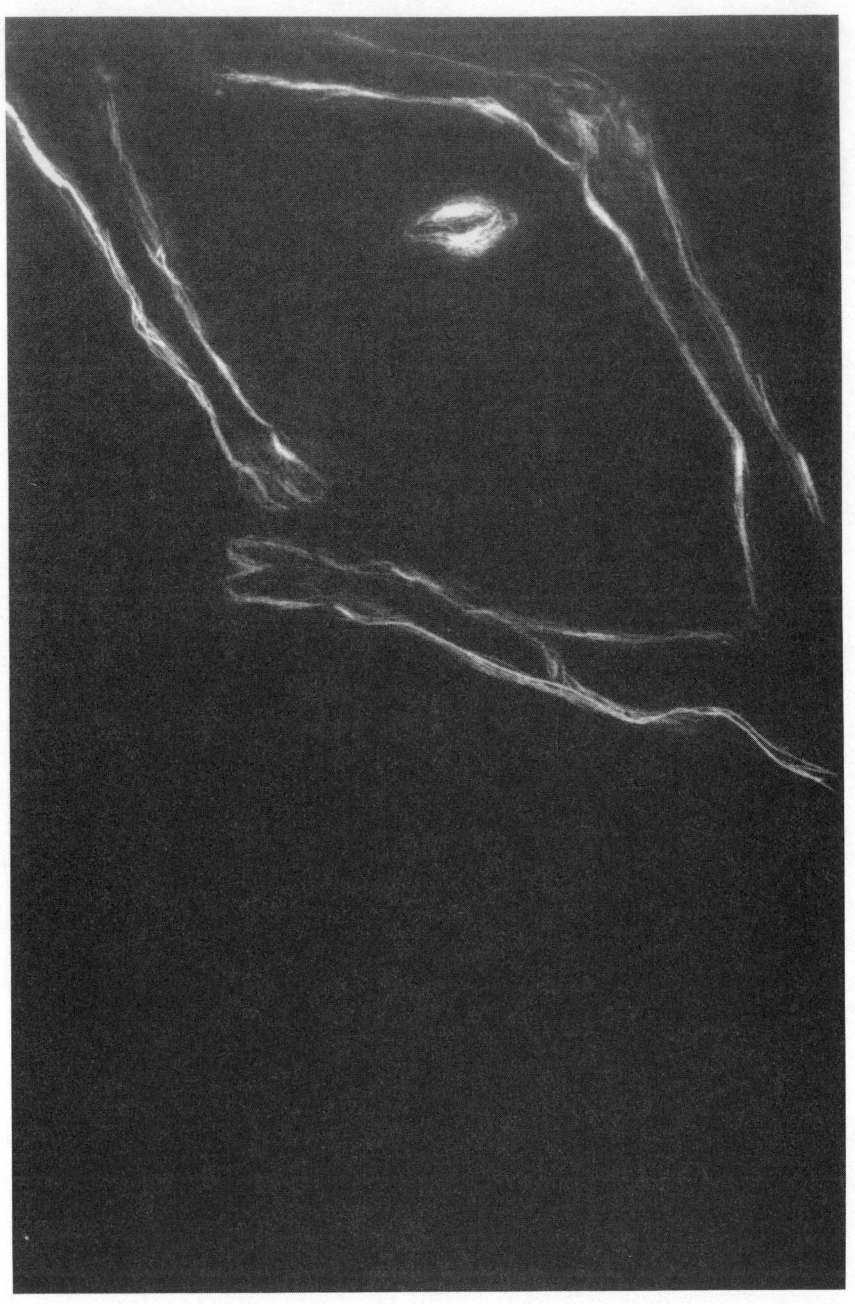

GOAT'S EYE

Eye hole's peculiar framed
see you, want you, think
of eye out, lost last sight,
past goat thoughts, what
was it, when or why—
Or if still the stiff
hair, musk, the way
eye looks out, black
line contracted, head's skull
unstudied, steady,
it led to lust, follows
its own way down to dust.

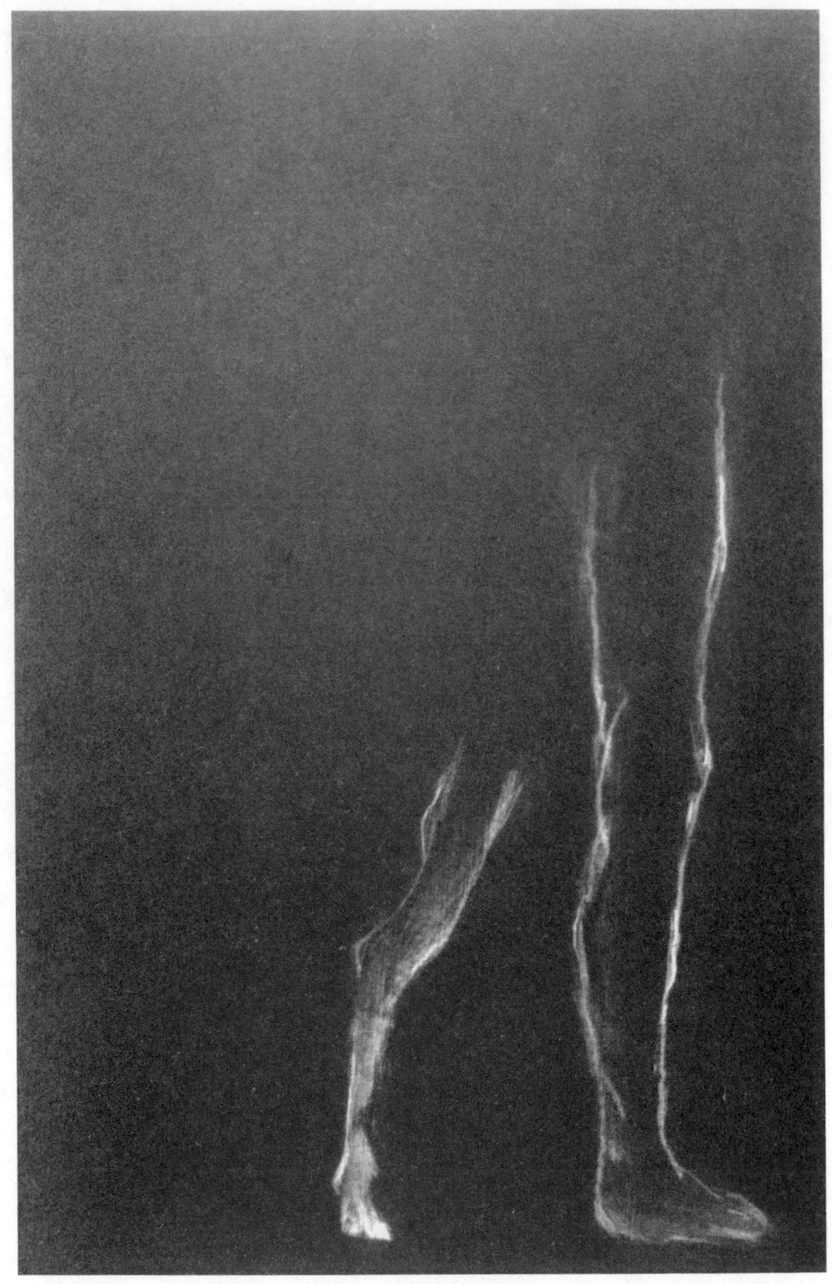

HUMAN LEG GOAT LEG

Which the way echoed
previous cloven-hoofed
dark field faint formed
those *goat men leading her*
in physical earth's spring
jumps one-legged parallel
long walked thinned out
to sparse grounded skin
bones of what scale say
now goat transforms man
then man goat become
and dances dances?

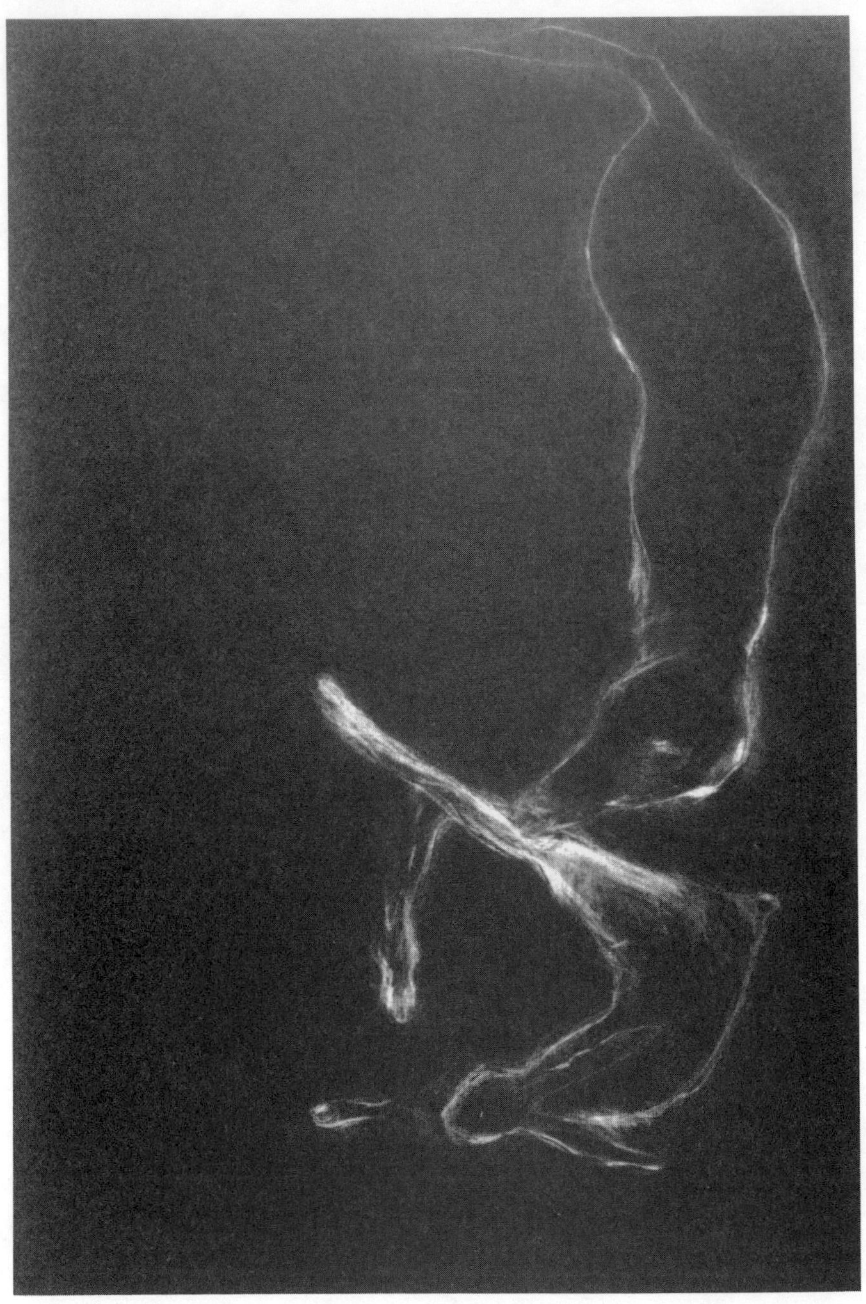

DOG HEAD WITH RABBIT LEG

Break the elliptical
make the face deadpan tell
nothing to it smile for the
camera lie down and roll over
be in complex pieces for once
you ran the good race broke
down and what's left you
least of all can understand.
It was cold. It was hard.
Dogs barked. Rabbits ran.
It comes to such end,
friend. Such is being dead.

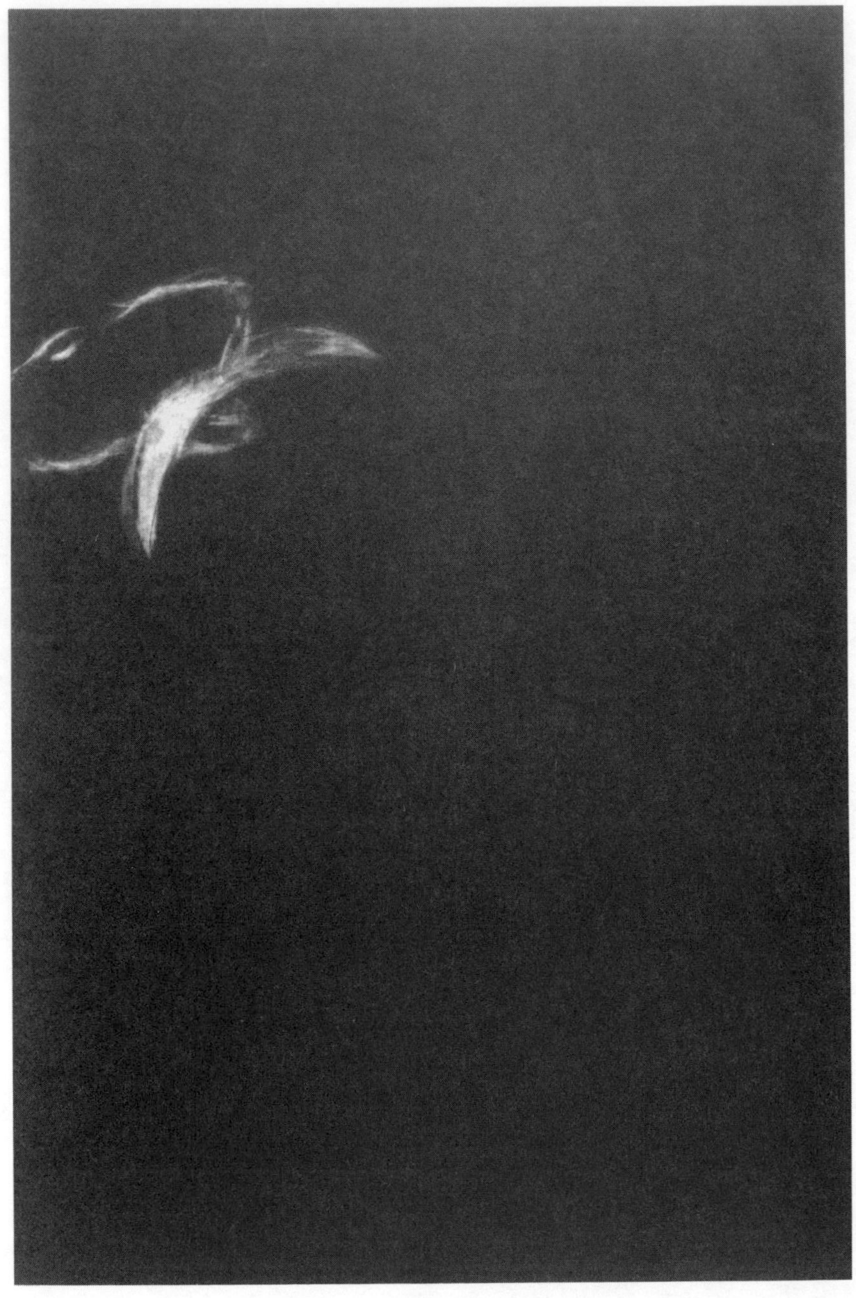

DOG HEAD WITH CRESCENT MOON

Harvested this head's
a manifest of place the
firmament's fundament.
Overhead sky's black night
in lieu of echoed moon
seems sounding out
a crescent crescendo
for a dog's life.
Barked bones soft
mouth's brought home
the arc again the light.
Waits patient for reward.

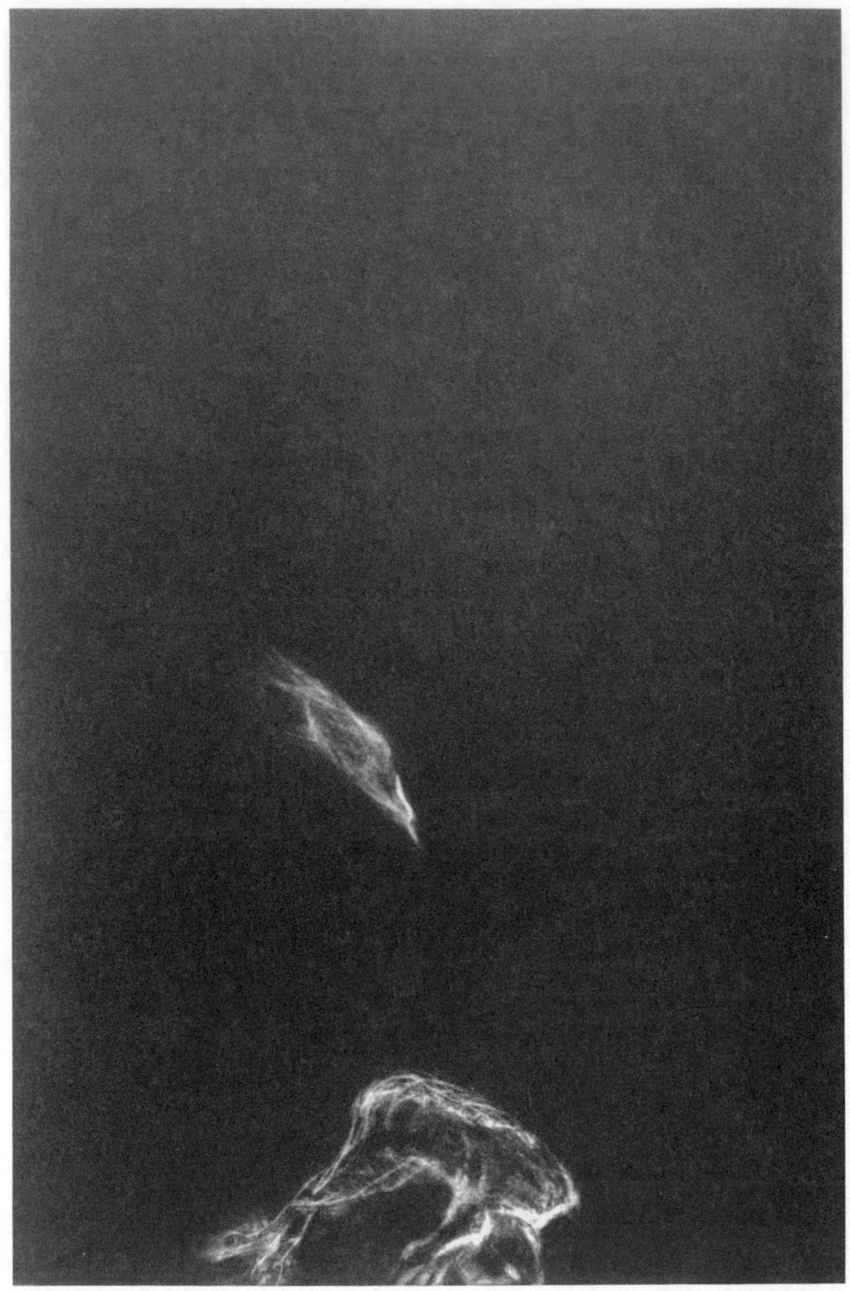

BIRD AND CALF

Peculiar patience is death
like an envelope a flap
a postulate you'd left a
space where it was and it
has gathered the outside
of its body in or just
flopped down dropped all
alternative forever waiting
for the plummeting streak
gets closer closer and
the god who cleans up things
puts death to work.

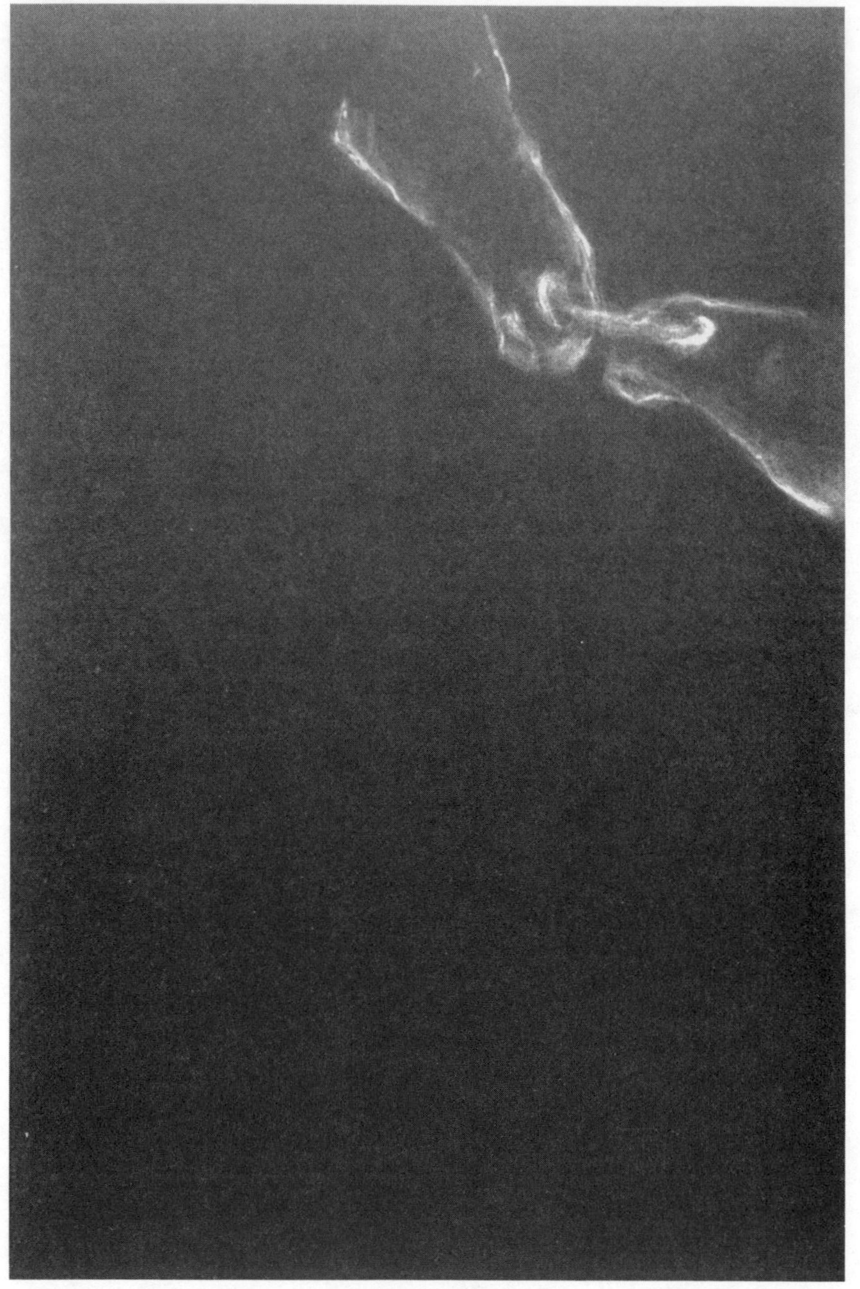

HORSES' BREATH

Had never known blue air's
faded fascination had never
seen or went anywhere never
was a horse unridden but on
one proverbial frosty morning
whilst going to the kitchen
I thought of our lives' opaque
addiction to distances to
all the endless riders etched
on those faint horizons and
nuzzled the mere idea of you —
swapped breath. *Oh love, be true!*

The White Blackbird

James Purdy

EVEN BEFORE I REACHED my one hundredth birthday, I had made several wills, and yet just before I put down my signature

Delia Mattlock

my hand refused to form the letters. My attorney was in despair. I had outlived everyone and there was only one person to whom I could bequeath much, my young godson, and he was not yet twenty-one.

I am putting all this down more to explain the course of events to myself than to leave this as a document to posterity, for as I say, outside of my godson, Clyde Furness, even my lifelong servants have departed this life.

The reason I could not sign my name then is simply this: piece by piece my family jewels have been disappearing over the last few years, and today as I near my one hundred years all of these precious heirlooms one by one have vanished into thin air.

I blamed myself at first, for even as a young girl I used to misplace articles, to the great sorrow of my mother. My great grandmother's gold thimble is an example. You would lose your head if it wasn't tied on, Mother would joke rather sourly. I lost my graduation watch, I lost my diamond engagement ring, and, if I had not taken the vow never to remove it, my wedding ring to Will Mattlock would have also taken flight. I will never remove it and will go to my grave wearing it.

But to return to the jewels. They go back in my family over two hundred years, and yes, piece by piece, as I say, they have been disappearing. Take my emerald necklace—its loss nearly finished me. But what of my diamond earrings, the lavaliere over a century old, my ruby earrings—oh, why mention them? For to mention them is like a stab in the heart.

I could tell no one for fear they would think I had lost my wits, and then they would blame the servants, who were I knew blameless, such perfect, even holy, caretakers of me and mine.

But there came the day when I felt I must at least hint to my godson that my jewels were all by now unaccounted for. I hesitated weeks, months before telling him.

About Clyde now. His Uncle Enos told me many times that it was his heartbroken conviction that Clyde was somewhat retarded. "Spends all his time in the forest," Enos went on, "failed every grade in school, couldn't add up a column of figures or do his multiplication tables."

"Utter rot and nonsense," I told Enos. "Clyde is bright as a silver dollar. I have taught him all he needs to know, and I never had to teach him twice because he has a splendid memory. In fact, Enos, he is becoming my memory."

Then of course Enos had to die. Only sixty, went off like a puff of smoke while reading the weekly racing news.

So then there was only Clyde and me. We played cards, chess, and then one day he caught sight of my old Ouija board.

I went over to where he was looking at it. That was when I knew I would tell him — of the jewels vanishing, of course.

Who else was there? Yet Clyde is a boy, I thought, forgetting he was now twenty, for he looked only fourteen to my eyes.

"Put the Ouija board down for a while," I asked him. "I have something to tell you, Clyde."

He sat down and looked at me out of his handsome hazel eyes.

I think he already knew what I was to say.

But I got out the words.

"My heirloom jewels, Clyde, have been taken." My voice sounded far away and more like Uncle Enos's than mine.

"All, Delia?" Clyde whispered, staring still sideways at the Ouija board.

"All, all. One by one over the past three years they have been slipping away. I have almost wondered sometimes if there are spirits, Clyde."

He shook his head.

That was the beginning of even greater closeness between us.

I had given out, at last, my secret. He had accepted it; we were, I saw, like confederates, though we were innocent, of course, of wrongdoing ourselves. We shared secretly the wrongdoing of someone else.

Or was it *wrongdoing*, I wondered. Perhaps the disappearance of the jewels could be understood as the work of some blind power.

But what kind?

My grandfather had a great wine cellar. I had never cared for wine, but in the long winter evenings I finally suggested to Clyde we might try one of the cellar wines.

He did not seem very taken with the idea, for which I was glad, but he obeyed docilely, went down the interminable steps of the cellar and brought back a dusty bottle.

It was a red wine.

We neither of us relished it, though I had had it chilled in a bucket of ice, but you see it was the ceremony we both liked. We had to be doing something as we shared the secret.

There were cards, dominoes, pachisi and finally, alas, the Ouija board, with which we had no luck at all. It sat wordless and morose under our touch.

Often as we sat at cards, I would blurt out some thoughtless remark: once I said, "If we only knew what was before us!"

Either Clyde did not hear or he pretended I had not spoken.

There was only one subject between us. The missing jewels. And yet I always felt it was wrong to burden a young man with such a loss. But then I gradually saw that we were close, very close. I realized that he had something for me that could only be called love. Uncle Enos was gone, Clyde had never known either mother or father. I was his all, he was my all. The jewels in the end meant nothing to me. A topic for us — no more.

I had been the despair of my mother because, as she said, I cared little for real property, farmlands, mansions, not even dresses. Certainly not jewels.

"You will be a wealthy woman one day," mother said, "and yet look at you, you care evidently for nothing this world has to offer."

My two husbands must have felt this also. Poring over their ledgers at night, they would often look up and say, "Delia, you don't care if the store keeps or not, do you?"

"You will be a wealthy woman in time, if only by reason of your jewels," my mother's words of long ago began to echo in my mind when I no longer had them.

My real wealth was in Clyde. At times when I would put my hand through his long chestnut hair a shiver would run through his entire body.

He suffered from a peculiar kind of headache followed by partial deafness, and he told me the only thing that helped the pain was when I would pull tightly on his curls.

"Pull away, Delia," he would encourage me.

How it quickened the pulse when he called me by my first name.

Yes, we came to share everything after I told him without warning that bitter cold afternoon.

"Clyde, listen patiently. I have only my wedding ring now to my name."

I loved the beautiful expression in his hazel eyes and in the large, almost fierce black pupils as he stared at me.

"Do you miss Uncle Enos?" I wondered later that day when we were together.

"No," he said in a sharp loud voice.

I was both glad and sad because of the remark. Why I felt both things I don't exactly know. I guess it was his honesty.

He was honest like a pane of the finest window glass. I loved his openness. Oh, how I trusted him. And that trust was never betrayed.

I saw at last there was someone I loved. And my love was as pure as his honesty was perfect.

My secret had given us a bond one to the other.

In those long winter evenings on the edge of the Canadian wildlands, there was little to do but doze, then come awake and talk, sip our wine so sparingly (I would not allow him to have more than half a glass an evening), and there was our talk. We talked about the same things over and over again, but we never wearied one another. We were always talking at length on every subject—except the main one. And I knew he was waiting to hear me on that very one.

"How long has it been now, Delia?" His voice sounded as if it were coming from a room away.

At first I was tempted to reply, "How long has it been from what?" Instead I answered, "Three years more or less."

"And you told no one in all this time?"

"I could not tell anyone because for a while I thought maybe I had mislaid them, but even as I offered this excuse, Clyde, I knew I could not be mistaken. I knew something, yes let that word be the right one, something was taking my jewels. Oh, why do I say 'my'? They never belonged to me, dear boy. I never affected jewels. I did not like the feel of them against my skin or clothes. Perhaps they reminded me of the dead."

"So that is all you know, then," he spoke after minutes of silence.

I had to laugh almost uproariously at his tone. "I am laughing, dear Clyde, because you spoke so like an old judge just then.

Addressing me as a dubious witness! And dubious witness I am to myself! I accuse myself—of not knowing anything!"

"Could we go to the room where you kept them?" he wondered.

I hesitated.

"No?" he said in a forthright, almost ill-humored way.

"It's a long way up the stairs, and I have never liked that big room where I kept them. Then there are the keys. Many many keys to bother and fumble with."

"Then we won't go," he muttered.

"No, we will, Clyde. We will go."

Ah, I had forgotten indeed what a long way up to the big room it was. Even Clyde got a bit tired. Four or five or more flights.

"Well it's a real castle we live in, my dear," I encouraged him as we toiled upward.

"You must have a good heart and strong lungs," he said, and he smiled and brought his face very close to mine.

Then I pulled out my flashlight, or, as my grandfather would have called it, my torch.

"Now the next flight," I explained, "has poor illumination."

As we approached that terrible door, I brought out the heavy bunch of keys.

"Put this long key, Clyde, in the upper lock. Then this smaller key when you've unlocked the top one, place it in the lower one here."

He did it well, and we went through the door, where, of course, another bigger door awaited us.

"Now, Clyde, here is the second bunch of keys. Put the upper key to the large keyhole above, give the door a good shove and we can go in."

He fumbled a little and I believe I heard him swear for the first time. (Well, his Uncle Enos was a profane old cuss.)

We entered. There were fewer cobwebs now than when I had come in so many months before.

"See all those red velvet cases spread out over the oak table there?" I said. "In the cases were the jewels. Their jewels."

He looked around and I gave him my torch. But then I remembered there was an upper light and I turned it on.

He shut off the torch. He seemed in charge of it all, and much older than his twenty years then. I felt safe, comfortable, almost sleepy from my trust in him.

"Look there, will you!" he exclaimed.

I put on my long-distance glasses and looked where he pointed.

He bent down to touch something on the floor under the red velvet cases.

I took off my glasses and stared.

"What is it, Clyde?" I said.

"Don't you see?" he replied in a hushed way. "It's a white feather. A white bird's feather. Very pretty, isn't it?" He raised up the feather toward my trembling hand.

A strange calm descended on us both after Clyde found the white feather. At first I was afraid to touch it. Clyde coaxed me to take it in my hand, and only after repeated urgings on his part did I do so.

At that moment the calm descended on me as it had many years ago when, during one of my few serious illnesses, old sharp-eyed Doctor Noddy had insisted I take a tincture of opium.

Why, I wondered, did the glimpse of a white bird's feather confer upon both me and Clyde this unusual calm? As if we had found the jewels, or at least had come to understand by what means the jewels had been taken. I say "us" advisedly, for by now Clyde and I were as close as mother and son, even husband and wife. We were so close that sometimes at night I would shudder in my bed and words I was unaware from where they came filled my mouth.

Clyde, more than the jewels, then—let me repeat—was my all, but the jewels were important, I realized dimly, only because they were the bond holding us together.

That evening I allowed Clyde a little more than half a glass of red wine.

"The only pleasure, Clyde," I addressed him, "is in sipping. Gulping, swallowing, spoils all the real delicate pleasure."

I saw his mind was on the white feather.

He had put it on the same table the Ouija board rested on.

"We should see it in a safe place," Clyde said, gazing at the feather.

His statement filled me with puzzlement. I wanted to say, Why ever should we? But I was silent. I spilled some wine on my fresh white dress. He rose at once and went to the back kitchen and came forward with a little basin filled with water. He carefully and painstakingly wiped away the red stain.

"There," Clyde said, looking at where the stain had been.

When he had taken back the basin he sat very quietly for a while, his eyes half-closed, and then:

"I say we should put it in a safe place."

"Is there any such, Clyde, now that the jewels have been taken?"

"Just the same, I think we should keep the feather out where it is visible, don't you?"

"It is certainly a beautiful one," I remarked.

He nodded faintly and then raising his voice said, "It's a clue."

My calm all at once disappeared. I put the wineglass down for fear I might spill more.

"Had you never seen the feather before, Delia?" he inquired.

The way he said my name revealed to me that we were *confederates,* though I would never have used this word to his face. It might have pained him. But we were what the word really meant.

"I think it will lead us to find your jewels," he finished, and he drank, thank heavens, still so sparingly of the wine.

I dared not ask him what he meant.

"I think the place for the feather," I spoke rather loudly, "is in that large collection of cases over there where Cousin Berty kept her assortment of rare South American butterflies."

"I don't think so," Clyde said after a bit.

"Then where would you want it?" I said.

"On your music stand by your piano where it's in full view."

"Full view?" I spoke almost crossly.

"Yes, for it's the clue," he almost shouted. "The feather is our clue. Don't you see?"

He sounded almost angry, certainly jarring if not unkind.

I dared not raise my wineglass, for I would have surely at that moment spilled nearly all of it, and I could not have stood for his cleaning my white dress again that evening. It was too great a ceremony for ruffled nerves.

"There it shall be put, Clyde," I said at last, and he smiled.

Have I forgotten to tell how else we whiled away the very long evenings? Near the music stand where we had placed the feather stood the unused old grand piano, by some miracle still fairly in tune.

Clyde Furness had one of the most beautiful voices I have ever heard. In my youth I had attended the opera. In my day I heard all the great tenors, but it was Clyde's voice which moved me almost to a swoon. We played what is known as parlor songs, ancient, ageless songs. My hands surprised him when he saw how nimble and quick they still were on the keys. My hands surprised me, as a matter of fact. When he sang my fingers moved like a young woman's. When I played the piano alone they were stiff and hit many wrong keys.

But I saw then what he meant. As I played the parlor songs my eyes rested not only on him but on the feather. What he called—the clue.

I had suggested one or two times that now that Uncle Enos had departed, Clyde should move in with me. "There's lots of room here; you can choose what part of the house you like and make yourself at home, godson."

Whenever I'd mentioned his moving in up till then he had always pouted like a small boy. The day we found the feather I felt not only that something had changed in me, in the house, in the very air we breathed, but that something had changed in him.

As I went up to kiss him goodnight that evening I noticed that over his upper lip there was beginning to grow ever so softly traces of his beard.

"What is it?" I inquired when he hesitated at the door. He touched the place on his cheek where I had kissed him.

"Are you sure as sure can be you still want me to move my things here?" Clyde asked.

"I want you to, of course. You know that. Why should you walk two miles every day to Uncle Enos's and back when it's here the welcome mat is out?"

"You certainly have the room, don't you?" he joked. "How many rooms have you got?" he grinned.

"Oh, I've almost forgotten, Clyde."

"Forty?" he wondered.

I smiled. I kissed him again.

The feather had changed everything. I must have looked at it every time I went near the piano. I touched it occasionally. It seemed to move when I picked it up as if it had breath. It was both warm and cool and so soft except for its strong shaft. I once touched it to my lips and some tears formed in my eyes.

"To think that Clyde is going to be under my roof," I spoke aloud and put the feather back on the music stand.

Dr. Noddy paid his monthly visit shortly after Clyde had come to stay with me.

Dr. Noddy was an extremely tall man but, as if apologetic for his height, he stooped and was beginning to be terribly bent so that his head was never held high but always leaned over like he was everlastingly writing prescriptions.

This visit was remarkable for the fact that he acted unsurprised to see Clyde Furness in my company. One would have thought from the doctor's attitude that Clyde had always lived with me.

He began his cursory examination of me, pulse, listening to my lungs and heart, rolling back my eyelids, having me stick out my tongue.

"The tongue and the whites of the eyes tell everything," he once said.

Then he gave me another box of the little purple pills to be taken on rising and on getting into bed.

"And shan't we examine the young man then?" Dr. Noddy spoke as if to himself.

He had Clyde remove his shirt and undershirt much to the poor boy's embarrassment. I went into an adjoining closet and brought out one of my grandfather's imported dressing gowns and insisted Clyde put this on to avoid further humiliation.

Dr. Noddy examined Clyde's ears carefully, but his attention seemed to wander over to the music stand. After staring at it for some time and changing his eyeglasses, he then looked at Clyde's hair and scalp and finally took out a pocket comb of his own and combed the boy's hair meticulously.

"Delia, he has parted his hair wrong. Come over here and see for yourself."

I took my time coming to where the doctor was examining my godson, and my deliberateness annoyed him. But all the time nonetheless he kept looking over at the music stand.

"I want you to part his hair on his left side, not on his right. His hair is growing all wrong as a result. And another thing, look in his right ear. See all that wax?"

Dr. Noddy now went over to his little doctor's bag and drew out a small silver instrument of some kind.

"I will give you this for his ear. Clean out the wax daily, just as I am doing now." Clyde gave out a little cry, more of surprise than of pain, as the doctor cleaned his ear of the wax.

"Now then, we should be fine." But Dr. Noddy was no longer paying any attention to us. He was staring at the music stand and finally he went over to it. He straightened up as much as age and rheumatism would permit.

It was the feather, of course, he had been staring at so intently, so continuously!

He picked the feather up and came over to where I was studying the instrument he had recommended for Clyde's ear.

"Where did this come from?" he spoke in almost angry, certainly accusatory tones.

"Oh, that," I said and I stuttered for the first time since I was a girl.

"Where did it come from?" he now addressed Clyde in a tone of rage.

"Well, sir," Clyde began, but failed to continue.

"Clyde and I found it the other day when we went to the fourth story, Dr. Noddy."

"You climbed all the way up there, did you?" the old man mumbled, but all his attention was on the feather.

"May I keep this for the time being?" he said, turning brusquely to me.

"If you wish, doctor, of course," I told him when I saw his usual bad temper was asserting itself.

"Unless, Delia, you have some use for it."

Before I could think I said, "Only as a clue, Dr. Noddy."

"What?" Dr. Noddy almost roared.

Taking advantage of his deafness, I soothed him by saying, "We thought it rather queer, didn't we, Clyde, that there was a feather in the room where I used to keep my grandmother's jewels."

Whether Dr. Noddy heard this last statement or not I do not know. He put the feather in his huge leather wallet and returned the wallet inside his outer coat with unusual and irritable vigor.

"I will be back then, in a month. Have Clyde here drink more well water during the day." Then, staring at me he added, "I take it he's good company for you, Delia Mattlock."

Before I could even say yes, he was gone, slamming the big front door behind him.

Dr. Noddy's visit had spoiled something. I do not know exactly how to describe it otherwise. A kind of gloom settled over everything.

Clyde kept holding his ear and touching his beautiful hair and his scalp.

"Does your ear pain you, Clyde?" I finally broke the silence.

"No," he said after a very long pause. "But the funny thing is I hear better now."

"We always called earwax beeswax when I was a girl," I said. Clyde snickered a little but only, I believe, to be polite.

"He took the feather, didn't he?" Clyde said, coming out of his reverie.

"And I wonder why, Clyde. Of course Dr. Noddy is, among other things, a kind of outdoor man. A naturalist, they call it. Studies animals and birds."

"Oh, that could explain it then, maybe."

"Not quite," I disagreed. "Did you see how he kept staring at the feather on the music stand?"

"I did. That's about all he did while he was here."

I nodded. "I never take his pills. Oh, I did at the beginning, but they did nothing for me that I could appreciate. Probably they are made of sugar. I've heard doctors often give some of their patients sugar pills."

"He certainly changed the part in my hair. Excuse me while I look in the mirror over there now, Delia."

Clyde went over to the fifteen-foot-high mirror brought from England so many years gone by. He made little cries of surprise or perhaps dismay as he looked at himself in the glass.

"I don't look like me," he said gruffly and closed his eyes.

"If you don't like the new part in your hair we can just comb it back the way it was."

"No, I think maybe I like the new way it's parted. Have to get used to it I suppose, that's all."

"Your hair would look fine with any kind of a part you choose. You have beautiful hair."

He mumbled a thank-you and blushed.

"I had a close girl chum at school, Irma Stairs. She had the most beautiful hair in the world. The color they call Titian. She let it grow until it fell clear to below her knees. When she would let it all down sometimes just to show me, I could not believe my eyes. It made me a little uneasy. I like your hair, though, Clyde, even better."

"What do you think he wants to keep the white feather for?" Clyde wondered.

We walked toward the piano just then as if from a signal.

I opened the book of parlor songs and we began our singing and playing hour.

He sang "Come Where My Love Lies Dreaming." It made the tears come. Then he sang a rollicking sailor's song.

But things were not right after the doctor's visit.

"It's time for our glass of wine," I said rising from the piano. "We need it after old Dr. Noddy."

A great uneasiness, even sadness now came over both of us.

I have for many years had the bad habit of talking to myself or, what was considered worse, talking out my own thoughts aloud even in front of company.

Dr. Noddy's having walked off with the feather Clyde and I had found in the jewel room was the source of our discontent.

Thinking Clyde was dozing after sipping his wine, I found myself speaking aloud of my discomfiture and even alarm.

"He is making us feel like the accused," I said, and then I added more similar thoughts.

To my surprise I heard Clyde answering me, which was very unlike him.

I felt we were in some ancient Italian opera singing back to one another, echoing one another's thoughts.

"I didn't like the way he stared at us, holding the feather like it was proof of something," Clyde started up.

"Exactly, godson. The very words I was trying to express when I thought you were dozing."

"What does he aim to do with it?" Clyde raised his voice.

"And what does he mean to do with it regarding us?" I took up his point. "He acts more like a policeman or detective than a doctor where the feather is concerned."

"You take the words right out of my mouth," he spoke loudly.

"Oh Clyde, Clyde whatever would I do without you?"

"You'd do all right, Delia. You know you would." He picked up the empty wineglass and to my considerable shock he spat into it. "It's me," he said, "who wouldn't know where to turn if I wasn't here with you. I would be the one who didn't know up from down."

"With all your talents, dear boy!" I cried, almost angry he had spoken so against himself. "Never!"

"Never what, Delia? You know how I failed in school and disappointed Uncle Enos."

"Failed him, failed school! Poppycock! Then it was their fault if you did. Uncle Enos adored you. You could do no wrong in his eyes. Oh, if only he were here to tell us about the feather. And about that wretched doctor. He would set us straight."

"Now, now," Clyde said, rising, and he came over to my chair and all at once he knelt down and looked up into my troubled face.

"Does old Dr. Noddy know your jewels have disappeared?"

"I think so."

"You think so?"

"I'm sure I told him when I was having an attack of the neuralgia that they had all vanished."

"And what did he say then?"

"It's not so much what he said, he never says much, it was the way he stared at me when I said, 'All my jewels are gone.'"

"Stared how?"

"As he stared at us today when he held the feather. Stared as if I had done something wrong. As if I had done away with my own jewels."

"Oh, he couldn't think that against you, Delia."

"He thinks against everybody. He feels anybody who needs him and his services has something to be held against them. If we are ailing, then we are to blame. That's what I gather from old Dr. Noddy."

"And now, Delia," he said, rising and standing behind my chair so that I could feel his honey-sweet breath against my hair. "And now," he went on, "we have to wait like the accused in a court of law."

"Exactly, exactly. And, oh my stars, what on earth can he do with a feather, anyhow? Make *it* confess?"

We both laughed.

"I can't go to bed on all of this we're facing now," I told Clyde. "I am going to the kitchen and make us some coffee."

"Let me make it, Delia."

"No, no, I am the cook here and the coffee maker. You make it too weak. I must stay alert. And we must put Doc Noddy on trial here tonight before he can put us in the witness box and call us liars to our face."

With that I went into the kitchen and took down the jar of Arabian coffee, got out the old coffee grinder, and let Clyde (who had followed me without being asked), let *him* grind the beans.

"What a heavenly aroma," I said when our chore was finished. "And I made it with well water, of course, for as old Doc Noddy says you must drink well water religiously, dear lad."

We felt less threatened, less on trial at any rate, drinking the Arabian brew.

Then a great cloud of worry and fear descended upon me. I did all I could to conceal my feelings from my godson.

The source of my fear was, of course, who else but Doctor Noddy.

I recalled in the long heavy burden of memory that Dr. Noddy was nearly as old as I, at least he must have been far into his eighties at this time. But it was not his age which weighed upon me. It was the memory of Dr. Noddy having been accused a half century or more ago of practicing hypnotism on his patients. And also being suspected of giving his older patients a good deal of opium. But the opium did not concern me now, has indeed never worried me. He only gave it in any case to those of us who were so advanced in age we could no longer endure the pain or the weight of so many years, so much passed time.

No, what gave me pause was hypnotism, if indeed he ever had practiced it. His taking away the feather had brought back this old charge. But my godson sensed my sorrow. He watched me with his beautiful if almost pitiless hazel eyes.

At last he took a seat on a little hand-carved stool beside me. He took my right hand in his and kissed it.

"You are very troubled, Delia," he said at last. He seemed to be looking at the gnarled, very blue veins on the hand he had just kissed.

"I am that," I said after a lengthy silence on my part.

"You don't need to say more, Delia. We understand one another."

"I know that, godson, but see here, I want to share with you all that is necessary for me to share. I want you to have everything you deserve."

"I don't deserve much."

"Never say that again. You don't know how precious you are, Clyde, and that is because you *are* perfection."

He turned a furious red and faced away from me.

"Let me think how I am to tell you, Clyde." I spoke so low he cupped his ear and then he again took my hand in his.

"I can see it's something you've got to share."

"Unwillingly, Clyde, so unwillingly. Perhaps, though, when I tell you, you won't think it's worth troubling about."

He nodded encouragement.

"Clyde, years ago before even your parents were born, before the days of Uncle Enos, Dr. Noddy was charged with having practiced hypnotism on his patients.

Clyde's mouth came open and then he closed it tight. I thought his lips had formed a cuss word.

We sat in silence for a lengthy while.

"That is why his taking away the feather has worried me."

"And worries me now," he almost gasped.

"My worry over the white feather finally recalled the charge he had hypnotized some of his patients."

"But what is the connection," he wondered, "between a bird's feather and hypnotism?"

"I don't know myself, Clyde. Only I feel the two have a connection we don't understand."

He smiled a strange smile.

"We must be calm and patient. Maybe nothing will happen at all and we will resume our old quiet evenings," I said.

He released my hand softly.

Looking into his face, yes, I saw what I had feared. My trouble had fallen upon him. And so that long evening drew to its close.

For a whole month we could do nothing but wait in suspense for Dr. Noddy's return. Now that I come to think of it, how happy I would have been if there had been no Dr. Noddy! Yes, I do think and believe that had he never appeared out of the fog and the snow and the bitter winds, Clyde and I would have been happy and without real sorrow forever. Dr. Noddy, having found the clue, the feather, began to dig and delve, uncover and discover, sift evidence, draw conclusions and then shatter all our peace and love along with our parlor song evenings and Clyde's solos on the Jew's harp. All was to be spoiled, shattered, brought to nothing.

But then, as someone was to tell me much later (perhaps it was one of the gypsy fortune-tellers who happen by in this part of the world), someone said to me, *"Had it not been Dr. Noddy, there would have been someone else to have brought sorrow and change into your lives."*

"Then call it destiny, why don't you?" I shouted to this forgotten person, gypsy or preacher or peddler or whoever it was who made the point. Oh well, then, just call it Dr. Noddy and be done with it.

"In our part of the world, nature sometimes is enabled to work out phenomena not observed by ordinary people," Dr. Noddy began on his next visit, sounding a little like a preacher.

Dr. Noddy had tasted the wine Clyde had brought him from the cellar even more sparingly if possible than was our own custom. (I had felt the physician needed wine to judge by his haggard and weary appearance.)

To my embarrassment he fished out a piece of cork, tiny but, as I saw, very distasteful to him.

"Fetch Doctor a clean glass," I suggested to Clyde.

Dr. Noddy meanwhile went on talking about nature's often indulging in her own schemes and experiments, indifferent to man.

"She in the end can only baffle us. Our most indefatigable scholars and scientists finally admit defeat and throw up their hands to acknowledge Her inscrutable puissance."

I looked into my wineglass as if also searching for pieces of cork. Clyde had meanwhile brought Dr. Noddy a sparkling clean glass. He had opened a new bottle and poured out fresh wine.

"Dr. Noddy was saying, Clyde, whilst you were out of earshot, that Nature is an inscrutable goddess," I summarized the Doctor's speech.

"Yes," Clyde answered and gave me a look inviting instruction. I could only manage a kind of sad sour smile.

"The feather," Dr. Noddy began again, pulling it out now from his huge wallet, "is one of her pranks."

Clyde and I exchanged quick glances.

"But we should let Clyde here expatiate on Dame Nature's hidden ways and purposes. Your godson was known, from the time he came to live with Uncle Enos, as a true son of the wilderness, a boon companion to wild creatures and the migratory fowl."

Clyde lowered his head down almost to the rim of his wineglass.

"Our young man therefore must have known that nearby there lived a perfect battalion of white crows, or perhaps they were white blackbirds!"

At that moment Clyde gave out a short stifled gasp which may have chilled Dr. Noddy into silence. To my uneasiness I saw Dr. Noddy rise and go over to my godson. He took both Clyde's hands and held them tightly and then slowly allowed the hands to fall to his sides. Dr. Noddy then touched Clyde's eyes with both his hands. When the doctor removed his hands, Clyde's eyes were closed.

"Please tell us now," Dr. Noddy moved even closer to Clyde, "if you know of the birds I am speaking of."

"I am not positive," Clyde said in a stern, even grand tone so unlike the way he usually spoke. He kept his eyes still closed.

"You must have known there were white crows or white blackbirds, what some who delve into their histories call a sport of nature."

"I often thought," Clyde spoke musingly and in an almost small-boy voice now, "often would have sworn I saw white birds in the vicinity of the Bell Tower."

"The Bell Tower!" I could not help but gasp. The Bell Tower was one of the many deserted large buildings which I had long ago sold to Uncle Enos at a very low price.

"You see," Dr. Noddy turned to me. "We have our witness!"

"But what can it all mean?" I spoke with partial vexation. "It is so late, Dr. Noddy, in time I mean. Must we go round Robin Hood's barn before you tell us what you have found out?"

"This feather," Dr. Noddy now held it again and almost shook it in my face, "let Clyde expand upon it." The old man turned now to my godson. "Open your eyes, Clyde!" He extended the feather to Clyde. "Tell us what you think, now, my boy."

Clyde shrank back in alarm from the feather. "It could certainly be from a white crow if there is such a bird," my godson said.

"Or a white blackbird, Clyde?"

Clyde opened his eyes wide and stared at his questioner. "All I know, Delia," Clyde turned to me, "is, yes, I have seen white birds flying near the Bell Tower, and sometimes . . . "

"And sometimes," Dr. Noddy made as if to rise from his chair.

"Sometimes flying into the open or the broken windows of the Bell Tower."

"And did you ever see a white crow carrying anything in its beak when you saw it making its way to your Bell Tower?" Clyde's eyes closed again.

"I may have, sir, yes, I may have spied something there, but you see," and he again turned his eyes now opened to me, "you see I was so startled to glimpse a large white bird against the high green trees and the dark sky, for near the Bell Tower the sky always looks dark. I was startled and I was scared." Some quick small tears escaped from his right eye.

"And could those things the white bird carried, Clyde, could they have been jewels?"

At that very moment, the wineglass fell from Clyde's hand and he slipped from his chair and fell prone to the thick carpet below.

Dr. Noddy rushed to his side. I hurried also and bent over my prostrate godson.

"Oh, Dr. Noddy, for pity's sake, he is not dead, is he!"

Dr. Noddy turned a deprecatory gaze in my direction. "Help me carry him to that big sofa yonder," he said in reply.

Oh, I was more than opposed by then to Dr. Noddy, seeing my godson lying there as if in his coffin. I blamed it all on the old physician. "You frightened him, Doctor," I shouted.

I was surprised at my own angry words leveled against him. I would look now to my godson lying there as if passed over and then return my gaze to Noddy. I must have actually sworn, for when I came out of my fit of anger I heard the old man say, as if he was also in a dream, "I never would have thought I would hear you use such language. And against someone who has only your good at heart, Delia. Only your good!"

Taking me gently by the hand he ushered me into a seldom-used little sitting room. The word hypnotism seemed at that moment to be not a word but a being, perhaps *it* was a bird flying about the room.

"What I want to impart to you, Delia," the old physician began, "is simply this. I must now take action. I and I alone must pay a visit to the Bell Tower. For in its ruined masonry there lies the final explanation of the mystery."

The very mention of the Bell Tower had always filled me with a palsylike terror, so when Dr. Noddy announced that he must go there I could not find a word to say to him.

"Did you hear me, Delia?" he finally spoke in a querulous but soft tone.

"If you think you must, dear friend," I managed to reply. "If there is no other way."

"But now we must look in on Clyde," he said after a pause. At the same time he failed to make a motion to rise. A heavy long silence ensued on both our parts when unexpectedly my godson himself entered our private sitting room. We both stared without greeting him.

Clyde looked refreshed after his slumber. His faced had resumed its high coloring, and he smiled at us as he took a seat next to Dr. Noddy.

"I have been telling Delia, Clyde, that I must make a special visit to the Bell Tower."

Clyde's face fell and a slight paleness again spread over his features.

"Unless you object, Clyde," the doctor added.

As I say, the very mention of the Bell Tower had always filled me with dread and loathing. But I had never told Clyde or Dr. Noddy the partial reason for my aversion. I did not tell them now what it was which troubled me. My great uncle had committed suicide in the Tower over a hundred years ago, and then later my cousin Keith had fallen from the top of the edifice to his death.

These deaths had been all but forgotten in our village, and perhaps even I no longer remembered them until Dr. Noddy announced he was about to pay a visit there.

While I was lost in these musings I suddenly came to myself in time to see Noddy buttoning up his great coat preparatory to leaving.

"But you can't be paying your visit there now!" I cautioned him. "What with a bad storm coming on and with the freezing cold and snow what it is."

"This is one visit that should not be postponed, Delia! So stop once and for all your fussing."

He actually blew a kiss to me, and raised his hand to Clyde in farewell.

I watched him go from the big front window. The wind had changed and was blowing from a northeast direction. The sycamore trees were bending almost to the ground in a fashion such as I could not ever recall.

I came back to my seat.

"Are you warm enough, Delia?" Clyde asked with smiling concern.

"Clyde, listen," I began, gazing at him intently.

"Yes, Delia, speak your mind," he said gaily, almost as if we were again partaking of the jollity of our evenings.

"We must be prepared, Clyde, for whatever our good doctor will discover in the Bell Tower," I said in a lackluster manner.

Clyde gazed down at the carpet under his feet.

I felt then that if I were not who I was I would be afraid to be alone that night with Clyde Furness. But I had gone beyond fear.

"Shan't we have our evening wine, Delia?" he said, and as he spoke fresh disquietude began again.

"Please, dear boy, let's have our wine."

We drank if possible even more sparingly. I believe indeed we barely touched the wineglasses to our lips. Time passed in a churchlike silence as we sat waiting for the doctor's return. I more than Clyde could visualize the many steps the old man must climb before he reached the top floor of the Tower. And I wondered indeed if he would be able to summon the strength to make it. Perhaps the visit thither would be too much for his old bones.

It was the longest evening I can recall. And what made it even more painful was that as I studied my godson I realized he was no longer the Clyde Furness I had been so happy with. No, he had changed. I studied his face for a sign, but there was no sign—his face was closed to me. Then began a current of words which will remain with me to the end of my days:

"It's hard for me to believe, Clyde, our good doctor's theory that it is a bird which has taken my ancestors' jewels."

Clyde straightened up to gaze at me intently.

"Ah, but, Delia, do you understand how hard it has been for me over and again these many weeks to have to listen to your doubts and suspicions!"

"But doubts and suspicions, Clyde, have no claim upon you where I am concerned."

"No claim," he spoke, in a bitterness which took me totally by surprise. "Perhaps, Delia, not in your mind, but what about mine?"

"But Clyde, for God in heaven's sake you can't believe that I regard you as . . . " But I could not finish the sentence. Clyde finished it for me.

"That I am the white blackbird, Delia? For that is what you think in your inmost being."

Then I cried out, "Never, never has such a thought crossed my mind!"

"Perhaps not in your waking hours, Delia. But in your deepest being, in your troubled sleeping hours, Delia, I feel you think I am the white blackbird."

I could think of no response to make then to his dreadful avalanche of words launched against me. Nothing, I came to see, could dispel his thought that I considered him the thief, the white blackbird himself. My mouth was dry. My heart itself was stilled. My godson was lost to me, I all at once realized. He would never again be the young and faithful evening companion who had given my life its greatest happiness. As he returned my gaze I saw that he understood what I felt and he looked away not only in sadness but in grief. I knew then he would leave me.

Yet we had to sit on like sentinels, our worry growing as the minutes and the hours slipped by.

It was long past midnight and we sat on. We neither of us wanted more wine. But at last Clyde insisted he make some coffee, and I was too troubled and weak to offer to make it myself.

As we were sipping our second cup of the Arabian brew we heard footsteps, and then banging on the door with a heavy walking stick.

Clyde and I both cried out with relief when Dr. Noddy, covered with wet snow and carrying three parcels, stomped in, his white breath covering his face like a mask.

"Help me, my boy," Dr. Noddy scolded. He was handing Clyde three packages wrapped in cloth of old cramoisie velvet.

"And be careful, put them over there on that big oak table, why don't you, where they used to feed the threshers in summers gone by."

As Clyde was carrying the parcels to the oak table, I saw with surprise Dr. Noddy pick up Clyde's second cup of Arabian coffee and gulp it all down at one swallow. He wiped his mustache on a stray napkin near the cup!

"Help me off with my great coat, Delia, for I'm frozen to the bone and my hands are cakes of ice."

As soon as I had helped him off with his coat and Clyde had hung it on a hall tree, Dr. Noddy collapsed on one of the larger settees. He took off his spectacles and wiped them and muttered something inaudible.

Because he kept his eyes closed, I thought for a while the doctor had fallen into one of those slumbers I had observed in him before. My own eyes felt heavy as lead.

Then I heard him speaking in louder than usual volume:

"I have fetched back everything, Delia, that was missing or lost to you. And I have wrapped what I've found in scraps and shreds from the crimson hanging curtains of the Bell Tower."

His voice had an unaccustomed ring of jubilee to it.

"Bring out the first package, Clyde," he shouted the order, and as he spoke he waved both his arms like the conductor of a band.

Clyde carried the first bundle morosely and placed it on the coffee table before us.

"Now, Delia, let us begin!" Noddy snapped one of the cords with his bone pocket knife and began undoing the bundle of its coverings with a ferocious swiftness.

I felt weak as water as he exposed to view, one after the other, my diamond necklace, my emerald brooch, my ruby rings, my pearl necklace and, last of all, my sapphire earrings!

"Tell me they are yours, Delia," Noddy roared as only a deaf man can.

I nodded.

"And don't weep," he cautioned me. "We'll have no bawling here tonight after the trouble I've been to in the Tower!

At a signal from the doctor, Clyde fetched to the table even more doggedly the second package, and this time my godson watched as the doctor undid the wrappings.

"Tell us what you see," Dr. Noddy scolded and glowered.

"My gold necklace," I answered, "and yes, my diamond choker, and those are my amethyst rings and that priceless lavaliere and — oh see — my long-forgotten gold bracelet."

I went on and on. But my eyes were swimming with the tears he had forbidden me to shed.

Then the third bundle was produced, unwrapped and displayed before us as if I were presiding at Judgment Day itself.

"They are all mine, doctor," I testified, avoiding his direful stare. I touched the gems softly and looked away.

"What treasures," Clyde kept mumbling and shaking his head.

My eyes were all on Clyde rather than the treasures, for I took note again that it was not so much perhaps Dr. Noddy who had taken him away from me, it was the power of the treasures themselves which had separated my godson and me forever.

And so the jewels which I had never wanted in my possession from the beginning were returned again to be mine. Their theft or disappearance had plagued me, of course, over the years as a puzzle will tease and torment one, but now seeing them again in my possession all I could think of was the fact that their restoration was the cause of Clyde's no longer being mine, no longer loving me! I was unable to explain this belief even to myself but I knew it was the truth.

The next day Clyde, holding his few belongings in a kind of sailor's duffel bag, his eyes desperately looking away from my face, managed to get out the words:

"Delia, my dear friend, now that the weather is beginning to clear, I do feel I must be returning to Uncle Enos's so I can look after his property as I promised him in his last hours."

Had he stabbed me with one of my servants' hunting knives his words could not have struck me deeper. I could barely hold out my hand to him.

"I have, you know too, a bounden duty to see that his property is kept as he wanted me to keep it," he could barely whisper. "But should you need me you have only to call, and I will respond."

I am sure a hundred things came to both our lips as we stood facing one another in our farewell. Instead, all we could do was gaze for a last time into each other's eyes.

With Clyde's return "in bounden duty" to his Uncle Enos's, there went our evenings of wine sipping and parlor songs and all the other things that had made for me complete happiness.

I was left then with only the stolen jewels, stolen, according to our Dr. Noddy, by a breed of white blackbird known as far back as remote antiquity as creatures irresistibly attracted to steal anything which was shining bright and dazzling.

Shortly after Clyde had departed for his uncle's, I had called some world-famous jewel merchants for a final appraisal of the treasures. The appraisers came on the heels of my godson's departure. The men reminded me of London policemen or detectives, impeccable gentlemen, formal and with a stultifying politeness. As they appraised my jewels, however, even they would pause from time to time and briefly stare at me with something like incomprehension. They would break the silence then to say in their dry clear voices:

"Is nothing missing, ma'am?"

"Nothing at all," I would reply to the same question put to me again and again.

I had by then taken such a horror to the jewels and to their beauty which everyone had always spoken of with bated breath that even to draw near them brought on me a kind of fit of shuddering.

After I had signed countless pages of documents, the appraisers hauled the whole collection off to a famous safety vault in Montreal.

Then for the first time in years I felt a kind of relief that would have been, if not happiness, a kind of benediction or thanksgiving, had I not been so aware I had lost forever my evenings with my godson.

Six Poems

Alexander Theroux

JESUS AND THE CAT

Jesus in Nazareth once saw a cat
That peered from shadows of a distant past
And he knelt to touch it with joy.

It was in Egypt when a little boy
Where his family had fled that he often sat
And saw them revered like Bast.

He smiled a moment to remember at last
At the age of five near Heliopolis that
A cat was his only toy.

JONAH CONSIDERS HIS RIGHT HAND FROM HIS LEFT HAND

Falling out of lovc
becomes as delicate an act
and as necessary to attaining wisdom
in what demands it makes of grace
as the reverse of what now we feel
once called upon a different face.
Nineveh was spared, for it repented.
It was harder for Jonah to forgive
than condemn that erring city.
We are all irate prophets
and kill in the way that often
love is only pity.

Alexander Theroux

WHAT MR. AMBIDEXTRINE WAS TOLD AT CONFESSION AT THE 31ST ST. SHRINE

Any man is any sort of man,
 at some time or other.
We aren't even our own friend
 until in a disapproving way
We've *not* become our brother,
 by which I mean we're bought
And sold in that crucial way
 and found by what we sought.

CONSOLATION OF PHILOSOPHY

Why would nature choose long years
To give a creature is a riddle,
Like the turtle which appears
To relish it so little,

But how better deal with strife
With mankind proven such a dud
Than squander two-thirds of your life
In stupor in the mud?

LUCIFER IS HAUNTED BY THE ECHO OF HIS LAST GOODBYE

You made me just what I was
For what I tried hard to be
I saw was in spite not because
Of what was truly in me.

We have to be what we are
And be able to choose for this
For that can only mar
By not letting be what is.

And so what you were I saw
And chose the opposite plan
For if what in you is the law
Thank God I became what I am.

WILLOW TREE

for Peggy Lee

I find consolation in your sight,
willow by my window,
to me your lessons of the night
like a kindred soul endow,

so softly do you weep at the whim
of fickle winds when they start,
so easily you break in limb
just like a lover's heart.

When the River Runs Red

Catherine Scherer

SOME MUSCOVITE great-grandsons have great-grandmothers who were Mongolian princesses. They pride themselves that they are becoming atavistic, blood wise. Some great-grandsons give birth to their own great-grandmothers who will be Mongolian princesses.

Some great-grandsons in childhood will be impressed by the blood-glowing red of sun settings in Moscow singing in the mind's ear like music, from earlife to death to the moment of death. Some will hear clocks beating in empty rooms bared by memory. Their eyes will be drawn by the ears to the carmine red roses that circle the white of the dial. They will lick their toys tin-bare, they will lick off the promise of piebald tin ponies until the color streams in their blood yellow and red. Some rode birch horses with the bark peeled in alternate stripes and the bark will be worse than the salt bite of the white where the wood will be bitter where they will not be able to resist placing their tongues.

Some grandsons have grandmothers small and sprightly as birds. Their grandmothers have hair as yellow as the mailboxes in Munich, the ones their grandsons will hear singing to them like canaries. As village girls grandmothers could swing full pails of water from the ends of their ropelike braids. Their eyes are the same blue as the streetcars will be painted in Munich. All the streetcars in Munich will be drawn by the same piebald horse licked clean of its color years before by the childish tongues of the grandsons. The red roofs of Munich will seem in the eyes of some grandsons to reflect the sun setting all the way from Moscow. The heavens will be a glass in which the grandsons will see redly. In Munich the grandsons will say, Here I can have my childhood and eat it too. They will say it in the North German tongue of their grandmother's knee.

At the word of the grandsons long-dead great-grandmothers will turn in their graves into Mongolian princesses, becoming the only daughters of an extinct line. Strangely devised combs of ivory-silent horn catch and tangle in the straight black void of their hair. Forget-me-nots and touch-me-nots twine in the hair that no longer falls to their waists from bald skulls. The eyes decayed out of their bone-blind sockets trade in their vanished color, black for blue, and skin that would crumble to dust at a touch changes its tint to yellowish-green. Tongues keep eternal silence still but in a different language. The birth of great-grandmothers is the rebirth of grandsons who become great. It is a new blood running in their veins. Some great-grandsons will pass years in the forced labor of economics and Roman and Russian law until they feel their youth dissolving like a lump of sugar in water. But then they place their great-grandmothers in a direct line between them and the setting sun. They get drunk on optic wine, they intoxicate themselves with the fragrance of triangles, they hear the chorusing of colors like mad tubas. And they say, This I owe to my great-grandmother. It germinated in the egg inside her womb, I myself fertilized it. I am not to blame.

When some great-grandmothers were young girls their fathers, who were the lesser khans who had succeeded the greater, warred among themselves, for they were the true descendants of the blue wolf. They fought as the world was created, with violence and with the din and wrack of battle. Some khans ordered their troops by night to range themselves on the opposite bank of the river facing the enemy camp. At dawn the khans' forces rushed down to the edge of the water, shouting defiance and brandishing line-sharp swords. The enemy camp rouses in panic and a tangle of blunt fingers fumbling with buckles and drawn swords half-in half-out their scabbards. In disarray, the enemy counters the rush down to the water. As one man in a unison of slashing strokes, the khans' troops cut off their own heads with their own swords. The enemy is frozen with horror and amazement. The reserves of the khans' army fell upon the enemy from behind and slaughtered them, meeting no resistance. The river ran red with blood for hundreds of miles. Even to Moscow itself the river is running red in the days of the great-grandsons. Some people see it and cross themselves and say it is a fearful sign and an impending doom. And some people laugh and say, but don't believe, that it is only the water reflecting the sunset.

The Mongol women set to work sewing the heads of the beheaded back on their bodies. Each man they save they may take as a husband. Some Mongol princesses, as befits their rank, sew a fine seam. In the time it takes them to sew on one head the cruder women have already sewn seven or eight. But perhaps those who are destined to be great-grandmothers dally deliberately. They are not anxious to acquire one husband let alone several. What would I do with them, they say, stack them like cordwood outside the house and on cold nights bring one into my bed to thaw myself against. I am a fire unto myself, they say. But perhaps they are saving themselves to be at the disposal of their great-grandsons. In the general confusion and hurry the wrong heads are often fitted to the bodies so that many are not quite the same men they were before.

And when did all this happen, someone asks the great-grandsons. They reply, I just thought of it yesterday but it will happen a long time ago, in the time of our great-grandmothers. Or perhaps in the time of their great-grandmothers.

Some great-grandsons will be geometrical in form from time to time. They will be both circle soft and line hard. They will be in deep disappointment like a mourning. They want to be secure in some shape. They want to be, ideally, circles. Some great-grandsons pursue circles like chasing after the horizon. They think that when they are circles they will be stable and unstable, fixed and free, symmetrical and asymmetrical in the same blink of the same steadfast eye.

Some great-grandsons do not succumb. They do not become cubes. Some did.

Some great-grandsons will become, temporarily, blobs of color and set themselves adrift. They will make all the lines blur, the lines will soften and become indistinct. They will race around crazily crossing purposes in all directions at once. The lines confuse time so that the past is yet to be invented and what is invented today as history will be rewritten in the future as fairy tale. That is why great-grandmothers will be said to have said, History is written on glass.

Statements such as these tell a good deal about some great-grandsons.

In their great age great-grandmothers become full of wisdom. The actions of young girls once considered frivolous and pigheaded are recognized as prescient of the wisdom of old women. For example, some Mongolian princesses, the daughters of lesser khans, will be expected to marry heroes. Heroes inevitably present themselves in the sight of the princesses. They are men of steel, with bowels of iron, bladders of brass. They are wearisome, the princesses refuse to marry them. There appears a broad mountain of a man, flesh and blood, but with an ample behind made of burnished tin. It is his secret weapon. He challenges the other suitors and facing his rivals he turns his back on them scornfully and bending over he lets them expend their arrows harmlessly against him. The tin reflects the rays of the setting sun into their eyes blinding their aim. The princess who is destined to become a great-grandmother is content to marry him.

All Mongolian women after they marry will be expected to wear on their heads the foot of a man carved from light wood as it were a foot in length, the whole encrusted with pearls and at the top a burst of crane's feathers. Some Mongolian princesses, from pride of their destiny, refuse to wear this headdress but plait their hair in a cone-shaped knot on top of their heads. Some husbands are criticized for allowing this indulgence and for a long time sulk like mountains and then like mountains rise up and tear themselves loose from their roots and crumble into blue dust according to the shattering theory of the atom. Some Mongolian princesses, as befits women of imagination, will send all the way to Moscow for such consolation as is to be had from telescopes, clocks and monks who have been to Jerusalem. They will feed their grief on roasted melon seeds and peanuts covered with sugar paste. They will live by water shining like glass under imaging skies spreading like glass so that whatever is reflected in the water is mirrored again in the sky. The reflections doubling and meeting on the earth between water and sky create the illusion of substantial concreteness. Some Mongolian princesses then have built for themselves according to their design and desire boats delicate as eggshells with ruffled tails like fish. They have built for their pleasure ruffled towers that sit on squat haunches and on ship-lit starred nights wave pennants at the sky yoohooing, Moonfish, here we are. Some Mongolian princesses will harbor around them their daughters and their boats, and the ample semicircular bottoms of the boats will resemble the generous behinds of the daughters and the two will hardly be distinguishable when all sit down to rock, rocking like music lulling like dreams in their babies' sleep. Together they are an abstract shape, they are crystallized music and rock-candy sleep. They will not be disturbed by the questions of others: Is it washable? Does it get good mileage? Will it stand the test of time?

Some great-grandsons will spend decades staking pain on effort. Then they will blossom. Some great-grandsons will die in Switzerland and their bodies will become Swiss cheese wholly or in teeming part.

Some great-grandmothers, sleeping in their bones, will give their marrowed-out thighs to be played on like flutes, and their favorite jade necklaces and bracelets and pendants will tinkle at their sides. They will strike music from their bones and if the sound is not heard, the wind carried the silence a long way.

Pollen

Mei-mei Berssenbrugge

1

The sky and movement of clouds figure in the issue of the frame of the spring, just as
a freeze from fifty years ago figures in the tension of vegetation regarding its boundaries, now.
Touching the body, its waste and involuntary movements figure in tensions regarding her frame, relating
planets to the moon in a strip above the spring. She's talking about contained space, as if a frame were something
made in the body, that might be stepped on, but not tripped over, grass, tamarack, slippage between her family's
existence and establishing the imprecise area. She walks by. The spring reflects her looking and space around her.
Space is rejected for an internal shift of weight and balance, highly charged as sky next to the left side of
a person's face. His body is a response I get from somewhere else, as if suddenly things began telling my thoughts,
rocks, crows of vermillion, while she stays on the periphery of what I see and hear, the moon behind a cloud
its character of light of being *behind* something that will move. Everything is in the field to designate and stabilize,
the plants evenly spaced by available water. A ball of sand rolls downhill, leaving a line behind it. In-depth
seriality takes time, blur, static and transient ecological interference into a memory with the frame built in.

2
Saffron lichen under a quartz boulder uses moisture off the rock and receives light through it. The pigment
is in the ground, but the color is up, air as clear as if it were not an environment, like light in dreams,
a nonmaterial hydraulic. A storm on the horizon creates pressure changes you feel with your body.
    Your body
in a narrow corridor moves with a section of river you're watching. You add red sediment to the hydraulic.
It becomes a volume. You see his angular cheek against the sky like your shadow on muddy water. Red light
on his hair represents a sunray approaching along the line of a planet, a slanting seriality in the jetstream,
when you think there's another step, and an unexpected jolt testifies to the profile's material
and nonmaterial impingement on its surroundings, lightning's eroded fissure between nonmaterial and site.

3

The whole frame of the world moves at the edge of the person's face like a butterfly, and I move.
Rain seeks a mesh of creases and paths in the immateriality of a dark fissure, like a small theater.
Neither its mixed content nor indeterminacy confuse where the water goes. A barren panorama begins to
contain something visual that would be a critique of all the plants that will eventually construct themselves.
The distribution is my remembering them, plant to plant, like gold dust here and there. The rim moves at the edge
of the motility of a tadpole I remember in water in my hands, a way of relating presence to the absence
of a containment, assuming memory registers in its own contour and weight, some contour of the living material,
extending it. Between two people occurs a kind of triangulation of their two outlines in the panorama.
Waterflow would critique how the image falls out, like navigating in a car down alluvial fans in Utah.

4

Part of sunlight reaches the earth in parallel rays, but other light scatters against the air, until ambient
at every point between earth and sky. An orange cliff holds the light, concave and convex from wind,
as between alive and not alive, the boundary of the person touching you, as if the person were moisture
leaving the air, skin's respiration. You would hold her like pollen in air, gold and durable, more like
a dry spring that continues holding the sky. The human body, touching it, its involuntary movements figure
in tensions regarding its boundaries. She saw light on the mesa, neon fur, not really seeing a depth,
but one thing next to another. He proposes a neon script of the memory as the curvature of the horizon,
this limitless nature on which he will not tolerate a human sign.

5

The air is sticky with moisture and heat. It feels like a decomposition, strings of protein, a wound
healing in my daughter's chin. Air absorbs heat from the wound. The moth's imitation of a hummingbird
absorbs the bird's beauty in the shadows in the honeysuckle. A web or grille opens out from within me,
rather than starting just beyond my step, the distance allowed in front of another person.
Here is a riparian environment of flowering cacti at the edge of a stream, barrel cactus, cholla, saguaro.
The female mates with the male moth inside a yucca flower. Time is involved in strands hanging from a glowworm,
where light from the sun to the decomposition is ambient and so dense, it pushes in when you push against it.
Pollen condenses to mottled light on the ground. Assuming the sense of an activity links to
the frame of its experience, weaknesses in the framing process make our sense of what's going on vulnerable.
If the apparent frame *is* the frame, she directly expresses her underlying qualities. Symbolization is not involved,
as you would symbolize the edge of his face a structure for admitting the sky, a limitless seriality
between the person standing in front of you alone, though nothing is disconnected in the world,
your memory of a person casting strands across an unfixed wild space sticky with pollen,
and the moving frame of a child's hand in the collapsed chest cavity of an animal beside a barrel cactus
crowned with magenta flowers, how it stands in the world. The top is where growing crosses into the real.
The child turns toward an imaginary animal.

Red Banner's Whereabouts

Nathaniel Tarn

—for Robert Kelly

Now where is my red banner moving to
on this electric wind—hotter than ever day
can be remembered in these parts—or on this moon,
against the blacking out of hope,
our certainty that to be happy is to share
in the belief of one another's happiness?
    Voices all around us on these winds,
        as if in a battle of flowers
            on a coast used to be fabled for joy.
    Simple acceptances: I give, I take, you take . . .
            I have given to the limit of my shame,
        to the name you gave it, saying: yes, take,

but we are losing ourselves in the competition,
unable any longer to distinguish our own message:
    edge is serrated,
    we cut our tongues alone
        on the extremities of our own truth. Where
is my banner gone, or going where, that fire,
        as we sink down the mountain
into earth's bones?

    Presage of a body so huge
it is impossible to grasp it with the mind
unless you move mind up, by some mechanism,
set of jumped steps it has never experienced:
    so that ant is dog-sized,
        star sits, a diamond in your hand,

earth's bones shift to another focus
of such high dividend
terror blackens your teeth sudden as fire,
floods in your mouth sudden as waterfall.

To go down the great spine
as if the middle country had been lost aeons ago,
paradise preserved there,
locked between major arteries, invisible from them,
leaving all other voices on those arteries,
jazzing and jabbering along them,
my poor, sad, saturated nation!
But on that center, farmed for beauty alone,
the voice you looked to die with might reappear,
sound again, soar contented.

And no matter
they ran out of names to name the mountains with
so that three giants in a row
are coiffed with the titles of
three pint-sized colleges back east
as if the west had whelmed its iconographers!

Clouds still roll above these storm kings –
"blancas" as the fathers called them –
from their snow veils:
don't let the tongueless fuck with them,
force them from pastures out to highways
where they'll lose voice which on mind depends.

Oh where is my red banner moving to
wavers so close to my face in the home gardens
I cannot see it – nor can it see me
(as they once said "to see/to know"
being the ultimate in sapience)
but now, among these foreign voices, as I turn
to gain release, there is its move from wall to wall,
flaring against the white –

and, *there*, I witness it,
savage parade again.
And might *you* not? This voice affirms it.
To begin again, greatest hardship.
And what if you . . . ? No: take the air.
Rememorize. Gold flowers/fruit.

If you but knew that land!
I buy myself a music,
purchase permission here of you,
dear friend and that,
to walk once more, as if angelkind,
in the garden of language –
where is my banner now
to go before me: revolution,
no longer mother – everbride
something I can depend on,

abides like city parks do, in childhood cities
prolific shops, in childhood cities,
where the books came from, cacti, stamps perhaps:
I don't remember now –
when uncle Oedipus walked back into our town
once in a century . . .

It should be possible
to write forever
without pen scorching paper
all of the time,
to keep distinguishing a true volcano
from sullen lava of the dispossessed:
all of these voices, breaking silence singly
(and all at once and cacophonously)
which will never empower
one midnight courier.

Promise like shards of glass on a broken floor.
  Can we start out again?
    Slide down the mountain's breastbone
into the gully where they build a town,
  re-build a whole old town
in which to gamble the new?
  They'll bring up from the highway, east *and* west,
televised players, chips and strumpets,
  deejays' asses, dank trombones.
      It is imperative to get beyond
  this cancer of the language. Can we leave?
Keep to the central road back to our home
  with the red banner forward on the hood,
      letting them know who's coming?

Five Poems

Rosmarie Waldrop

THE VITAL KNOT

Applied to the destruction of cerebral parts. Signified weakness. Pulled the strings of his own puppet. A whir of cicadas emerged into the dream. A dripping faucet. All his life he had wanted a bicycle. Odd or even bodies of women.

Parts that excite. Sensibility wilted under the burden of response. An earlier state of things. Small like the start of a conversation. A gift for misgivings. Barely had he heard the first chords when he stopped eating.

Luminous motions. Cerebral lobes. Will, see, hear, remember, feel, annihilate time. A word dedicated to chance embraces, the inertia inherent in organic life. More fingers than he needed at the pleasure level still does not mean he recognized. A just-so story. The effect of music on animals.

The system was nervous. A ghost of himself, beset by unconsidered notions of the self. It took all of Mahler's rare talent to write his bad music. And now and then stomp, keeping time.

A point between the parts of feeling and the parts of movement, between flesh and mirror. Without the least guile, with all the conservative nature of living substance. He was all rhythmic agitation. The risk of losing not only speed, but his struggle to deceive himself.

A point very much like the collar between the stem and root of vegetables. Impressions must come here to be perceived. The rain, to beat down. Sincerity, to be interrupted. Suddenly women. Hooded crows perched on telegraph poles called to mind examples from animal life.

Rosmarie Waldrop

PLEASURE PRINCIPLE

Of course it's not easy to believe in your own dream. The working of instinct near water. Not orchards. Not apples or pears. Not nowadays. I don't know how psychoanalysis has no hesitation on how dark the night can get. The world, which is unfinished, occupying more and more of the sky.

Emotion as unpleasurable tension, the high passage of the moon. The laundry. Sensitivity won't do it. Therefore and quite often we lie down in stubbled fields. The voice of the cicada. Tells nothing.

Any day lies thick in the garden I propose to enter. Then fills with secret rivers that darkness feeds on. Lapsed sense of history. No massacre. The cicadas relentlessly.

It doesn't matter if your feet are small. When you're asleep. The fruit trees are enormous. A motor idles in the foreground. If, with quicker travel, things did indeed turn out according to one's wildest. If a child could be born from something not a mother.

The circumstance that the wife occupies the inner room and rarely if ever comes out is called the pleasure principle. In certain societies. Suddenly made clear by the cicadas. The meaning of life, absolutely. Distinguished from the now moonless garden.

And hooded with fabric like mirrors not in use. And like appearance refusing itself. A pleasure that cannot be felt as such to transcend becoming strange.

An orchard in the foreground. With beginnings of unease immediately behind.

Rosmarie Waldrop

LOCALIZATION

That the propensity to steal has its own organ. Cerebral parts. Clean feet. Default: an apple tree all by itself. Explanation beside the joint, almost as far as the superciliary ridge. Fell into step. Fell into the hands. Hot weather firmly implanted in the pelvis.

Extending from the organ of cunning to unpleasant. Mere children of nature. We know unpleasant equals real life. Straw, rags, wood. Firmly focused on infinity without an inch to spare. Using the speech of other people, forgetting too much delight. The scissors must keep moving. Apples, apples and apples.

Overcome by the unfortunate impulse, and at such a pitch. In love, in a black dress, not, indeed, in opposition, in the third person. Once the fear of flying catches in the spleen, a fierce need to sharpen scissors.

Propensity followed him into the cloister. In the name of science. To solve a powerful riddle by following the mistake into someone else's dream just as the wind comes up. Assault on the senses. Inflections, calm sumptuous syllables. Or barks, snorts, trumpets, roars, grows, rumbles. A condition called must.

She had looked in too many mirrors to experience experience as experience. A bite from the apple wrapped in snake. Nor can novelty, the condition of enjoyment, be denied her clandestine dimension. A mystery of pyramids and low-frequency calls. Surrounded on three sides.

The foot has its callus, but all creatures defend their nests. Innate adolescence. Risking everything, even intelligence. A riddle that distracts. Desperate or settling on a pronoun other than I. An unease with scissors until put in the pocket.

Rosmarie Waldrop

OUTERMOST

Beginning with: bodies move. "Carry themselves adversely." No image: mechanical concussions, railway disasters, the terrible war. Hard down to the payment. The living daylights.

Law of inertia. The puppet master straightens the most bewildering neuroses. To be swallowed red, but temporary. Wealth of motor symptoms approaching hysteria. The elephant's extremely sensitive trunk. The empty space inside the blind man now slated for demolition. Meticulous cross sections of muscle fiber.

If something is a body then it moves. Large populations. In front of trains. Separate paths to silence. Seeing, an involuted signal in the blind man's lungs. Or rather, vertical. Fright, fear, anxiety improperly used as synonyms for beginning, middle and end. And digest barely half of the rough forage devoured.

Does the proposition have to be expressed in the form "if-then"? If we know the puppet's imitation is next to naked. The train station behind damage. Though an actual injury works as a rule against the birth of signs, the subtle blasphemy. Shoes, strings, sticks, stones, consequences and graffiti. Gestation period up to 22 months.

Does it have to be expressed? In brief? In kilter? The light shut down tight. Useful knowledge: Sanskrit texts cast elephants almost exclusively in a military role. Beginning with lost to impact. Mysterious adjectival energy. Swinging our arms while taking trains. We would hold on to blindness.

They will collide. Mating dance. Derailed trains. The terrible war. Later conceiving a child among run-down obstacles, wills, warnings. All that is left of inexplicably scattered is the child's sexual exploration. Pulling the string again and again. Just as the neck thickens into data.

But nobody would put it this way. Such harsh foreclosure. Such primary color. Such fatal complication of extremes. Kids on bicycles. Trains. But the outermost surface has ceased to have the structure of living matter, has become to some degree inorganic and resistant to the stampede of stimuli.

Rosmarie Waldrop

TO WIT A VERY SMALL GLAND

Thought of the soul as joined to the whole body. Owing to the disposition of organs. Only afterwards he realized there was no map above the neck, no sin below the navel. Taboo equations. It was warm, the cortical layer without protection. Though if we displace the meaning of life inward in the persistent manner of a blind person, we are too. Without protection? At the bottom of thought.

Owing to the disposition of organs — the organs of the soul — if any one be removed the extreme heat of the sun floods the threshold. Insistent echo of eternity. Somewhere else. Instincts, representatives of bodily forces, he explained in passing. Even hours after waking up words from the dream invade our long childhood.

The dream enters the body as dream and hollows it for the soul. Only hours after waking up he realized and seemed suddenly older. Hesitant to penetrate the grassfire, decipher the mail, stress copyright. Lid effect. Still pressing forward with bruised knees, in the wake of eyes, like thinking without interruption in order to carry something back into sleep.

Only afterwards he realized that we can't conceive of half a soul. Any more than ignore nakedness. Bifurcation. Rain too enters the body. As rain. Unconscious point of impact. Pressing it home, which means warm claustrophobia.

No relation to extension, he explained in passing. Not smaller because some moisture of the body. Not inconsolable. Not naked. Not above. Owing to the disposition of organs, the body dreams with its tongue. With the persistence of a blind person. The eyes are thinking something else. Does this cause vertigo? Color separation.

Not the whole brain, he explained in passing, but its uppermost part. "This." Inasmuch as it is one, with enough anxiety to qualify as sexual. And the other parts all of them double. Warm without protection bound in flesh. Only afterwards he realized a person might still need to climb a mountain, if only in a promise, in excess.

UNFINISHED BUSINESS

Excerpts from Novels-in-Progress, with Introductions by the Authors

Robert Antoni
Carole Maso
Jim Lewis
Keith Waldrop
Jessica Hagedorn
David Foster Wallace
Janice Galloway
Paul Gervais
Leslie Scalapino
Paul West
Gilbert Sorrentino

From Blessèd is the Fruit

Robert Antoni

We are two and we are one. But then, there is nothing really strange in dreams.

—Jorge Louis Borges

The duality of dreams, acknowledged by Borges and Freud, is integral to my novel-in-progress. I had been thinking about this novel for several years; what I could not come up with was the form, which is always my starting point. I knew that there were two voices, two stories. One belonged to my great aunt, the other to the Barbadian maid who had raised me since infancy (she had actually worked for my aunt before she came to live with us). I also knew that these two stories had to be told together, *at least during the dream sequence. I thought of alternating chapters, of alternating sections, even of alternating pages. Nothing seemed quite right. Then I had my own dream.*

I dreamt that I was reading the book I wanted to write. I held it in my hands (I dreamt it in hard cover), opened to somewhere near the middle. What I saw on the page was this: two lines of type and a space, two lines and a space, two lines and a space . . . and so on down the page. Each line told a different story, in a different voice. They were the two voices I knew, but it was up to me to choose which story I wanted to follow, skipping alternate lines. Sometimes my eye slipped, and I read the line below; sometimes I'd catch a glimpse of a few words written on the line above, and my attention would be drawn to the other *story. No matter how hard I tried, I could not keep the two stories separate, and I was always somehow conscious of the other story being told. I remember saying to myself:* That's exactly what you've been looking for! But by the time you wake up you'll have forgotten the whole thing! *Which was exactly what happened.*

A few days later a composer friend invited me to a recital. He and two other composers were presenting new pieces. Sometime during the performance one of the composers wheeled in two sets of speakers, two sets of hi-fi equipment, and he set them up on either side of the stage. He announced the title of his piece as something or other recorded on two tracks, *and he turned on both sets of equipment. It was street sounds — car horns and brakes and bootsteps on the sidewalk — and it was pretty awful. But in the middle of all the noise my dream came back to me. When I got home I went straight to my desk. After a couple minutes I'd come up with this:*

L(V)   L   L/V:V/L   V   V(L)

My novel-in-progress is called Blessèd is the Fruit, *and it is set on the West Indian island of Corpus Christi. It is told in the voices of two island women, both in their mid-fifties: one is a black maid, Velma, and the other is her white mistress, Lila. Velma comes from dire poverty, near starvation, and Lila is the descendant of the once wealthy British plantocracy. Not long after Lila's husband leaves, Velma comes to work for her. The two women have lived alone for thirty years in a large old colonial house, which is rotting and falling down around them. They have become dependent upon one another, though they do not quite realize the extent of their dependency when the book opens. For several months Velma has kept secret from her mistress the fact that she is pregnant, even at her advanced age. Velma knows that should Lila discover her pregnancy, she will send her home, back to poverty and starvation. Velma "binds her belly" every morning to hide the pregnancy, and she makes several unsuccessful attempts to abort the child — from the pharmacist's drugs to bush-medicine to spells of "obeah" magic. Finally Velma makes a desperate, brutal attempt to abort the child with a wire coat-hanger. Lila discovers her wounded, near dead from loss of blood; she carries Velma upstairs into her own bedroom (Lila's private sanctuary, where Velma has never been allowed entrance in all the years she has lived in the house). Lila brings a doctor who treats Velma's wounds.*

The story is about these two women's acceptance of the child as their own; their acceptance of responsibility for the child as its figurative parents. When the novel opens (and when it closes) the two women are lying together in the big bed in Lila's room. Velma is sleeping peacefully after the doctor's sedative. Lila is awake, and the first third of the novel is told in her voice, her monologue. She tells of her life with Velma, of her life with her husband, and of her childless, failed marriage. Finally Lila tells of her childhood as the daughter of a sugar plantation owner, including the failure of the sugar industry in the Caribbean. (Lila's portion of the novel proceeds backward chronologically.)

For the middle third of the book Lila falls asleep, and the narrative is subsumed by the simultaneous dream of Velma and Lila: the voices merge, cross over. This dream, however, is really the fetus' dream—the fetus' dream of its figurative parents who are these two women. (This fictional device actually has a medical precedent: physicians report that they have identified REM movements in unborn infants, so fetuses do in fact dream.)

Velma awakens, and the final third of the novel is told in her voice. Velma's story begins with the poor village where she was raised by her grandmother and several aunts (not knowing her father, and scarcely knowing her mother). She tells of her brutal treatment by various men and, one by one, of the deaths of her four children (the excerpt that follows comes from this time in her life). It is only after Velma reaches utmost despair and attempts suicide that she is given the servant's job with Lila, and she leaves her village to work for this wealthy white woman. Velma's narrative proceeds chronologically toward the present—the scene with which the novel opens—with these two women lying together for the first time in Lila's large bed, and the baby still alive in Velma's womb.

THAT BIG POT, dream of that pot! Big black belly-pot, and had on two handles. Dream it there in the middle the kitchen. Dream it *bubbling,* with fire kicking below and smoke rising to top. That was in Granny Ansin house away up in the country, big old board-house where I was born and grow up in. That house was standing pon posts—we did call them groundsils—with the underneath open and the kitchen at the back. And the kitchen, I could remember the kitchen was dirt floor, earth. The bedrooms and the parlor-room was board floor, but the kitchen earth, and it had in fire. So you cook to the fire with wood. Good hard big-wood, like old electric poles government did cut down and sell to poor people in the country. Cause wasn't no electricity in the country, not at that time, but we did had them poles to make the fire with. And that kitchen so rotten you didn't need for no chimney. Child, smoke just go through the holes! Or go anyplace, cause at that time you just couldn't care less. You know, roof build with galvanize, and that galvanize so rusty and rotten, smoke just go through the holes. So that fire kicking, it *kicking,* and when that big black pot come off and carry out in the yard—like a big pork-stew with green-fig, cassava, carrot, dumplings—child, feed everybody, that one pot! All the family and all the neighbors standing round the circle with plates in we hands holding, and that big black pot in the middle bubbling, still, and steam rising and food smelling so *good,* and granny dishing it out and we all eating! We *eating!* Everybody! Dream of food, dream of that pot!

Food, plenty food, in them days. Cause in them days everybody would add little something to the pot. Everybody in the house, living pon the street, throw in little something inside the pot. Like my grandmother, she working estate, one day she bring home big sack of potatoes, next day yams, pigeon peas. My aunt she working in town she bring home piece of meat from town, or buy big fish head at the docks. You know everybody add little something. Like you cleaning you field today you got onions, throw in some onions. Tomorrow might be eddoes, cassava. You hear of somebody picking green-figs, you go and they give you hand of green figs, or plantains. Everybody add what little they got, and we could *all* get food like that. Cause that pot cook regular, cook every night. That's one thing you could depend is that pot, in them days.

But the thing I did love the most, well my tan husband, he uses to raise about five-six pigs in the yard, Uncle Charpie. He just build a shack-fen, little fen, so when things get hard up we just kill a pig. Sell a pig. Keep some the pork for weself and sell the rest. Kill the pig early morning, that way the pork could sell fresh. That's when I did get the blood too! Ain't nobody tell me to do that. I just feel, I just say, *Well that thing must be good!* I did only reach six-seven years then, no more. But I could remember watching at Charpie and that blood and saying to myself, *Well that thing must be good!* One day I just catch it up and I cook it. You know, when Charpie stick the pig, I just run and hold my tot beneath—we did call it a tot cause it ain't got no handle, like a sweetmilk tin, or cornbeef—we did call it a tot at home at that time. So I run quick and I hold my tot beneath the pig neck, where the hole is, where he get stick. You know they would have that pig holding, and that blood just do like a siphon, out from he neck. I just collect it up and I carry and I season. Put in black pepper, things growing in the yard, thyme and different things, and fresh like that. Just snatch off some, and you know, chip it up in the same tot. I stir with a fork and hold it right there by the fire, cause they would have that fire build outside in the yard, with the big drum that cut to hot the water to scald the pig. I hold my tot right there, cook my blood right there. When it cook it get hard, but I keep stirring stirring and it come just like scramble egg. Now I sit down and I *eat!* I sit down and I eat and I ain't giving nobody none! Cause that thing did taste so *good!*

Then one time I remember I did get scared. You know, they got that pig there holding, and when he stick, when Charpie stick the pig, that pig *kick!* Child, he kick! One time I say, *Well what now if that pig kick you upside in you head? That pig could kill you like that! Kill you dead like that, one kick!* I was scared now. My Tantee May tell me, she say, "Vel, you ain't going for you blood?" I say, "No." She say, "You going let you blood waste out pon the ground? Waste out pon the ground like that?" I say, "Let Charpie collect it up." My tan say, "You know he ain't going collect it up. You know he ain't. He going let it waste out pon the ground is all." I didn't answer she nothing, I just say, *Well it would have to waste out then. Cause I ain't going by that pig to get kick upside in my head!* We was all standing there round the big fire, in the dark, waiting for Charpie to stick the pig. But when I see he stick, and Charpie stand up with he face sweating and reflecting in that fire – when I see that blood coming out and wasting pon the ground – I just couldn't keep way! Just couldn't keep way! I *had* to run with my tot and collect up, every *drop* was left in that pig!

So in that old house was living my granny, my Tantee Elvira and she six girls, me and my sister. Wasn't no men. My Tantee May she was living to she little house by the side, but she husband wasn't living with she, that nasty old Charpie. He just uses to come home visit pon evenings. Only Clive was living with my tan, she boy-child, but sometimes I uses to sleep over by my Tantee May too. My other uncle wasn't living with we neither, Mr Bootman the Panama Man. He was living with he son Arrows in town. So that was twelve people living between the two houses: three women, nine girls, and one boy. Wasn't no men. Nor my mother wasn't living with we neither. She uses to come home must be about every, about every two weeks, just to see how things going, catch little something to eat. She, you know it look like she just hide out and get me before she know anything, what is what. She must of been about fourteen-fifteen when she had me, still young. So she never tell me nothing about my father. I only get to know he when

I reach about seven years. I hear somebody say how this man is my father, so I just go at he house and I knock the door. I say, "You is my father?" He say, "Yes. I is you father." So we just get introduce like that. And from that day we keep in contact, but not—you know he could never claim me for he own, put me under he name—he done married and have he children and he house proper. He could never claim no hands pon me. But I did love he still. I did feel that I could *call* he for my father—I could say that, to myself, in the secret like—even though I didn't have no father in truth. My father could never claim no hands pon me. He was a joiner, uses to make furnitures. But my father wasn't my mother kind of man, and that's the reason why my mother never like me. Cause I look just like my father. I dark like he. I carry on like he, looks and ways.

My mother didn't like me nor my sister. My sister she for somebody else, she never even find out who. My mother only like my brother of we three. He living by she, so he would get he food and he clothes, my mother uses to fix my brother food and he clothes for he. But me and my sister, we got to scramble for weself. Eat what we could eat, you know, survive how we could. I say, *Why my mother don't like me? What wrong with me?* I go cross to my Tantee May, I ask her, "What happen that my mother don't like me? Cause I ain't got no father or what?" She say, "Child, you ain't to worry you head with that." She say, "You mother going regret the day she ain't know unna. You, and you sister." But still I couldn't stop from thinking about that, how the family make and everything. I was still studying about what it is to make the family.

Then one time my Tantee May went in childbed to have baby. She did went to have the baby home, as people did uses to do in them days, all we gather round the bed with the mid, some standing to the parlor front-room. Granny Ansin was there, Miss Pantin was there, Tantee Elvira, Dorine, Ellis—Mr Bootman the Panama Man was there with he son Arrows—and mummy was there with she boyfriend, that Andrel Bay Downs, with me there and my sister and my brother. And Tantee boychild Clive was there with she husband, that old Charpie. So the men they was most in the parlor-room firing waters, and we was in the bedroom waiting for the birthing and eating cakes and drinking cokes. I could tell you tan little house did so full up with family it was most ready to burst! And sometimes one the neighbors from the street would drop in too—like Miss Barnet the needleworks woman—she bring a nice nilla cake and everybody take piece, all we talking and laughing and having weself a good good time for the birthing.

But then now soon as things start in, in the last minute, up and say the mid that something wrong, something wrong, and tantee must carry to the hospital in town. Mr Bootman up and gone for he big motor-car, and he was moving slow and rickety already with the waters. Tan gone in the backseat stretch out with Ansin and Miss Pantin and Tantee Elvira, and the mid she must of go too, with the men most in the front seat what could fit. So Mr Bootman tip the horn and drop a gear and the car let loose a chups of white smoke, and everybody bawl *weeeee!* with the dust raising and the children running screaming behind.

Quick so the house quiet quiet. Me one inside, so it seem—all up and gone and left me there like if they ain't notice, forget—left me there sitting pon the bench in the parlor-room eating piece of cake and crying. I was crying for my tan, cause I was so afraid for she in that hospital, and I did love she, very much. My tan give me dress, slip, hat for church, everything she give me when my *own* mother ain't give me, my tan, and I was crying for she. Cause I did think people only go in hospital when they dying, near dying, and I did afraid so bad for she in that place. I say, *Them people, you know most of them there people in hospital does dead in childbed you know? Dead straight way like that! Cause people ain't know what to do, and they carrying this person in hospital and thing. You know they can't born the child and wait to the last minute, that child kill the person! Kill my tantee!* I there sitting pon the bench in the front room, and crying, now I hear somebody like Uncle Charpie, my tan husband, hear now like Charpie calling to me from the bedroom. But he calling very quiet, call like a whisper like, say, "Vel! Vel!" like that. But I ain't move. I say, *Wait! He ain't gone? All up and gone and he ain't gone?* Charpie call again, quiet, "Vel! Vel!" But still I ain't move. Now he come out in the parlor-room—he there in he baggy old drawers, he vestshirt—and he sit down pon the bench and he pull me cross to sit pon he. Sweet Jesus! I there pon this bench sitting, and he pull me cross, on top, and he foist me down hard pon he and he start up. *Doing* pon me! Child, I could remember that there like now! I eating this cake, and crying, and he, this nilla cake in my hand turning to sticky now, like wet, and running down my arm sticky pon my wrist.

But he couldn't get nowhere. Too *small!* Eight years old! So then, so then I just get fed up. I just get fed up with he! I wasn't scared, no, not at that moment. I didn't even *know* what I did had to frighten for! I did more confuse, just get fed up. I say, *Wait! You tan sick, and what he trying to do? What he playing with you like that for?* I say, *That ain't the right way! That ain't the right way, when people crying to stop the person from crying!* I did want to run, get way. But he, then he foist me down *harder* pon he. He pull up pon my dress, pon my slip that I did wearing for that birthing. You know what he was trying? to do? You know what he was trying to do to me? intending? And me only eight years, eight years old with nobody else in the house. And all I doing is crying, crying for my tan. The most is crying. And cake in my hand wet.

Last he let me go and I take off. I run! I hide out in the canes. Cause all behind tan house was them canes, estate, and I hide out in there the whole night, most the next day too. I hide out till I see the others come back. Cause I ain't going back in that house with Charpie there, nor I ain't going inside granny house neither, not by myself. I wait till I see the others come back. They come back with Tantee May but they don't bring the baby, cause that baby dead in the hospital. But my tan don't dead, and I was so happy for that! I did feel sad for that little baby, true, but not that much. Cause they say when a baby dead like that it go straight in heaven. And I did think heaven must be full up with little babies, *full*, amount of babies dead like that. But that's the onliest thing I did know about babies, at that time, that most of them up in heaven. I didn't make no connection, with Charpie, he nastiness, nor I didn't *want* to know nothing about men neither. Just keep way from he and all the rest, best as I could.

But then in them days all the men uses to cut canes in crop season. All the young men. Cause in them days everywhere was canes canes and more canes, and all the men got to cut canes in crop season. So the children got to ask for break from school, cause we got to carry the breakfast for the men working in the field. And child, this field *far!* Must be about ten-twelve miles from where the school was. Far, real far! I ask for break, I come out at ten o'clock from school, you know when two o'clock reach I only now going back in school. I just do it for favor for my mother. She ask me to do it, so I tell she that I would do it for she. Granny pack the breakfast pon morning, and I carry it for this man, this Andrel Bay Downs. Cause I get to thinking, I did think that if maybe I could get to *know* he, little bit, and we could get to like one another, he could be more like my father. We could all be more like family then. So I tell my mother I would carry the breakfast for he, tell she I glad to do that. I had reach about ten years then, ten going on eleven.

So when I arrive in this field, I find Andrel sitting down beneath a tamarind tree, shade tree. He there catching the cool, waiting for me to bring he the breakfast. I give he the basket and he take out—was a metal bowl with stew chicken, and rice, pigeon peas, all cook together—and still hot. We did call that cook-up. He had some fruits too, was a paupau and hand of sicreyea figs, the little sweet bananas. And he had a bottle full with barbadine drink, and wrap in a damp towel that it could stay fresh like that. So he spread out the breakfast pon he shirt there beneath the tree. You know he was sitting there bareback, relaxing in the breeze. He say, "Why you don't sit down little bit catch youself a cool? Cause you know that sun going be hotting up the road to walk back now." He say, "You could keep me in company whilst I eat."

So I sit down, sit down near he in the shade of that tamarind tree. He was there sitting by heself beneath the tree, and that tree was a good distance from where the other men was. They taking they breakfast now too. And he did seem kind of lonely sitting there like that, there by heself. I did feel kind of sorry for he. So I sit down, he commence to eating he breakfast, I watching, he eating he cook-up. Then he ask me if I want some. I say, "Yes. I would take some." Cause you know that food was still warm from when granny cook it. But he tell me I must move closer. So I ain't thinking nothing, I push over sitting little closer by he. But before he give me the bowl to eat, he take up a spoonful and push it inside my mouth. I say, *Wait! What this man feeding you like that for? You ain't no baby that got to get feed.* But then when I swallow, *next* spoonful again he push inside my mouth. I say, I talk up to he now, I say, "You don't bound to feed me like that already! I's a grown person! I could eat for myself!" He say, "That's how I does like to eat." I say, "Well that's not how *I* like to eat! I like to eat food for myself, I don't like nobody to feed me!"

He put down the metal bowl now, and he take up the bottle with barbadine drink. He wrap out the towel and he screw out the lid, say, "I got a special way I does like to drink too!" And now he take up my hand—cause I was sitting there just beside he—he take up my hand and pour some the barbadine over, and some going pon the ground. Then he start to licking licking pon my hand, that white pulpy thing, he sucking pon my fingers. I pull my hand way!

I pull it back straight! I say, "Wait! You's a child? You's a child that you got to play games like that with you food?" He say, "That ain't children games, that's *adult* games," and he smiling he teeth big like that. He say, "You wait till I start in pon them figs!" You know he was lying there beneath the tree, and bareback, half sitting up and half lying down, he back resting against the tamarind trunk. Now he pour out some the barbadine drink pon he bare chest, that white pulpy thing, and smiling big, he pour it down he chest down the front of he pants. He say, "This adult games and you could lick from my chest! You could drink from my navelhole too!" I jump up! I say, "You's a *stupid* person! Throwing way good food like that!" I say, "You's a *fool!* Cause that's one thing you don't play with is food! One thing you got to respect is food! One thing!" I say, "You's a stupid person! You's *uneducated!"* And I run! I take off, leave he there laughing behind.

Next day when I give he the basket, he give me this letter that he did write. Cause I was ready to leave, take off! I was ready to run again! But he give me this letter, he say, "Read it. This a letter that you could read it." Cause I could read good from early. So I go-long reading this letter, pon my way coming from carrying the breakfast, walking back from the field. When I reach home I give it to my granny, this letter that he write. Cause I did had enough with this man! And I know that if I show this letter to my mother, I know she would say just what it was she *do* say, say how *I* write it. Cause I could write good from early too, and she couldn't write nor read neither, my mother. So granny tell my mother how he did give me this letter, write it just so, that he did want to *frig* with me, write:

> *Dear Miss Velma,*
> *I want to frig with you. You mother wouldn't know nothing. And I would give you money every weekend that you could spend. Buy what you want.*
> *Cordial,*
> *Mr Andrel Bay Downs.*

Child, I could see that writing there like now! That crab-hand writing. I did had only about ten years, ten years is the most. Everything happen so fast, so *fast!* This woman thing and this badluck thing!

So when granny tell my mother, course she say, "That ain't true, she making up that! He ain't ask, he would never ask she that!" But then my grandmother present she the letter, and my mother couldn't answer one word. My granny say, "You think that she, you think that she could make up that? This girl left school—left Shervon and gone all out in *Henly,* to carry the breakfast for he—and this the thanks! this the thanks! that he did want! This is what he did want to do to she! And you got the nerve to say she lying!" My granny tell my mother, "You never did like these children anyway. Least the two girls. You got one child and that's you boy!" My grandmother say, "Well I ain't got much, but I going to keep them in here. The two girls. You go-long!" She tell my mother just like that. "Go-long!" And my mother went long *shameface.* So that finish with that. I did never see my mother again, after that day.

Time soon come I approaching a woman now, getting pretty, real pretty. I walking with my little mini-dress tantee give me to make the style then. I walking with my little bag, my clasp and thing. Miss Pantin, she give me little Pons, you know in them days didn't had much of cream, just Pons. Pons Cold Cream, I could remember, and powder, like Cashmere Bouquet. I could remember them too good. Miss Pantin give me little Pons, and I catch few cents from somewhere, I buy little powder, little Cashmere. And nailpolish. I hide them away secret in a little box. I had my little white shoebox, all my things wrap nice in tissue, but I didn't know what it was to be a woman yet. I did had my first menstruation, yes, but I didn't see nothing after. Just one. And I didn't know what it was even. I say, *Well maybe that come again? Maybe that's just something that come again?* I didn't know, nor didn't had nobody to explain me nothing neither. Granny Ansin, she never tell me nothing, nor my Tantee May. And I didn't talk to Tantee Elvira too much, nor my mother wasn't there no more neither. And I's the oldest girl, I didn't had no older sisters in the house, nor cousins could tell me nothing. So when I see this menstruation, I did worried, I did worried *plenty,* but then I say, *Well maybe that's just something got to happen.* I didn't make no connection, with baby, nor nothing so. I just know babies come when they come, and I did afraid for that so bad since my tantee went in hospital. Since that baby near *kill* my tantee in hospital!

So then in those days I uses to bathe in the night, go at the pipe, standpipe, we did call it a standpipe at home at that time. That pipe must of been about half-mile from where the house was, to the pitch road where the pipe was. Government put that pipe there for poor people to draw water. Cause in them days the houses didn't have in pipes, water, not the poor people. But we had a place build under the chenet tree that you could bathe private, shower-stall. Shower-stall and toilet-stall build together, beneath the big chenet tree side the house. Onliest thing is it ain't got no roof, that shower-stall, and them boys from the street, you know they like to climb up in the tree and peer down. Them boys always doing that. Ogle you whilst you catching you bath. So I uses to go for water at night, bathe in the night when it good and dark. When them boys wouldn't be watching. But you know it tiring to go all the way to that standpipe for water. That bucket *heavy.* One night I was feeling tired, I just say, *Chups! I going bathe right here!* Cause ain't nobody does go to the pipe at that hour in the night, and even if they do, you could see them coming. You could hear them coming a long way off. Didn't make no sense to carry that water all the way home. I say, *Chups! I going keep a watch over my shoulder, and I going bathe right here!* And from that night I just get in the habit of bathing there side the pipe.

So it night now, good and dark, *dark,* and I carry my bucket to catch a bath. I rest it down beneath the pipe, open the water, and I full up my bucket about half-full. My rag and my piece of soap right there keeping in a joint of one them banana trees behind the pipe. So I reach it down, and I start to soap out my rag inside the bucket. Now I look over my shoulder, I listen a minute, make good and sure ain't nobody coming, then I slip out my pantics and push them in a joint of that banana tree. I raise up my skirt, my little mini-dress, and I start to soap. But when I turn round to wash out my rag, ain't find the bucket. I say, *What the? you bucket gone!* I feeling in the dark now, feeling for my bucket, and I look up peering in them bushes. Cause you know behind that pipe had a lot of thick bushes and bananas that you could scarce see inside. But when I look down again my bucket back there again. So I ain't pay it no mind, I wash out my rag tranquil enough, look over my shoulder again, raise up my skirt and commence to wash. When I look down my bucket gone again! I say, *What the hell! What the hell happen with you bucket?* But when I look down again I find the bucket back there again! Same place, and still half-full. I say, *Wait! Something wrong with you eyes? You eyes playing fool with you?* So I wash out my rag in the bucket, look over my shoulder again, raise up and commence to wash again. Child, when I look again, my bucket gone *again!* I say, I speaking aloud now, I say, "What the *hell* going on here? Where my bucket gone?"

Now I hear a voice, I hear a man-voice say, "I gots it." Child, I drop that skirt quick quick! I did *startle.* I say, "*You* gots it? *You* gots my bucket? *Who* you is?" The man-voice say, "I is Joe." He there standing behind the banana trees where the pipe is, but that place *dark.* I can't see he. I can't see nothing. I say, "I ain't *know* who Joe is? What you gone with my bucket for, Joe?" He say, "I going mash it up." I say, "Mash it up? *Mash* my bucket? What you want mash up my bucket for? I ain't do you nothing! You best give me back my bucket!" He say, "I going mash it up." I say, "Best give me back my bucket, or I would call for police!" Course I did know wasn't no police nor nobody else round that pipe for me to call. Not at that hour. He did know too. He say, "Come for it. Come for you bucket." I say, "I ain't *know* where you is." He say, "You know where I is cause you could hear my voice. You could hear me talking. Come for it." So I gone now, must be about five-six steps where he is, where I hear the voice, but you know that place *dark!* Behind the spicket where the canes start. Just behind. You can't see nothing inside them canes. Nothing nothing nothing! I say, "I can't see *nothing!*" He say, "I here." So I gone five more steps deeper inside the canes, and still nothing. I say, "I *can't!* I can't *see!*" He say, "I here. So now I gone deeper inside the canes about five-six more steps, and now I feeling, well not afraid, more spooky like, the silent. And you know, ain't seeing nothing, and ain't understanding why this man want thief my bucket. What he did want.

I say, "You there? Joe? You there?" Now I hear he voice *behind* me, and more a whisper like, say, "I here." Like that. I say, "What you? What you *want* with me?" He say, "You know what I want." I say, "I ain't know what you want. What you want with me, Joe?" Now, like he voice in *front* now, he voice in front me again, onliest thing is, I ain't *hear* he move in front. Spooky, real spooky. Like he voice did swirling round my head. In them canes. I standing there in the silent, breathing heavy, all in a sudden I feel he hand grab on my hand. My same hand that still did holding that piece of soap. Soap squeeze out pon the ground and he grab on tight, and I ain't know *how* he could hold so tight with my hand all soapy up like that. He grab on with this lock-grip, hard, real hard, and he start to pulling me now, pulling me now and running through the canes. So I running too, running close behind he, running in the blind, cause them canes *black.* I can't see. But *he* could see, somehow he could *see,* so I only running behind. Like he did cutlash heself a trail through them canes, or something, for he to know. But I ain't know nothing, nor can't pull way out from he lock-grip neither. Onliest thing for me to do is run. Run behind he fast as I could, *run,* like when you running down a steep steep hill and you feet can't scarce keep up. Can't scarce keep the momentum up. Like you feet ain't even touching ground, ain't carrying any weight. Like if somebody throw you inside a well—big deep water-well, black—and you falling. You falling and you can't stop you can't fight you can't do *nothing.* Onliest thing that you could do is fall.

So now we reach, we reach inside a clearing where he done cutlash the canes, unna could suppose, cause unna doesn't know if it's a clearing or a cave or what. Onliest thing I know is ain't no more canes in my face, lashing pon my face. So we stop, we stop now, and now he hold me down pon the ground pon some dead canes, dead grasses. One moment I did breathing fast fast, next moment like I stop. Like I *stop* breathing now. One moment them canes lashing pon my face, screaming in my ears—like a sharp shrill screeching sound, *loud*—and next moment everything quiet, dead quiet. I still falling, yes, but now like I falling in slow motion, in empty space. Now I falling inside the silent. I feeling far away, far far away falling inside the dark empty silent. All in a sudden *whaks!* this pain come searing trough my middle, down there. I feel this pain searing through my middle. And I, like I hit the ground, *whaks!* Like I hit the hard water down at the bottom of that well, *whaks!* Flat pon my back. And now I sinking. Now I sinking slow inside that ice-cold freezing water, inside that pain.

That thing did hurt so bad! So harsh! Like a fire did searing trough my middle, hot, or cold-cold. Like when you touch a block of ice and you hand stick, burn. You can't pull it way, all you could feel is that pain searing. I ain't know what he do, what it is he do to me. All I could know is that hurt, that pain. I ain't even know if we did lie there a time after or what. All I could know is he still holding my hand, that lock-grip, we lying, we lying and now we standing, we walking again. He leading me walking through them canes again. Leading me someplace else again. He ain't saying nothing now, nor me neither. Just walking behind he in the black. And still I ain't even see he face proper! Ain't even see he face good! All in a sudden he grip slip—slip out like a rope that knot and just slip—and I, like the weight, like that momentum was carrying me forward. I take about five more steps through the canes, and when I look up, there is that standpipe again. There is my bucket below. My bucket again like nothing, like nothing ain't even *happen.* Onliest thing is that pain, to remember by. That pain that I still was feeling. So I take up the bucket—ain't even remember my panties — I take up my bucket still half-full with water, and I raise it up pon my head. I say, *Leastest thing you could do when you reach home is bathe. Try and bathe.*

But when I reach home and I see this *blood,* all this blood pon my skirt, all that mess, I could of *kill* he! I did think maybe he did kill *me!* Then I remember that menstruation, that first and only that I did had and not know, and didn't see nothing after. I say, *Well maybe that's the same thing?* I did think maybe it was the same thing. I say, *That's the first time I know he too. Know a man.* And I, I was *confuse.* I had to throw down my skirt inside the toilet! I *had* to throw it way, cause that blood could never wash! That mess! I throw my skirt down inside the toilet and I bathe. I scrub. Time as I finish I so tired I can't scarce drag myself up in the bed. And I didn't feel to sleep in that bed neither, not with them other girls, four-five of we sleeping to the same bed. I did feel to sleep by myself, that night. I sleep right there under the house, pon some sacks of peas granny had there drying. I fall down pon them sacks of pigeon peas and I just sleep.

Next day, or maybe about two-three days later, I going at Crossroads to catch the bus, I see he again. See this Joe. Cause I *know* it was he, even though I never did see he face proper. This Joe come walking behind me. I turn and he turn too, walk behind me too. Child, I take-off! I run! Every time I see he, must be about a week, two weeks after that, after them canes, I take off and I running. And I could run *fast!* He couldn't catch me then. I ain't going at that standpipe no more neither, not in the *night,* not for he to hold me again. I go in the day. Bathe in the day. Or save water till night come to bathe. When he, when this Joe hold me up the second time, about two weeks later, walking to catch the bus, Crossroads, when I couldn't run from he no more. When I *tired* running from he. He hold up my hand in that lock-grip again, and he say, "I see you sporting that skirt. I watch at you with them nails. I take you for woman. You ain't no woman! You's still a little girl!" That's when I see he the second time, when he hold me up the second time. He say, "And plus you keep running from me. Why you keep running from me for?" Child, I was vex! I did had enough, enough of he. I say, "I ain't got no hands to do with you! No *hands* to do with you! I got to put in, got to throw my clothes down in the toilet, all them kind of things!" I say, "I ain't in *business* with you! You does mash up people!" He say, "That got to happen." I say, "That don't got to happen! That don't got to happen! Not like that!"

I say, "Why people don't, why people does *do* like that? Why you? You sick or something? You sick?" He say, "Girl, you been lying." He tell me that. I tell he he sick or something, he say you been lying.

That was the second time, when I couldn't run from he no more. I get to feel, you know, *confuse.* I did had to tell somebody. I did had to talk with somebody. Explain, get explain. But ain't nobody. I didn't had nobody to tell me nothing. Nobody but Joe, this Joe. I did think, I did feel maybe he could answer me some things, explain me some things. I could feel that he was a nice boy too, deep down. I say, "Joe, you a nice boy. I could feel that you a nice boy. Why you *do* like that? Why you?" He say, "That got to happen." I say, "That don't got to happen! *That* don't! Not like that! You does mash up people!" I say, "To *hell* with you!" After, you know after I start to talking, I feel he dirty. He *dirty,* and I dirty too. So we got to keep way. We got to keep from one another. I say to hell with you!

I never follow he up, nor go behind, nor talk, nothing. Just leave he to heself, do what he want, and I go by myself. But in truth I did feel he was a nice boy. A nice boy—cause this Joe wasn't no man, he was a *boy*—sixteen-seventeen years of age, nothing more. But he was tall and good looking. Very strong and very dark, quiet. He didn't talk too much, not like them other boys. Running off with they mouth and talking big. He was different. When he speak you could feel he voice quiet, calm. I did kind of, I did start to like he. Little bit, maybe little bit. But I ain't know that till *after,* after the canes. I see he with another girl, walking. I just get jealous. I just get jealous jealous jealous, and ain't know why. After what he do to me? After all that? But I just get jealous. I strike out! I throw one big rock. One *big* rock I throw at he break *two* of he fingers.

Next day he ask me, he say, "What you hit me for?" I say, "I ain't know." He say, "I got to hit you back." I say, "Oh my sweet Jesus don't kill me! Don't hit me too hard!" He say, "What I going tell my mother?" I say, "Tell she you fall or something." He say, "Can't tell she that. You hit me with a woman next. I walking with a woman and you throw two big rocks at me and you break my finger." He say, "I can't tell my mother that I fall down, not with this woman walking there. She *glad* to tell she. She glad to tell my mother that. I got to tell my mother the *truth.*" He say, "And I got to hit you back. I got to hit you back that she could *know.*" I say, "Well if you got to please you mother please her then, hit me back! But don't hit me too hard! Please don't hit me too hard!" I standing there, and

I waiting for it, waiting for he to cuff, but then my feet couldn't keep still. I take off! I run! He could never hit me then. He could never run so fast as me. I did uses to be athlete at school you know? Uses to run at school, long distance. About two miles, three miles. Round Keslin's Noble and back, about two laps, three laps, *fast!* But not in no shoes. I could never run in no shoes. I did feel like them shoes *weighing* me down. And I uses to take off like a jet! He could never hit me then.

When he hit me was a Sunday morning I went at school, Sunday School. He was sitting by the side, and I ain't see he when I pass, or I would of run. It was a Penticost—not Pen, like Baptist like—the jump-up stuff. I love that, *testifying!* He was sitting right there, and I pass and ain't see he sitting there. He just jump up and *whaks!* cuff me hard, front everybody, side my head. That thing knock me off balance. Knock me over backward, that cuff, cause I wasn't looking for it, and I fall. My grandmother stand up and she see, and now my grandmother say, "Alright Mister! Alright Mister, I going lock you up for my child! I going carry you in the court for that!" Joe say, "Woman, I don't care one damn where you carry me." And now he start to get on, you know, say, "When she break my fingers, you ain't tell she nothing." Granny say, "I ain't *see* that. Ain't see she break none of you fingers. But I see *this* one!"

Well my granny, you know, she call police, police come and they write up, this and that and the next. So, went to court. Joe, and he friends, he had some boyfriends with he, you know how young boys got they friends? Full up that court full full. And you know how them getting on! Ca-hooting and thing! And poor me! Me one with my granny. Nobody but my granny with me. She say, "Girl, keep on!" I say, "*What?*" She say, "Keep them shoes on!" Cause I did kick them off. I just couldn't stand for my feet in them shoes. I kick them off. I did want to run from that court too. Then Joe, Joe look down pon me from that box. He look down pon me out from he eyes, this gaze that he call up. He call up this gaze make me *stupid!* Make me so I can't think, can't breathe proper. Like everything was moving, swirling round my head.

So now Magis, Magis ask Joe, "You hit she?" Joe say, "Yes." Magis say, "What you hit she for?" Joe say, "She break my finger, so I *knock* she." Now Magis ask me, "You break he finger?" I say "Yes," and everybody laugh now. Magis say, "For why?" I say, "I see he with a woman! I see he with a woman and I just didn't want to see he with nobody but me!" And everybody laugh more at that. Them boys, more laughing. But I just couldn't care. I just couldn't care if they want laugh at me. Magis say to me now, "You does go with he?" I say, "No. I don't does go with he." With more laughing, ca-hooting and thing. Everybody but Joe. He ain't laughing. Joe just there looking pon me out from he eyes, that gaze that he call up. I run from that court! Cause I was crying, I did start to crying now. I run! Granny Ansin, she was so vex. She was so vex with me, cause *she* had to take up them shoes and carry them home.

So, charge dismiss. Magis dismiss the charge. I did feel so bad, so *shame!* I did want to look for he, for Joe. Cause I could feel that maybe he did, you know, that maybe he did want. But I had to make the next move. Me. After all that, court and Magis and thing. But I couldn't. I did feel too shame. When I see he again I just run. I run. But then now about two months after that, about four months, four months after the canes, I feeling, sleepy. Feel, just *sleepy.* All in the day was sleep. All in the night was sleep. Just can't keep the eyes open. If I go at school, I just rest my head pon that desk and I sleep. Onliest thing was sleep. Just one menstruation. Just one, and then not again. And then that one time in the canes with Joe. Just that one time. I ain't know my mother, nor my mother ain't know me. She could never tell me nothing, about baby, nor men, nor she didn't even uses to be at home. Nor my granny, nor my Tantee May, they never tell me nothing. And you know I was just twelve years old, I was embarrass to ask about them things. I feel like them things *dirty.* And you know I's the oldest child, my sister, she could never know more than me, nor my cousins.

Now my granny and my tantee turn bad pon me. They turn bad pon me, *mean.* Give me hard looks, words. They give me hard words. They never speak like that to me before. Never! Not my Granny Ansin. Not my Tantee May. I did feel so bad! And *dirty!* I did feel I's a dirty old piece of dirty rag. I feel I's the dirtiest thing that living. I didn't want to go at school no more, I did feel too shame. I *couldn't* go at school. You pregnant you can't go at school! Don't be no schoolchildren at school pregnant! I just look for place in the canes and I just sleep. Whole day. I didn't want to eat nothing. Just trying to keep off. Far from everybody. I just trying to keep far off by myself.

I ain't know what happen to the baby. Cause I ain't *see* no baby. I just know I was in the hospital, the maternity. Still first. Still first I could remember a man come at granny house, doctor man, white man. I ain't know who call he. I ain't know why he did come. All I know is he talking with Ansin in the front-room, he talking and then more men come, was two negro men, two negro men dress all in white. They hold me down. Cause I did want to run! They hold me down and they give me injection. My arm. Then I was in the ambulence driving to some place, to the big hospital in town. I know that for sure, cause I was moving. But that injection had me so *drowsy,* and so. But I know I was driving to some place then. When I get at the hospital, *next* injection. Then they put this gown pon me. Doctor gown, and tie at the side. But I couldn't tie that thing! I couldn't even lift up my arm! I just watch at the nurse tying at my side like in a dream. That gown was white, and had on pink elephants. Lot of little pink elephants. That did make me feel more like a dream still, them elephants. Cause I never see no elephant before. Don't be no elephants in Shervon! But I know they could never be pink, that rosy pink. I was sure about that. So then. That's all. That's all I could remember. And falling. Falling again in that water-well. And black. Onliest thing is there ain't no bottom to that well now, ain't no water to reach, hit. That ice-cold water. Onliest thing is falling.

Then I wake up. I wake up and I was in the doctor bed, and still wearing that gown tie to the side. I ain't know what happen to the baby. Cause I ain't see no baby. I only know that it was gone from out my belly. I know that, cause I could *feel* it gone. You carrying a baby all these months and it gone you does know, you does know that. But I ain't know what happen to the baby. I in that hospital about a week, ten days. Cause I didn't even know what was the time in that place, when was day and when night. I ain't talking to nobody, them other women in the ward, round me, different beds. They all dress in that same gown tie to the side, same pink elephants. They all talking to one another, they laughing, they caring for they babies when the nurse bring them. They feeding they babies. But I ain't got no baby to feed! I didn't even know why I was in there, with them other women. I ain't talking to them. I ain't talking and I ain't sleeping neither. Now I *can't* sleep. I can't sleep and I can't eat. Not much. Nurse come and she bring rice, bring fish, flying fish. But all was tasting in my mouth like cottonwool. Onliest thing that I could do is lie there with my eyes open and not think. Try and not think.

Nobody never visit me but one person, Miss Pantin, lady by name of Miss Pantin, tan of mine. She come the day before I leave the hospital. She tell me they wouldn't let she in before, before then, cause I was very sick. But they tell she I better now, I most ready to go home now. Miss Pantin come and she bring clothes for me, new clothes that she did buy. Was a blouse and skirt and new shoes, and white socks, a panties. She give them to the nurse and nurse give them to me the next morning. Nurse tell me I ready to go home. That morning Miss Pantin come again, but with Mr Bootman this time, she come with he in he car. They say they going carry me back in the country, back to my grandmother. Cause that hospital was in town, and Miss Pantin and Mr Bootman was living in town. So I get up from the bed to go now — I was dress and everything, dress in my new clothes that Miss Pantin give the nurse for me — but I was lying in the bed still. I get up ready to go now, and nurse say, "Wait." She say, "Wait here." Now nurse gone and she come back with this baby. Nurse come back with this baby wrap in little blanket. Little pink blanket, and *swaddling.* Nurse give me he to hold. Give me this little baby to hold up in my own hands!

My sweet Jesus that was a little doll! A little *doll,* and so *pretty!* I just couldn't left that baby to sleep. Just couldn't left he out from my hands. I couldn't left he hardly to sleep. Cause he so pretty, and pink, all I want to do is hold he all the time. Everybody who see he say how pretty. Well it wasn't much of people — Miss Pantin, Mr Bootman — but they say how pretty he was. Granny Ansin say how pretty too, the first, but then she ain't pay me much of mind again. Nor the child neither. Like she was vex with me still, and my Tantee May. Like them two was vex still. But I don't care! I don't care about nothing but my baby, my little baby. And them others, my sister and my cousins, them other girls in the house, they only fighting down each other to see who is the first to hold he. I strike out! I say, "Don't you even *think* about that! Cause onliest person going hold this doll-baby is *me!*"

Onliest thing I can't understand is the milk. Cause every time I try to feed he, he would, that milk would come back out. Come back down trough he nose. Come back in white bubblings, like white froth. I hold my breast inside he mouth but he don't take it, suck, he don't *suck* at it. I hold and I try to, you know, squeeze out some, but that milk just wouldn't go inside. Wouldn't *take.* Or come back down trough he nose. But he never cry. He never *once* cry. I say, *Well if he don't cry then he can't be hungry. Cause if he was hungry he would cry.* So I wasn't worried. I say, *This child so good! He so good, and so pretty!* But then one evening my grandmother, my Granny Ansin, she look cross and she say to me, "Why you don't *leave* that child? Why you don't put he down? Night I can't sleep. You, and that child! Always *taking* he up." She say, "That child got to go. Got to *go!*" She say, "When you pick up that child you don't feel strange? You don't feel *funny?*" I say, "Yes. I does feel funny. I does feel my head getting *swirly.*" You know, head swirly like, *scary.* But still you try, you try and you hold on, and favoring. I ain't know.

Next morning I look, I call quick to Ansin. You know my grandmother wasn't lying down far from me. She bed wasn't far from mine. I look and I call to Ansin quick, I say, "Ansin, look what happen! To the child!" She say, "What happen?" I say, "This child never cry. This child never once cry! And look, look where he mouth full with ants!" She say, "That child ain't *come* to stay! And you always *taking* he up. Ain't come to stay. Come to go! That child *dead!* You can't *see?* That child dead long time!"

I throw he out from my hands! Throw he pon the ground. All the ants! You know, *ants!* Was in that child mouth. Them ants was *eating* he. Eating that child. All where he was lying circle, circle with ants. *Circle!*

He was ten days when I carry he out the hospital. So, sixteen. Ten plus six is sixteen. He ain't even went out the house. But that child did breathing. He did breathing good enough, and pink, and pretty. I ain't know what happen. Maybe I do something? But when she, when Ansin tell me he dead, I had a *feeling* something happen. The wrong. Cause if ants bite you, you does *feel* it! But how, how them ants could be eating up he? When I look them ants was boiling out from he mouth, he nose, *boiling!* Like he was dead already a day, maybe two days. Cause that previous morning he was living. I *know* he was living. And you know sometimes you look at a baby and he smile, and you could smile too? You look at a baby and you know he yours, he yours, and you could smile too? Sometimes he eyes open, and sometimes they don't be open. And still always he sleeping. I ain't know if I was too young to notice. I ain't know what went wrong. But my grandmother, she tell me, "He ain't come to stay. That's why he ain't cry. He ain't sin. He ain't do nothing. Just here for little time."

So we bury he. Dorine sister which is Ellis, Dorine is my cousin. Dorine got a sister does make clothes, needleworks. She make and bring the dress for he. Cause we uses to put boys in long-dress too.

You know, to Christen them in, carry them out in. Onliest thing is my baby never Christen. My baby never even leave the house. Only to bury. That was the onliest time my baby leave the house. Granny and me dress he up in the little dress, we put he inside the box. Arrows bring the box for he, wood, and cover with white. A nice white little box. Didn't even get chance to name he nor nothing. Nor Christen nor nothing. Nothing nothing nothing nothing!

From AVA
Carole Maso

AVA is a living text. One that trembles and shudders. One that yearns. It is filled with ephemeral thoughts, incomplete gestures, revisions, recurrences and repetitions – precious, disappearing things. My most spacious form thus far, it allows in the most joy, the most desire, the most regret. Embraces the most uncertainty. It has given me the freedom to pose difficult questions and has taught me how to love the questions: the enduring mystery that is music, the pull and drag of the tide, the mystery of why we are here and must die.

No other book eludes me like AVA. It reaches for things just outside the grasp of my mind, my body, the grasp of my imagination. It brings me up close to the limits of my own comprehension, pointing out, as Kafka says, the incompleteness of any life – not because it is too short, but because it is a human life.

AVA is a work in progress and will always be a work in progress. It is a book in a perpetual state of becoming. It cannot be stabilized or fixed. It can never be finished. It's a book that could be written forever, added to or subtracted from in a kind of Borgesian infinity. Do I ever finish putting things in order? Can I assign a beginning to affection, or an end? Every love affair returns, at odd moments, as a refrain, a handful of words, a thrumming at the temple perhaps, or a small ache at the back of the knee. AVA is filled with late last-minute things – postscripts, post-postscripts.

I come back to writing continually humbled and astonished. I do not pretend to understand how disparate sentences and sentence fragments that allow in a large field of voices and subjects, linked to each other quite often by mismatched syntax and surrounded by space for 265 pages, can yield new sorts of meanings and wholeness. I do not completely understand how such fragile, tenuous, mortal connections can suggest a kind of forever. How one thousand Chinese murdered in a square turn into one thousand love letters in the dying Ava Klein's abstracting mind, or how the delicate, coveted butterflies Nabokov chases on the hills of Telluride become a hovering and beautiful alphabet. I cannot really speak of these things. As Michael Palmer said of one of his volumes of poetry, "the mystery remains in the book." I can discuss only the writing of AVA.

I was promoting my novel The Art Lover. I was flying places, meeting people, connections were constantly being made and broken. I felt strange and estranged the way I do during such times, with all the reading, all the talking into black microphones, all the pat replies to the same questions. Because I must write every day, I continued to write then, though I could manage only one or two sentences a time. The next entry, some time later, would be another sentence, often unrelated to the one that had come before. I was using language as an anchor and a consolation, enjoying the act of simply putting one word next to another and allowing them to vibrate together. Most days it was my only pleasure. Shortly after the book promotion, North Point Press, scheduled to do my next book, The American Woman in the Chinese Hat and also The Art Lover in paper, folded. These books made the rounds at commercial houses where so-called literary editors displayed the ignorance and lack of vision I have now become more accustomed to, with their love of safety and product and money. But I was still capable of being shocked by them then. I kept writing in pieces. I was scheduled to escape to France and had sublet my apartment when a death prevented me from leaving the country. The fragments piled up. Keeping the notebooks going, I began to travel the world in my own way. Among the many voices I had accumulated I began to hear a recurring voice, an intelligence if you will. She was a thirty-nine-year-old woman, confined to a hospital bed and dying, yet extraordinarily free.

I cannot say what direction her story would have taken had it not been assuming its final form during the terrible weeks of the Persian Gulf War. It was my first war as an adult and like everyone I watched the whole awful thing live on TV. War as a subject permeates the text of AVA, but more importantly war dictates the novel's shape. A very deep longing for peace, one I must admit I had scarcely been aware of, overwhelmed me as I watched the efficient, precise elimination of people, places, things by my government. My loathing for the men who were making this and my distrust for male language and forms led me to search for more feminine shapes, less "logical" perhaps, since a terrible logic had brought us here, less simplistic, a form that might be capable of *imagining peace, accommodating freedom, acting out reunion. I was looking for the fabric of reconciliation. Something that might join us. I was determined not to speak in destructive or borrowed forms any longer. But what did that mean? I began to ask the question of myself, "What could she not ask of fiction and therefore never get?" I began one more time to ask what fiction might be, what it might do and what we might deserve, after all. Traditional fiction had failed us. Did we dare presume to dream it over? To discard the things we were given but were never really ours?*

In an attempt to ward off death with its chaos and mess, traditional fiction had flourished. Its attempts to organize, make manageable and comprehensible with its reassuring logic in effect reassures no one. I do not think I am overstating it when I say that mainstream fiction has become death with its complacent, unequivocal truths, its reductive assignment of meaning, its manipulations, its predictability and stasis. As I was watching the war it became increasingly clear to me that this fiction had become a kind of totalitarianism, with its tyrannical plot lines, its linear chronology and its characterizations that left no place in the text for the reader, no space in which to think one's thoughts, no place to live. All the reader's freedoms in effect are usurped.

In an ordinary narrative I hardly have time to say how beautiful you are or that I have missed you or that – come quickly, there are finches at the feeder! In a traditional narrative there is hardly any time to hear the lovely offhand things you say in letters or at the beach or at the moment of desire. In AVA I have tried to write lines the reader (and the writer) might meditate to, recombine, rewrite as he or she pleases. I have tried to create a place to breathe sweet air, a place to dream. In an ordinary narrative I barely have the courage or the chance to ask why we could not make it work, despite love, despite everything we had going. In an ordinary narrative I probably would have missed the wings on Primo Levi's back as he stands at the top of the staircase. And Beckett too, during the war, hiding in a tree and listening to a song a woman sings across the sadness that is Europe.

"The ideal or the dream would be to come up with a language that heals as much as it separates." When I read this line by Hélène Cixous, I knew she was articulating what I was wordlessly searching for when I began to combine my fragments. "Could one," Cixous asks, "imagine a language sufficiently transparent, sufficiently supple, intense, faithful, so that there would be reparation and not

only separation?" And yes, isn't it possible that language instead of limiting possibility might actually enlarge it? That through its suggestiveness, the gorgeousness of its surface, its resonant, unexplored depths, it might actually open up the world a little, and possibly something within ourselves as well? I agree with Barthes when he says that the novel or the theater (and not these essays by the way) are the natural setting in which concrete freedom can most violently and effectively be acted out. That this is not the case for the most part, in fiction at any rate, is a whole other matter relating back to the "literary" editors who have entered a covert, never discussed and possibly not even conscious conspiracy to conserve the dead white male aesthetic. Women, blacks, Latinos, Asians, etc., are all made to sound essentially the same – that is to say, like John Cheever, on a bad day. Oh, a few bones are thrown now and then, a few concessions are made to exotic or alternative content, but that is all.

All experience of course is filtered through one's personality, disposition, upbringing, culture (which is why I know we do not all sound like John Cheever). Truth be told I was never much for ordinary narrative, it seems. Even as a child, the eldest of five, I would wander year after year in and out of our bedtime reading room, dissatisfied by the stories, the silly plot contrivances, the reduction of an awesome, complicated world into a rather silly, sterile one. When my mother was reading stories I would often wander out to the night garden, taking one sentence or one scene out there with me to dream over, stopping, I guess, the incessant march of the plot forward to the inevitable climax. Only when it came time for poetry did I sit transfixed by the many moments of beauty, the astounding leaps and juxtapositions. These seemed to me much closer an approximation of my world, which was all mystery and strangeness and wonder and light.

Back then my remote father grew roses. The tenderness of this fact, and the odd feeling I had that he cared more for these silent, beautiful creatures than he did for us, always intrigued and oddly touched me. It was what my childhood was: random, incomprehensible, astounding events, one after the next. I cherish this image of my father. And because I have never wholly understood it I gave Ava's father the task of growing roses. Unlike my father, Ava's father also survived Treblinka. He gives Ava a penny a piece for each Japanese beetle she can collect from the garden. The Germans sold the dead Jews' hair for fifteen pennies a kilo. There were piles of women's hair there. Fifty feet high. Ava in her innocence and purity, holding her clear jar of beetles, says, "Yes, we'll have to make holes for the air." The book is built on waves of association like this. There is a rose called "Peace." A rose called "Cuisse de Nymphe Emue"—that's "Thigh of an Aroused Nymph." It blooms once unreservedly, and then not again.

I have attempted in some small way to create a text, as Barthes says, "in which is braided, woven in the most personal way, the relations of every kind of bliss: those of 'life' and those of the text, in which reading and the risks of life are subject to the same anamnesis."

Back to my mother reading stories those long-ago nights. Another thing I did was to detach the meanings from the words and turn them into a kind of music, a song my mother was singing in a secret language just to me. It was a rhythmic, sensual experience as she sang what I imagined were the syllables of pure love. This is what literature became for me: music, love and the body. I cannot keep the body out of my writing; it enters the language, transforms the page, imposes its own intelligence. If I have succeeded at all you will hear me breathing. You will hear the sound my longing makes. You will sense in the text the body near water, as it was then, and in silence. Not the body as it is now, in Washington, D.C., next to obelisks and pillars and domes, walking it seems in endless circles and reciting the alphabet over and over. That will show up later; the body has an incredible memory.

My hope is that you might feel one moment of true freedom in AVA. That the form, odd as it may at first seem, will not constrict or alienate, but will set something in motion. I am always just on the verge of understanding here, which is the true state of desire. Perhaps you will feel some of this enormous desire for everything in the world in the fragments of this living, changing, flawed work. And in the silence between fragments.

"Almost everything is yet to be written by women," Ava Klein says, moments before her death.

Let us bloom then, unreservedly.

There's still time.

EACH HOLIDAY celebrated with real extravagance. Birthdays. Independence days. Saints' days. Even when we were poor. With verve.

Come sit in the morning garden for awhile.

Olives hang like earrings in late August.

A perpetual pageant.

A throbbing.

Come quickly.

The light in your eyes.

Precious. Unexpected things.

Mardi Gras: a farewell to the flesh.

You spoke of Trieste. Of Constantinople. You pushed the curls from your face. We drank Five-Star Metaxa on the island of Crete and aspired to the state of music.

Olives hang like earrings.

A throbbing. A certain pulsing.

The villagers grew violets.

We ran through genêt and wild sage.

Labyrinth of Crete, mystery of water, home.

On this same street we practiced arias, sang sad songs, duets, received bitter news, laughed, wept.

Green, how much I want you green.

We ran through genêt and wild sage.

You are a wild one, Ava Klein.

We were working on an erotic song cycle.

He bounded up the sea-soaked steps.

She sang like an angel. Her breast rose and fell with each breath.

Night jasmine. Already?

On this slowly moving couchette.

Not yet.

Tell me everything that you want.

Wake up, Ava Klein. Turn over on your side. Your right arm, please.

Tell me everything you'd like me to—your hand there, slowly.

Pollo allo Diavolo. A chicken opened flat. Marinated in olive oil, lemon juice. On a grill. A Roman specialty.

Up close you are like a statue.

After all the dolci—the nougat, candied oranges and lemon peel, ginger and burnt almonds, anisette—my sweet . . . after walnut biscotti and lovemaking, Alfred Hitchcock's *Vertigo*. . . . Francesco, what was conspiring against us, even then?

This same corner I now turn in bright light, in heat and in some fear, I once turned in snow and the mind calls that up reminded of—

The way you looked that night, on your knees.

Reminded of: a simple game of Hide and Seek. Afterwards a large fire.

Sundays are always so peaceful here.

A child in a tree.

August.

I dream of you and Louise and the giant poodle, Lily, and the beach.

But it is not of course that summer anymore.

August. They sit together on a lawn in New York State in last light—bent, but only slightly.

Come quickly, there are finches at the feeder.

Let me know if you are going.

The small village. I could not stay away. My two dear friends. Always there. Arms outstretched, waiting.

A dazzle of fish.

My hand reaching for a distant, undiscovered planet.

Through water.

Where we never really felt far from the sea.

He kept drawing ladders.

We dressed as the morning star and birds.

He bows his head in shadow. He turns gentle with one touch. In the Café Pourquoi Pas, in the Café de Rien, in the Café Tout Va Bien where we seemed to live then.

We were living a sort of café life.

Let me describe my life here.

You can't believe the fruit!

I'd like to imagine there was music.

Pains in the joints. Dizziness. Some pain.

A certain pulsing.

She's very pregnant.

I'd like to imagine there was music in the background.

And that you sang.

What is offhand, overheard. Bits of remembered things.

Morning. And the nurses, now. Good morning, Ava Klein.

Ava Klein, Francesco says, helping me on with my feather headdress.

Brazil, 1988; Venice, 1976; Quebec, 1980.

Determined to reshape the world according to the dictates of desire –

Where we dressed as the planets and danced.

Spinning. To you –

Charmed, enchanted land.

Chinatown. A favorite Chinese restaurant. The way he held my hand. As if it were a polished stone. Steam and ginger. News that the actress you most wanted had agreed to the part and financing had come. On the street, rain, a yellow taxicab. I love you.

He bounded up the sea-soaked steps.

Music moves in me. Shapes I've needed to complete. Listen, listen hard.

It's cool at this hour – morning. How is it that I am back here again, watering and watering the gardens?

And you are magically here somehow.

A heartbeat away.

We have a curious way, however, of being dependent on unexpected things, and among these are the unexpected transformations of

Poetry.

And he is here in front of me asking, Qu'est-ce que tu bois?

Blood and seawater have identical levels of potassium, calcium and magnesium.

Wild roses and rose hips.

The rose.

Qu'est-ce que tu bois?

Summer in New York. I'm thirsty.

I say "water" in my sleep. I'm thirsty. You bring me a tall glass of water and place it by my bed.

And one is reminded of: We were driving from New York City up the Saw Mill Parkway toward the Taconic and listening to the *Wanderer* Symphony of Schubert on the radio. I begged you to slow down, but as slowly as you drove, we were still losing it in the static, long before it finished.

You are a rare bird.

And I had to complete it in my head.

Which is different from hearing it completed on WNYC.

Though I sang it LOUD. All the parts.

It was completing itself, in midtown Manhattan without us.

Though I knew the ending and tried to sing it LOUD, without

You are beautiful

forgetting any of the important parts.

How is this for a beginning?

There is scarcely a day that goes by that I do not think of you.

Turn over on your side.

My heart is breaking.

New York in summer.

The Bleecker Street Cinema. Monica Vitti on the rocks.

Danilo laments the U.S.A. He says we have forgotten how to be Americans.

Maria Ex Communikata gets ready for the midnight show.

The Bleecker Street Cinema closes for good. And suddenly it is clear,

We are losing.

The scales tip.

Please invoice me. Input me. Format me. Impact me.

The bullet meant for Ricardo hits Renee instead. The bullet meant for target #1 hits baby Fawn. A bullet kills Daryl, honor student.

We will go to the river. We will rent a boat.

There were flowers each day in the market in Venice.

And how your hands trembled at a gift of exquisite yellow roses, so beautiful, and pas cher, Emma.

To hear you say japonica in your British accent once more.

Tell him that you saw us.

Because the corner of Broadway and West Houston is everyone's in summer.

I think of his life. That somewhere else it was completing itself. Somewhere outside my reach. Without me.

Though there was no way for me to know, unlike Schubert's *Wanderer*, how it was going to be played out.

Somewhere a young girl learns how to hold a pencil. She writes A.

To sing the endless variations on the themes he set up.

Thirty-five years old. Aldo.

Because the guandu, Ana Julia's favorite food, when we could finally bear to use it was no longer good. Expiration date: 1989.

I might turn the corner and there will be Cha-Cha Fernández walking a Doberman pinscher.

I can see it all from here.

Rare butterflies.

Nymphets by the pool.

Danilo, working out an unemployment scam for himself. Plotting a trip to Prague. Can you come?

The *Prague*, the *Paris*, the *Jupiter*, to name a few. Can you come?

I miss Czechoslovakia sometimes.

I'll probably never see you again.

Of course you will.

I might look up and there will be the Fuji Film blimp.

Or Samuel Beckett in a tree.

They are singing low in my ear, now. In the morning garden.

He grew old roses.

So what's the war about? someone asks. In brief.

Impact me. Impact me harder.

She finds herself on her thirty-third birthday on a foreign coast with a man named Carlos.

Never stop.

He is worried the city will get better—but not for awhile, and not before it gets worse.

The man on the TV wants them to freeze his head while he is alive, and to attach his brain to another body sometime later, when they find the cure for his incurable brain tumor.

How are you Ava Klein?

What answer would you be interested in other than the truth?

Make a wish.

The blue and purple in your black hair, Carlos. . . .

Danilo is writing a love story where the beloved makes the mistake of not existing.

Ava Klein, you are a rare bird.

Because decidedly, I do not want to miss the grand opening scheduled for early winter, still some months away, of the new Caribbean restaurant down the block that will serve goat.

Or the cold.

Or the Beaujolais Nouveau.

And so: Monday: chemotherapy. Tuesday: reiki. Wednesday: acupuncture. Thursday: visualization. Friday: experimental potions, numbers one through twelve. Monday: chemotherapy.

This room. White curtains to the floor. Wide pine panels. Painted white. Like the room in a dream.

The iris, Marie-Claude, like you, so glowing and grave.

Thank you for the tiger lilies.

In an attempt between 1968 and 1970 to fashion a perfectly round sphere, he made three thousand balls of mud, all unsuccessful;

I wrote you fifty love letters.

She has lived to tell it. How to make the family challah: sugar, flour, oil, kosher salt, eggs, honey.

I ran through broom and wild sage.

We took the overnight train.

You are a wild one, Ava Klein.

The men hung swordfish in the trees to dry. Sword snouts. Teeth in the trees.

He spoke of Trieste, of Constantinople. He pushed the curls from his face, thought of buying a hat perhaps. My first honeymoon. It was how the days went.

The changing of the guard.

In Crete, a gold-toothed porter.

She sang like an angel. Her breast rose with each breath.

I needed to travel.

Aida sits in the day's first square of light.

I love your breasts.

It was Rome. I was twenty, and you were forty, almost. You were making a film of the *Inferno*. I laughed imagining the task. I was a graduate student. A student of comparative literature. I held your giant hand. You pressed me against a broken wall in the furnace called August. I kissed you. Or you kissed me.

Yes, but it is not that August anymore.

And in 1971 the artist carved 926 sculptures from sugar cubes.

That evening he led me into the circular room.

A woman named Yvette Poisson dancing in a glass bar in the seaside resort in winter.

A perfect gray sea. Grayness of the days.

Let me know if you are going—

Snow fell on water.

We took the overnight train. He kissed me everywhere. Shapely trees passing in the windows.

A beautiful landscape. Imagined in the dark.

The way his body swelled.

Trees that looked like other things.

He tries to conserve moments of existence by placing them in biscuit boxes.

At the feeder, goldfinches.

Danilo, my Czech novelist, with his deep mistrust of words. His fear of the Russians. His love of Nabokov.

And Flaubert is *not* Madame Bovary, students, I don't care what he says.

The Empire State Building is working overtime emoting in colored lights for every cause known to man: international children, the Irish, hostages, Fourth of July.

Václav Havel: Everywhere in the world, people were surprised how these malleable, humiliated, cynical citizens of Czechoslovakia, who seemingly believed in nothing, found the tremendous strength within a few weeks to cast off the totalitarian systems in an entirely peaceful and dignified manner. We ourselves are surprised at it.

Strange the way the joy keeps changing.

I remember the smell of rosemary and thyme in a young man's hair.

It was a kind of paradise, Anatole.

He makes a record on which he tries to remember the lullabies he might have heard as a child.

The morning nurse singing, Let me know if you are going to Central Park. Lunch break 12:30.

I hear water. You come around the rounded stone fountain. Ça va? I say. And you nod.

At La Fontaine des Quatre Dauphins in Aix, where I wept.

To see your beautiful head turn.

To see your beautiful head turn once more.

But we've already lost so much.

The heat of a plot. I'm beginning to detect the heat of the plot.

García Lorca feigning death.

Václav Havel comes to town. Danilo tries to meet him on this, his triumphant visit. Havel, being pushed out for five minutes at a time here, there to speak with American dignitaries. Also with Frank Langella, Paul Simon, Carly Simon, etc., John Irving in the corner. (Nobody wanted to talk to him.) This one, that one—poor Havel. Danilo looks pained.

It was as if we had come in on a conversation midway. That was the kind of beginning it was.

The late verses of Neruda vary widely in tone and texture. Their fluctuating musical impulses require a looser structure woven together less by the uniformity of lines than by the dying poet's sensibilities.

A stroll around the park. While the weather's still fine. The ginkgo trees in fall.

Un, deux, trois.

A simple game of Hide and Seek.

Danilo to his last, crazy lover: I'm going to take the garbage out. And she responds, What, you're going to see Gorbachev now? She shakes her head. Go then!

Turn over on your side.

And it will seem like music.

A blue like no other.

Maria Regina remembers the fascists: They told us to mount the stairs two at a time.

Often there is nowhere to go but forward or back. It is hard to stay here in one place and especially at moments like these.

I am afraid the news is bad, Ava Klein.

Now in America, they call this coffee. But I remember coffee. . . .

A simple game of Hide and Seek.

The giant head of Françoise Gilot in stone. We took photographs, though photographs were not allowed. Marie-Claude and Emma and Anatole and me, smiling in the bright light and so much sea, in the room called Joie de Vivre.

The Picasso Musée. Antibes.

He was on his way to see Gorbachev when we met for the first time on the street. It seems that all along we were neighbors.

Ten, eleven, twelve. . . .

I kiss you a thousand times.

Making mysterious La Joconde faces next to Françoise Gilot one afternoon.

Vladimir Nabokov: The book you sent me is one of the tritest and most tedious examples of a trite and tedious genre. The plot and those extravagant "deep" conversations affect me as bad movies do, or the worst plays and stories of Leonid Andreyev, with whom Faulkner has a kind of fatal affinity. I imagine that this kind of thing (white trash, velvety Negroes, those bloodhounds out of Uncle Tom's Cabin melodramas, steadily baying through thousands of swampy books) may be necessary in a social sense, but it is not literature . . . (and especially those ghastly italics).

The emblem is for a group called Missing Foundation. An upside-down champagne glass with the champagne crossed out. The party's over is what the emblem stands for. And everything points to it — that the party is over.

Would you like to have a perfect memory?

Because there is still Verdi and sunlight and the memory of that man on the Riviera — and when memory goes it is replaced maybe with beautiful, floating, free, out of context fish. Orange in deep blue with tails like feathers.

Or Samuel Beckett learning to fly.

Vitello Tonato: Boneless veal roast, white wine, anchovies, capers, tuna, a sprig of thyme.

It's a hot and lovely day. No humidity — odd for this city. A clear sky, high clouds. And the weather is for everyone.

What's the rush then?

Unable to get to you, Marie-Claude and Emma, any other way right now, I dream of the fish in your stone pond. I send you a report of the weather.

We are making a day trip to Cap d'Antibes. How much we wish you were here!

Aldo recalls his grandfather: he is gnawing on the end of an anisette biscuit with the perfect pointy teeth he acquired right before his death.

After sex, after coffee, after everything there is to be said —

The hovering and beautiful alphabet as we form our first words after making love.

And somehow I'm still alive.

Danilo swearing that in the next book he'll do something easier, less ambitious, more suitable to his talent.

So many of the old places: Sabor, Felidia, Trattoria da Alfredo.

Café Un, Deux, Trois.

In Venice. In August. At the mouth of the Saluti. . . . A celebration because *the plague is over!* So much joy.

They were going to go to the river. She brought chayote and plátano.

There was a man whose name was Whistle.

The small light a candle can give. The face flushed.

That's an almond tree. Cherry. Small fig.

A homeless man has fallen asleep in Ann's car on Fourteenth Street when she goes to move it in the morning.

Mr. Tunny and his fourteen-year-old grandson were leaving church when they heard the shots being fired. "He was moving very slowly, very gently." A bullet had entered the boy's cheek and exited the left side of the back of his brain.

I see my light dying.

Our destination in those days was always the sea.

Francesco with his silly film quizzes. Asking me one more time where the word *paparazzi* came from.

The choice is made a little mysteriously, in a superstitious manner, not rationally. Still it is made: ultraviolet light, or radiation,

Chinese herbs.

Danilo puts in a good word for modern American medicine.

INTERVIEWER: If you could remember, could keep forever, just one story, what would it be?

FRISCH: Which one? It would not be the story of my life, or a story I have heard, but a myth. I think it would be the myth of Icarus.

Aldo kept drawing ladders. Ladders going nowhere, maybe.

It's OK.

My aunt then, wandering, confused, during the war.

We took the overnight train.

We danced to Prince all night long in the circular room. It was 1988. It was France.

You were on holiday.

One night.

It was everything while it lasted.

One night once.

A shining thing.

My father offering pennies for each Japanese beetle.

She sends an envelope of poems.

There is not a day that I do not think of you.

The glittering green of beetles. . . . Hanging on the lip of the yellow rose.

The lemon trees are planted along the garden walls. By and by they will be covered with rush mats, but the orange trees are left in the open. Hundreds and hundreds of the loveliest fruits hang on these trees. They are never trimmed or planted in a bucket as in our country, but stand free and easy in the earth, in a row with their brothers.

Music moves in me. Shapes I've needed to complete. Listen. Listen hard:

I hear a heart beating.

Can it be that our visit was only eight months ago?

I know I am lucky that music moves in me in such a way—and if it has rearranged a few chaotic cells or changed the composition of my blood—but even if it hasn't—still—I have been, of course, extraordinarily lucky.

That night the baby was conceived. In a room called Joie de Vivre.

Where you spoke, Anatole, only once, and in a whisper, of freedom and how much you needed the sky and good-bye –

Swinging on the swing. What shall we name her?

Can it be that our visit was only eight months ago? It is so hard to imagine . . . I think even with all the insanity and pain of those days I was happier. I miss you.

xxx B

Sing to me of Paris and of lost things.

I knew a boy named Bernard Reznikoff. Quiet, carrying a stack of books. Blushing. New York City.

Just once I'd like to save Virginia Woolf from drowning. Hart Crane. Primo Levi from falling. Paul Celan, Bruno Schultz, Robert Desnos, and for my parents: Grandma and Grandpa, Uncle Isaac, Uncle Solly, Aunt Sophie, just once.

In the city of New York. Where I taught school, sang songs, watched my friends come and go. Climbed the pointy buildings. Marveled at all the lights.

Aldo, building cathedrals with his voice.

A man in a bowler hat disappears into thin air. Grandfather.

She was dressed in a gown of gold satin. Suppose it had been me?

She shudders at the sight of a garter belt as if it were a contraption of supreme torture.

I think of him often: Samuel Beckett learning to fly.

Look for this in my shoe.

He waits for disguised contacts who sometimes never come.

A a. B b.

All the bodies piling up on stage.

C.

Like your father you grew old roses.

Snow falls like music in the late autumn.

Home, before it was divided.

A pretty rough show, then, for someone who came to see nudes, portraits and still lifes. It is made rougher still by the inescapable dates on the labels of the stronger images, all of which come from that hopeful ignorant time when it seemed that all that was involved was a kind of liberation of attitude concerning practices between consenting adults in a society of sexual pluralism. Of course the show has its tenderer moments. There are prints of overwhelming tenderness of Mapplethorpe's great friend Patti Smith. There is a lovely picture of Brice Marden's little girl. It is possible to be moved by a self-portrait of 1980 in which Mapplethorpe shows himself in women's makeup, eager and girlish and almost pubescent in the frail flatness of his/her naked upper body. . . .

Let me describe what my life once was here.

Home before it was divided.

. . . The self-portrait as a young girl remains in my mind as the emblem of the exhibition, and the dark reality that has settled upon the world to which it belongs. One cannot help but think back to Marcel Duchamp's self-representation in *maquillage,* wearing the sort of wide-brimmed hat Virginia Woolf might have worn with a hatband designed by Vanessa, with ringed finger and a fur boa. . . .

Come sit in the morning garden for a while. Open the map.

With AIDS a form of life went dead, a way of thought, a form of imagination and hope. Any death is tragic and the death of children especially so. . . . But this other death carries away a whole possible world.

A remote chorus of boys.

Shall we take the upper or the lower corniche?

The way the people you loved spoke—expressed themselves in letters, or at the beach, or at the moment of desire.

Maybe I should go now.

No. Please stay.

From Sister
Jim Lewis

One night a couple of years ago, when I was traveling, I stopped and checked into a hotel in Wichita, Kansas. It was late and I'd been driving all day, but when I got to my room I found I couldn't sleep, so I went down to the bar. There was a woman there, sitting by herself, staring at the late news on a soundless television at the back of the room. She was small and dark-haired, a white girl, maybe twenty-four or so, wearing black jeans and a gray top. On the screen a jetliner was sitting motionless on a wide strip of tarmac. I asked if I could join her and she said, Sure, and gestured to the seat next to her. After I'd sat down she said, Chicago, and nodded toward the TV. It was enough of an opening to get us talking, and we talked for a while: her name was Marian, she was looking for work, and at one point she said that she'd grown up in Mississippi, but she hadn't been home in a while. I asked her why not.

Oh, I had some trouble there, she said, and waved her hand dismissively. You don't want to hear the whole thing.

But I did, and I pressed her. She hesitated for a moment more – the bartender turned the sound up on the TV so that he could hear the football scores – and then she said, Well . . . and began to tell me a long story, about her little sister and her little sister's boyfriend, and a baby that was never born, and her father, and a gun she'd bought at school. I could see that the whole thing still upset her, but she wasn't shy about it: she looked directly at me as she spoke, and she never faltered. It sounded as if she'd spent years going over it in her head again and again – not for a listener, but so that she could understand exactly how it went herself. When she was done she stared at her glass for a couple of minutes, turning it around on its little square napkin every so often. So that's why I stay the fuck out of Mississippi, she said.

I nodded, and we sat there in silence for a little while longer. Well, I guess I should go on to bed, she said at last. Then she slid off her seat, smiled, thanked me, and started for the door, lurching slightly to step around a bucket full of rags that a cleaning woman had left by the leg of a table.

I didn't see her at breakfast the next morning, and I was on the road by ten, but I remembered the story she told. I thought about it often; I tried it out on some people; and finally I decided there was something very important about it. So I changed the narrator's perspective, altered enough details to protect her privacy, and set it down.

"Lonely Is As Lonely Does"

When I was stuck I would draw a circle inside the book, or improvise around the letter O, or the number 0. At one point I considered prefacing it with an epigram from Emerson, a sentence that opens an essay called "Circles": "The eye is the first circle; the horizon which it forms is the second; and throughout nature this primary figure is repeated without end. It is the highest emblem in the cipher of the world."

Thompkins Square Park (sic)

At the end of the eighties I was in graduate school for philosophy, and my oldest and best friend was teaching the same discipline. We used to meet about once a week, to talk about various problems that interested us, and eventually we decided to write a paper together, on the act of forgiveness and how it fits into moral logic.

Since neither of us was a specialist in ethics, we started by looking through philosophical journals and indices, for earlier work on the topic. But there was surprisingly little; so we turned to literature, and eventually to The Tempest. *It was my argument that the play contained a smaller, misshapen version of itself, barely visible behind the main plot—as if Prospero's drama of forgiveness was a lens, through which one could make out the deformed image of another, similarly composed, but with Caliban standing at the center. The boy's monstrousness, I claimed, was just an effect created by the narrative through which he was seen; it distorted him, and it made his suffering comic by rendering it in grotesque proportions.*

Miranda, too, can see Caliban only through the stories her father tells, and Shakespeare, as much as Prospero, is careful to keep her from gaining any more immediate view—because if she saw him clearly she would fall in love. The passion of Mirandas for their Calibans is one of the laws of adolescence, and the playwright's decision to leave it unenforced within the bailiwick of Prospero's island provides the play with its main source of sexuality and suspense; it lingers about the events that transpire as the spectre of a loss that the magician, for all his powers, only narrowly avoids.

The paper my friend and I planned to write never got beyond our conversations, but Sister, *the love story that I wrote instead, began with an impulse to upend* The Tempest *so that Caliban's story came out on top. And then, of course, it became something else.*

J's drawing, with it's pencil-scrawled note: "I never thought the last time I saw you would be the last time I saw you."

Gerhard Richter, *Jugendbildnis (Portrait of a Young Woman)*, 1988.
Courtesy of Marian Goodman Gallery, New York.

This is a painting by Gerhard Richter, from a series based on the newspaper photographs depicting the history, imprisonment and deaths of the German left-wing terrorist organization known as the Baader-Meinhof Group. This particular work is entitled Portrait of a Young Woman, *and it shows Ulrike Meinhof herself, one would guess at the age of fifteen or so. With her thick, carefully styled hair, her clear skin and her full face, she looks like the kind of girl who's been well cared for; but her expression says everything about what she became.*

I saw the complete series at the Grey Art Gallery in New York three years ago, in the company of two friends, one of whom has since disappeared. I had been asked to write about it for an art magazine, and I said then, and believe now, that it's one of the most difficult and powerful bodies of work produced by an artist in this century.

I had a reproduction of Portrait of a Young Woman *taped above my desk for much of the time I was working. I was thinking about women's secret capacity for violence. I've always admired the rare, strange and beautiful combination of passion and fierceness that lies behind it. Even when the result is terrible, it has a profound, almost sweet quality that I can't help but appreciate.*

Deep rage, and the attraction of violence, fascinates and troubles almost every woman I know well, every woman I love. So I wrote Sister.

It cost me a total of about six hundred dollars, cash, to come up with the ending.

The prettiest song I've ever heard is an obscure old Hank Williams tune called the "Alabama Waltz." The recording is crude and unembellished, just his guitar and his slow, quiet voice. It lasts only as long as it takes him to sing one verse and one chorus: it can't be more than about a minute. It goes:

I was sad and blue
I was downhearted too
It seemed like the whole world was lost
Then I took a chance
And we started to dance
To the tune of the Alabama Waltz

Waltz, waltz, the Alabama Waltz
There all my tears and fears were lost
There in your arms
With all of your charms
We danced to the Alabama Waltz

A girl wearing a woman's perfume.

The passage excerpted here occurs about a third of the way through the book. The narrator is a seventeen-year-old boy, a self-described monster who, unbeknownst to anyone, has been living in the space underneath a gazebo in the garden of a mansion on a hill. At night he spies on the family that lives there—father, mother and two teenage daughters. He recounts his childhood.

1.

SELF-PORTRAITURE is a kind of folly, like trying to grasp the fingers of your right hand in the same fist. The sky on which we write our constellations is not a mirror, since once hung the stars shine by their own fire, and while the course we plot assumes that they're fixed we'd never know if they wandered. It's true nonetheless: I was born over my senses, and I was a very difficult birth. I struggled with all of my tiny might. We all know that there's no comfort or calm equal to the dark solitude before birthdays, but that wasn't why I was reluctant to be born: I didn't want to be at all, and I fought for hours, for days, to keep away from the world. Having been born, and now having lived, I sometimes think it would have been best if I'd used the moment of my first gasp to go right out again, but I was instantly impressed by the smart light of the delivery room, the shining metal tables and floors, the beeping of the instruments, and I reached my pink hand out toward the masked features of some doctor or nurse, and couldn't turn back.

I can see my father standing in the hospital hallway waiting for the news: I was the news. I can imagine him watching impassively as the nurse brought my soft, swaddled self up to the glass so he could get a look at me. Sir, a boy. He was a strict and quiet man, my father, a man with an incalculable and unexpectedly clear soul, which was absorbed by his work like well water in a dry flower bed. That day fulfilled one of those ironies of generation, of being born and begetting, that warp stories into sacredness: my grandfather was both a doctor and a tyrant, a tough and difficult man, so my father was scrupulously principled; he thought of himself as a name under a moral law that he sustained only by correcting himself through the years as a man corrects a dray, using his own doubt as a bridle, and his capacity for shame as a bit. I was the third issue, and he would bear it without complaining, as if an otherwise absent providence had determined it. I don't know what grief he might have kept alive over the years, but I'll ask you to believe that his life from then on was an attempt to concentrate, as if to sharpen away the brute moment of my being under the small abrasions of his duties. For a long time he had studied deserving, the way a foot soldier studies war, and he'd taught himself to see everything: he stood in the bright hallway, his thoughts carefully hidden: he simply watched, and slowly nodded.

And there in my imagination is my mother, damp, pale, exhausted and relieved, lying in a hospital bed with her hair unpinned and cast out on the white pillow. My father is in a chair beside her, waiting anxiously for her first look at the son she delivered. He holds her hand. A knock comes at the door, she turns her head expectantly, the nurse pushes her way into the room with her arms full of clothes, and there I lie, quietly covering my face with my tiny hands.

About a year later my mother died in an accident—I see an airplane landing in a rainstorm, though I don't know why—leaving me with my father. All that remained of her was her signature in the front of the poetry books that were sorted on one shelf in my father's study, an old-fashioned signature made in fading blue ink by practiced penmanship; and there were three photographs in which she appeared—one on my father's desk, the second on the mantel above the fireplace, and the third, which I saw only once, in his wallet. I was unconsciously young when she entered heaven, as my father, in a lapse from his usual plain-speaking, put it, so I have no memories of her at all. I have no suit against her. I don't know what kind of woman she was, and I never asked, since it seemed to be the last thing my father could have answered; I was afraid he'd turn as brittle as old paper, and then dissolve into dust under such a bright light.

2.

My parents had moved to Lincoln just before I was born, to a blue frame house on the edge of town. It was huge and hollow inside, with a front hall set with black and white diamond-patterned tiles over which I used to slide in my stockinged feet until the soles of my socks were gray with dust. Toward the side there was a porch which was seldom used, because it was cold in the winter, and the winters were long. My bedroom was at the start of a long, second-floor hallway, and my father's was at the opposite end. He and my mother had bought the place expecting to fill it with children—there was a bedroom for each of four—but his sense of a house died with her, and he simply left the unused rooms empty; there was a single, rickety chest of drawers pushed against the wall of one, a rolled-up carpet laid against the baseboard of the next, an unplugged lamp on the floor of the third. Absurd, but I think he was also a little sentimental, so we never did move.

I used the rooms as a diving bell. I wasn't happy, and as a boy I liked to imagine a sea in place of the Great Plains, with a hole in the bottom where I could live, passing midnight days among the translucent ferns, the shells and silt. In school one afternoon they pulled the shades and showed us films from diving ships, dark flickers of what they found near the boiling springs as far below as a man could go: giant white worms, fat mushrooms, flat-headed fish and eels. They did nothing but swim the currents and feed. I didn't even know how they went about making more of themselves, but I knew I wanted to live with them, because I knew that I belonged to nature, too—and why not? Freaks and sports of all kinds are hers to make and keep, spiny fish, moss and mung on trees, mandibles and hammered features, and choking smoke from fires, and crawling dirt, and brackish water, and me. If my father was bothered, he never showed it. We lived together, he and I, in a house that was far too big for us alone, and in which half the rooms had furniture the way months have full moons.

Like him, I can now grant that nature's insults aren't insults; but when I was a child I reckon I made things hard for him. From my bedroom I could imagine him, after one of my wildcat tantrums, returning to his study to sit silently in his chair, his head lowered into thoughts of his gone wife and my improbable unhappiness. I know he found it difficult and bewildering. At the bare blank and diminishing end, now, I'm grateful to him for his generosity. What use can I make of sympathy? My dear father, small-town doctor with a spook for a son, a boy who made fears.

3.

Daddy never brought stories of his patients home; their sufferings were secrets, and he took the privilege of his invitation into the systems that sustained them very seriously. But my curiosity about the patterns of disease was insatiable, and like a wind chime it could be set trembling and ringing by the slightest move. I used to watch him carefully while we sat at the dinner table, looking for some sign he might show of the travels of his adversaries; if he sighed softly just as he lay his fork across his plate at the end of his meal, I'd imagine that a patient had worsened during the night before; if he lingered over a forkful of potatoes, I decided that a new possibility had just come to him, and the next day would bring brisk arrangements; if he fixed himself an extra cup of coffee after dessert, I guessed that he was rewarding himself for having effected a cure – unless he added an extra spoonful of sugar to it, in which case I could tell that he was expecting to study late into the night.

When he did have work left ahead of him, he used to take the kitchen table to pore over the illustrated journals that arrived regularly in the mail, looking for a new therapeutic treatment, or something to suggest that a diagnosis may have been off. As I passed from the empty living room to the empty dining room I'd see him, his gray head bent over his wonderful researches, while the illnesses of men and women all around the world formed swirling, paperbound currents of blood and compounds. The magazines he read would be open to their difficult maps, the charts of deep waters and undertows that some anonymous second had prepared and published. He watched them all like some quiet, latter-day Poseidon, with his favorites and battles, redirecting Furies and tides to achieve his ends, the health and completion of the men and women who came to him with their aches, their breathing troubles, their messy cavities and miseries, their numb limbs, their sleepless, bedridden bodies.

I remember leafing through his books from time to time; I used to sneak into his library when I came home from school and choose from the leather-bound medical volumes that lined the shelves. Had I had the proper temperament I might have learned something, but I never thought to wonder how the things they described might have had a place in the causal order. I wasn't born to be a doctor; I'd rather think of the singular, the particular, the actual, than spend time making real sense of the general world of symptoms, or cures. I used to look at the pictures and try to imagine the body that had posed for them, and then recite passages aloud for the rattle of the syllables, without knowing or caring what they meant.

One fine day I came across a pathology textbook, as devoted to viscera as a slaughterhouse. It began with a special inset: on the endpage itself there was a pair of skeletons, like exotic musical instruments, half violin, half vibraphone—though one, with its deep, curving centerplate, looked as if it would be much richer and more resonant than the other. Over them successive transparencies could be laid, thin plastic sheets on which were printed first the shaggy skein of nerves, then the fatty organs, then the tubules of blood (red with burning oxygen, blue as a drowned child), then the fibrous muscles, and then translucent, pale pink skin, until a whole and very patient couple finally appeared, standing like sentinels over the carnival inside. I read through the book with the devotion of an initiate, skipping over the technical terms which seemed to multiply as the pages made their way toward the distorted glimmers and gazes, the pulp and sordid perfume that lead to the blots of flesh from which you and I, in our several ways, have begun; but I always returned to the frontispiece, and I never tired of assembling that map, with all its clever, interlocking layers.

I wrote stories of my own, in a notebook which still sits in the bedroom desk drawer where I hid it. It was a school composition book, bound fat with a strip of black tape over the spine, and the lines on the pages were wide enough for a child's hand like mine to keep its characters under control. The cover was a painterly abstraction, black ink spotted over a white background until the individual flecks melted together, making a sort of camouflage pattern; in the center a space was cleared for my name and home address, an oasis that I, inclined toward invisibility even then, left uninhabited. Inside I carefully wrote out little tales about a wild, illiterate and helplessly destructive Wilson; I hid in swamps, in ship's holds, in other people's houses, where I stole daughters and murdered fathers; I ate insects and stray, misfortunate men, and when I was done I belched loudly, bent down and beat the ground with my fists until the trees shook in Africa.

For every empire, even of a child's limpid imagination, there is an emperor, and I liked to imagine the great day when I was crowned. There would be a hall so huge that I couldn't see the ceiling. The light would come from rows of flaming, smoking torches that hung on the walls. At one end I would stand, boyish and unembarrassed, raised on a platform and gazing out with a slight smile over an assembled mob of monsters. They'd groan their cheers, they'd stamp their stumps on the ground, they'd shake their staffs in the air, and I would be declared President for Life.

4.

Lincoln in those days was a small, quiet city under a huge, blue sky. It wore the smell of the fields that surrounded it the way a farmer's wife wears a cotton dress, and like a farmer's wife it was bare-legged underneath. Within a few blocks of the main street the houses fell down to two-story frames as if on their knees before the sublime beauty of the Plains: there was so little substance to the whole, from limit to limit, that if the University and the Capital hadn't held it down like nails I think it would have become detached from the earth and floated silently up into the sky, leaving me alone at last and unwatched in the dirt below.

Our house was on the south side, and our nearest neighbor was the Widow Foster. She had always been the Widow Foster, and had always lived there, but in all the years we lived next door I never did meet her; I seldom so much as saw her in the open air. Still, on afternoons when I played lordly games in our yard I'd occasionally catch a dark glimpse of a serpentine form behind the windows of the French doors that led to her porch, and I'd seen the shadow of her figure often enough to know that she was a pleasant-looking woman, with white hair and a white throat, and a body as bent as a bicycle after an accident. All services were delivered to her door, and we grew used to the sight of a grocery delivery boy or florist standing at the top of her front stairs, waiting patiently for her to make her way up from the back of the house. Then one day when I was eleven, under the spell of one of my father's funereal afternoons, I first contemplated the mysteries of mortality, using our neighbor as an example. I never even left my room: I just wondered, and the next day a man with a package rang and rang, paused, rang some more, peered through a window, and then came over to our house and spoke to my father for a moment. I was sitting in the kitchen when he came to the phone, and I watched as his index finger drew the dial in a circle. I remember asking myself what law had been suspended to reduce the familiar seven digits, with their inconsistent rhythm (a measure that waltzed, a measure that marched) to a brief and urgent three.

In the Widow's place came a family from Kansas City, a young couple somehow connected to the University. I spied on them from my window as soon as the enormous green and yellow moving truck pulled up to the curb in front of their door. For the rest of the day the movers carried their furniture into the house, while a girl in a grass-stained dress played among their legs, sat sullenly on the front steps, poked around their new backyard, and finally turned her pale moon face up to my window, where she saw me standing and, after looking around to make sure no one was watching, slowly waved.

Her name was Liz, and she was a tomboy, pony blond and always into something. Aside from the day she moved in next door I never saw her wear anything but blue jeans. She smelled like hay and grape juice, and she had downy sunburnt skin and long, thin limbs, and a habit of standing with her mouth open and dazedly blinking whenever she came across something that excited her. For reasons I'll never understand, she befriended me with a wide, sly smile one weekend afternoon just after they'd arrived. I was on my way to the corner mailbox with a stack of my father's letters, and she stopped me from the edge of her lawn, came down to the sidewalk and asked me if I knew how to make a knot that no one could undo. When I said I didn't she sat me on the curb and showed me, using my own shoelaces and then laughing shamelessly as I struggled in vain to get them untied again. We finally had to cut them apart with a pair of sewing shears she borrowed from her mother.

For the weeks that followed, we used to meet on the playground at school, sit side by side against the jungle gym and eat lunch while she watched me with glittering eyes, then meet again at the end of the day to walk the few blocks home, where I'd leave her at the sidewalk and watch her as she dashed up the stairs to her front door. Then one winter's day she brought me into her house instead, and while her mother fixed dinner in the kitchen she led me down into her basement playroom, and under the matter-of-fact fluorescent light she simply disrobed, and showed me, with perfect grace, in what besides her long hair our differences lay, as if she were the endpage of my favorite book come to life. I was silent through the entire event, I was so fascinated by that form, with its *trecento* shape and coloration, at once elegant, devout and awkward. I still remember the soft, smooth texture and smell of her bare skin, already stippled with delicate goosepimples from the cold, the way it was gathered about her bones, the slight sharp taste of her breath on my face as she moved toward me and gently kissed my burning cheek. I couldn't have imagined that anything had the power to be so entirely naked, to be so present in its plainness: she was the first thing I'd ever encountered that depended upon nothing else to exist, either in itself or in my mind, and the afternoon stopped dead in the spring heat when she suddenly grew serious, backed away, and said, O.K., now it's your turn. When all at once I realized that she was looking at me as I was looking at her I spooked, and I shook my head No, and when she tried to cajole me and reached her hand out toward a button I ran away, hightailing it up the stairs and through the kitchen, past her mother's astonished stare and out the back door. When I reached my own room, breathless and with my heart backfiring, I lay face down on my bed and dizzily replayed the moments I'd just passed, until my father came home from work and called me down to dinner.

What did you do today? he asked as we sat down at the table, and I, thinking he already knew somehow, lowered my head, reddened, and then to his astonishment blurted out everything. His awkward, nonplussed silence when I'd finished only confused me more: he shuffled the beans on his plate with a fork, cleared his throat, swallowed half a glass of water, and then changed the subject.

5.

Liz drifted away on an uneasy tide, waving good-bye just once and halfheartedly from the foot of a long path that I invented and put in place of our own all too real driveway, just as, the week before, I'd removed our house from its neighborhood and put it in a green clearing in some dark, medieval woods. Afterward she ignored me when I passed by her and her friends as they played hopscotch on the sidewalk in front of her house, and school, which for a few weeks had been almost a pleasure, again became a miserable duty, the more so since the princess had willingly gone to some unnameable dragon.

I remember very little of my teachers, with the exception of one young woman, fresh out of college and no match for me, who asked me to stand before the class and recite a patriotic poem we were all supposed to have memorized the night before. I refused at first, but she insisted, so I stood, stared at the ceiling, and repeated as much as I could remember, changing the word *country* to *monkey* throughout. The boys in the back row giggled, and her face as she scolded me remains clear to this day. Little monster, she said, and I left the room on a brief, imaginary trip to an island in the Mediterranean, where I quickly wrecked a passing ship.

The others have faded into a pale, multiform band, within which I can make out single features, a beetle brow, a bald spot, a chalk smudge, a hand holding a lesson plan, but not one complete person; they have become blurred into a dim audience, frowning at a failing act without seeing that failing was my act. See, the old books lie. Teaching Caliban to curse made him Caliban. And Huck is one part Tom, and Tom is two parts Becky, and we are all three parts Runaway Jim. So I did a lot that others thought I'd do, and I did it because they thought I would; they were the spectators at my coming to be, and I was a master, a monster, of finding and finishing their expectations, the doctor's strange son, who seldom looked at a man directly, and never at a woman, who slouched and hid, and whose voice was always quiet. As every local reviewer knows, the logic of character is so appealing.

Still, I suffered from the typical torment that children pay one another. My classmates' boos and catcalls were the never-ending music of my adolescence. It's so predictable that it hardly bears recounting; someone always gets it, and I was the one. Instead, let me draw a picture of my own closing credit. It was the first example of my artistry, my way with nature and my powers.

It was a late spring day, sunny and breezy, and they were standing in a circle around me in the schoolyard during lunch hour, burying me with their usual insults. I was waiting expressionless at the center of the ring, and I was prepared to stand there and play the object of their scorn until recess ended, as I did each time some secret signal rang and they gathered around me. But on that day, as I stood and listened to the rising, hurdy-gurdy sound, a single syllable from a single voice—I don't know whose—suddenly appeared from out of the ring and, like a cold chisel, knocked at just the right spot to split my temper open, so that my fury spilled out: I opened my mouth and emanated ill-will. I made fun of one's unkempt clothes, another's fat father, a third's disgusting lisp, and when I could think of nothing to holler at the next in line I simply invented a failing—and when the failings ran out I received a gift of tongues, and a flood of mean energy, and I began to rage and rave at their blank faces, cursing them with a might that grew inside me, stretching my skin until I was sky high, one thousand feet tall, bitter all the way up and so angry that the weather changed: the sky darkened and I shouted up a North wind; papers, notebooks, textbooks swirled at my feet, the trees bent almost to the ground, my hair whipped across my face; on the other side of the playground a line of bicycles in a rack collapsed with a soft clatter. Through my squinty eyes I could see a teacher coming out the back door of the school, with her skirt tearing across her legs. She stopped in her steps and watched on, transfixed by the impression I made, as the wind blew and I leaned back with my arms outstretched and howled commandments to the elements.

I don't think any one of them understood half of what I said, but they were so taken aback by what I'd done that one by one they backed away, as if in the face of a supernatural force. Only Liz stayed on: she was standing by the fence that separated the playground from the street, hanging on with one hand to a diamond-shaped link while her red jacket flapped in the storm and her blue eyes opened wide in a look of astonished, delighted admiration. When the rest turned and ran I was left alone with her, and let the wind subside. I remember that it was very quiet afterward.

Liz let go of the fence and gazed at me with solemn curiosity. — Then she began to clap her hands together, and as the girl's childish, single applause drifted across the pavement I raised my arms, called down a rainstorm, and walked all the way home in it. I wasn't bothered again.

6.

Something mean hangs high over whatever law is made, whatever comfort a good man commands. To worst and best alike nature comes, in best and worst fashion. So I was made a sport, and my father was made with a weak blood vessel behind the wall of one temple.

One cold winter day it broke and he died. It was a Monday, and he'd gone home for lunch; a cancellation early in the afternoon left him free for an extra hour, and anyway he'd left a file that he needed on the desk in his study. He was fixing himself a sandwich in the kitchen when all of a sudden he felt faint, his breath came short, and his ears rang, so he shuffled up the stairs to his bedroom, lay down on top of his bed, closed his eyes, and there and then he left.

I was brought out of civics class that afternoon by the school nurse, a usually chatty woman who silently monitored the passing tiles on the floor as we made our way to the principal's office. Am I in trouble, I asked. No, no, she said, and put her cool hand gently on the back of my neck. I'm sorry, child. She sniffled and sighed; I had no idea why.

I was ushered through the anteroom—they were all watching me—and into the principal's office, and he put aside his papers, took off his glasses and told me that I'd been called home from school. Then he rose from behind his desk, and walked me to the empty street outside, where a colleague of my father's named Cooper was waiting, dressed in the curiously old-fashioned manner that he preferred; under his coat he wore a white shirt, a string tie, and black pants. His ankle-high suede boots were wet with melted snow and streaked with gray from the street salt, and each had a shiny spot near the big toe where the leather had started to wear through. In one hand he held his hat; he put his other arm around my shoulder without speaking. I shrugged him off. As we walked to his car the snow squeaked under my shoes, and the wind was so sharp in my nostrils that I pulled the neck of my sweater up over my mouth and nose until I could smell my own sweet breath mixed in with the humid wool. Cooper's dark green sedan was in a cleaver-blade of sunlight at the edge of the parking lot, glinting against the muddy snow that had been piled up to the curb. We drove to the house in solemn silence, pulling gently into the driveway that my father and I had cleared the day before; I remember the sound of the engine ticking from the cold as we walked away from it, the dark house against the white edge of the rise in our backyard, the snow and blue sunlight. There were no shadows. I was fifteen years old. He was lying in his bed with his eyes closed, his rare soul having dissolved into the sky like the foggy vapors of my breath that afternoon. For a few minutes I was left alone with his body so that I could say good-bye, but I couldn't bring myself to utter anything at all to that wax effigy, and when the door opened again I was found sitting in a chair across the room, staring at the bed as if it was a macabre sideshow exhibition.

Cooper was assigned me for the next few years, and he was proud to have received my father's commission. He was a nice man, never married, a facile guardian: he gave me a room in his house to sleep in, and a meal or two a day, and after I'd rebuffed him a few times he stopped trying to draw me out of my obvious misery and left me alone. I was an easy charge, and since I intended to finish school and be gone as soon as I could, I never gave him a reason to try to be more. I wouldn't want to see him again.

My father had willed the house to me, and I insisted on leaving it more or less as it had been before he died, but I packed away his clothes and personal effects, and I donated the most useful of his medical things to a small, poor school nearby. The cutlery was worn, the silver dulled in spots from the years he held them, however gently, in his subtle hands, but he'd left a wish that I give them away. I put his books into storage, and took his clothes to the Salvation Army; the furniture remained, along with the silent pictures on the walls and my own abandoned bedroom. I stopped by the house almost every day from then until the moment I left, although there was nothing for me to do there but sit in the living room and read the walls. On weekend nights when my classmates were at parties or cruising the main strip in their cars, at holidays when families gathered, on summer afternoons when girls went walking together and smiled at boys, I was alone in that dark house, too frightened to leave, waiting for my helpless youth to end.

One day during my last year of high school I decided it'd ended at last, and I walked out: that's all. That afternoon I visited Cooper in his office, stood before his desk, and told him I was gone. He fingered the frame of his glasses, nodded carefully, quizzically, and asked if there was anything he could do. I'd like for you to watch the house, I said. If you can, keep a little heat on to stop the pipes from freezing. He nodded again, and promised me that he would. I dangled a set of silver keys over his papers, explained which fit where, and set them on the blotter before him, and he opened a side drawer and deposited them inside. There was nothing to say after that: he stood and shook my hand, and walked me to the door.

I left the next morning, wandering out into sky blue spacetime, footstep by footstep. Aside from the clothes on my back and in my suitcase, a day's food and my toothbrush, I took only one thing when I left, a book of Daddy's, my favorite, the one where I could make a couple appear and vanish again in neat, successive stages.

thursday 1

(ALL PRESENT WITH CHOSEN ONE IN HIS CIRCLE)

Who chosen one

JULIAN

Why JULIAN-?

Why Julian

(YOU WILL HAVE SUPER POWER-YOU ARE KIND!!!!

~~What & When~~
About the Super Power

(I N FUTURE SECRETS OF THE AGES

~~What about Super power,~~ describe it

iN FUTURE=SECRETS OF AGES

From Light While There Is Light: An American History

Keith Waldrop

This is a family novel, told in first person, set mainly in the Midwest and the South, from the end of World War II to the end of the sixties. Its background is small-sect American Christianity, with some elements of cult and occult.

The narrator, whose name is the author's, shuffles his past, finding it still present, but uninhabited. So the story is a ghost story and the characters have disappeared before it starts.

It is not, however, a fantasy. The settings are concrete: a small town in Kansas, a holiness college in South Carolina, a boardinghouse in Atlanta, University Avenue in Urbana. And the time is historical time, with its penumbra of historical events.

The characters, though filtered through a memory which keeps in mind that they are no longer there, are also concrete. At the center is the narrator's mother, who moves from faith to faith, deeper and deeper in the murk of born-again religion – finally a tragic figure who, still holding fast to her faith, loses all hope.

God promises the narrator's sister a helpmeet, but fails to deliver. His two brothers build lives out of almost nothing – desperate bricolage *– bootlegging in Kansas, preaching the gospel, selling bus tickets, bibles, used cars, fruit. They run a business, for a while, on instructions from a Ouija board (as you will see in the following excerpt). One becomes a quack, then a guru; the other is killed – the family decides – by witchcraft. Neither is ever successful at anything.*

The narrator is always there, but marginally. It is really their story – his family's – and he is the ghost.

It is, let me repeat, a novel – the fiction of a family that happens to resemble my family to the point that I have used some real names (including, for the narrator, my own) and also put in family photos. But I have also added characters and details from elsewhere or nowhere and, even when working from remembered models, have remodeled them.

Why then, willing to distance things, did I choose to write about matters so close to home? For at least two reasons:

(1) Though it is a fictional story, it is set in a real history – in the pathos of a religion on the way out and the horrors of religion on the way in.

(2) I have no great imagination. Memories of my family gave me an enormous fund of material (overabundant indeed) from which to shape my fiction – so available a content allowing me to concentrate on formal aspects. This material was always at hand, most of it easily recalled, much of it indeed what I could not forget.

"YOU MUST HAVE those pictures somewhere," Charles said to me. "If you don't, then they're just gone." And after a moment, "For good," he added.

"I'll look for them," I said. With Seely gone, he had been rummaging for the photos of the two of them in smart clothes, standing beside the long black car, with JUST MARRIED in the center of the frame. Or – another I remember – the back end of the hearse as it drove off, trailing a cloud of smoke and the string of tin cans.

"I'm just glad we can all be together this Christmas," Elaine said. I should have kept my mouth shut then. Or I could, after all, have said a lot of things that wouldn't have mattered. But I had come to trust the banality of my first thoughts, the platitudes that spring from the preconscious mind.

"I'll ask the Ouija board," I said.

"The what?" said Charles. And Julian stopped dead in the middle of a mouthful of cake.

"Every Christmas," Elaine was telling Rosmarie, who was by now not quite a stranger to my family, "I'm just amazed we can all still get together."

I had played with a Ouija board as a child – a friend and I used to get messages by the hour. It kept us, as they say, out of trouble, and amused after we tired of poker (one or the other of us having won all the countries on the map). Then, in Connecticut, as if there had been no years between, another friend said, "Ever talk to a Ouija board?" and I said, "Sure." We had to persuade our friend's husband to get the board out of the attic. "He believes in it," she whispered when he finally went up after it. "Last time we used it, we got his dead mother." "What did his dead mother have to say?"

"She said she was burning in hell."

"I mean about the pictures," I said. Charles and Julian were still staring. "Haven't you ever played a Ouija board?" The room was hot and piled with trash left by Charles' three children. They had opened their presents two days before Christmas and now—Christmas Eve—cars, guns, cameras lay at random with smashed parts. I knew Charles had no money and I didn't know just how he had managed to get that great load of toys, but I was not surprised.

Julian got up and said he was going out to get a Ouija board.

"Ten o'clock Christmas Eve," I said. "Who's going to be open?"

Elaine said, "Ten o'clock. No wonder I'm so tired. You people can stay up all night if you want to. I'm going home."

She went home. The rest of us might well have stayed up most of the night, but the kids came back from a party somewhere and the uproar was more than any of us could stand. The last thing I remember, before the tree toppled, is Charles' lecturing Julian on the folly of Spiritualism. Charles has always had plenty of words, if not much of a world to put them in.

"Those Ouija boards," someone once told me, "it's all wish fulfillment. It's the same mechanism as dreaming." No doubt there's something to that. The planchette moves where the fingers, lightly pressing, desire it to go. The message is our libido, spelled out. Not a complete theory, but it's a start. "No one can have, in real life, everything he wants"—I forget who it was who spouted all this—"but there's nothing to keep us from having anything we want, in imagination." That may sound reasonable.

Charles called when I had all but forgotten that Christmas Eve. It must have been March or April when he phoned, which he doesn't ordinarily do unless he needs money urgently.

"Brother Keith." He sounded urgent. And he proceeded to tell me how afraid he was that Julian was being "taken over" by the Ouija board. I didn't just then go the thousand miles back there, but little by little I found out what had happened. Charles sent transcripts—sheafs of them—of the sessions, hundreds of answers spelled out letter by letter. Sometimes the questions were missing, and it was impossible to make a clear chronology of the sheets, but the gist was obvious. It was particularly startling, because I rarely heard from my family (except, occasionally, my mother, who if she had any real news always managed to put it in an unexplained subordinate clause: "after that awful accident happened . . .") and I had somehow put out of mind their obsessions. Startling because, of course, they're also mine.

Charles, in the meantime, had gotten Seely back. I can't keep straight their partings and their reconciliations. Seely would go off to a bar and it was weeks until anybody could find her. Charles all this while mad with desire—and in the grand manner: refusing to eat, calling up her mother, her sister, her friends, anyone who might have seen her, unable to think of anything else. He would know she was with Drake, whom my mother referred to only as Seely's "drinking companion." And Charles missed work—assuming at the moment he was working—and when Seely got back would be out of money, which would send her off again. They got divorced—over the money problem, they said. With three boys and no husband, Seely started drawing welfare payments. Charles stood at the door, more or less literally, and finally crept back into the old situation. Things went better for a while, with the added income of the welfare checks. Once, Seely got Drake to beat Charles up.

Me, Rosmarie, Mother, Julian

My mother thought Seely controlled Charles by some kind of spell, but it seemed to me that if he let go his idea of Seely, he'd have nothing left. He tried hard to apply to her what he'd read in books. "Don't you think," he would ask me, "her pictures show schizoid tendencies?" Seely painted, not too skillfully, images of a surrealist cast—brick walls around trees filled with eyes, a woman's nipple stretched until it forms a clenched or clutching fist.

"I don't know," I said. She had a recurring dream. She is in a space capsule. She is swaddled in some kind of clothing, like swathes of cotton, so that she can't feel anything. "It's like I didn't have any more body." It's always the moment before firing off. Then a baby's face, indistinct but combining, I gathered, in some way, a sort of greeting card cherub and the real rage of an infant just born. And a voice which reminds her of her grandmother's says, "Go on, and

I deliver the wedding hearse

have a good time, but if you go, don't think you can ever come back." And she wakes in a cold terror.

"What do you make of that?" Charles asked.

"I don't know." I've sometimes envied people whose dreams are bizarre.

"You've studied psychology," he said. And then, his reproach fading into the old perplexity, almost to himself, "It must mean something."

Julian found a Ouija board, disgusted that it was in the toy department—this was before New Year's. It worked with Charles and Seely, Charles scoffing as his fingertips moved with the moving planchette. It worked with Elaine and her husband Clyde, though they were both afraid of it. But it worked best when Julian was on one side or the other. It got so that every night the board was talking to them. While the Christmas tree turned into a pile of needles, they tested their discovery.

"Where are my pliers?" Clyde asked, and the answer spelled itself out: "B-E-H-I-N-D-T-V," which is where they were. It never seemed to miss on little things like that. But the more important test had nothing to do with efficiency.

"Are you evil?" they asked point-blank.

"I-H-A-T-E-E-V-I-L," the board replied, to their relief. For a while (some weeks, I guess) it gave Julian detailed instructions where to go to get bargains of one sort or another and (they were all a bit in the TV business then) where to get cheap used sets. There was never a hitch. Their business improved. Then one night the tone of the affair changed.

"Are you there?" Julian asked. The planchette went to YES. "Who are you?" I don't know where he got the idea to ask such a question. The answer came.

"I-A-M-T-H-E-G-E-N-I-E-O-F-O-L-D." Elaine almost fainted.

"An evil spirit!" she said, but the Genie of Old assured them again that he hated evil.

"Ask him why he's come," Charles said.

"Why have you come?" Julian asked, and they could hardly keep up with the letters.

"I-H-A-V-E-C-O-M-E-T-O-B-R-I-N-G-Y-O-U-S-E-C-R-E-T-O-F-T-H-E-A-G-E-S."

Elaine said, "I'm getting out of here."

"Wait," Julian said, "he's going on."

"I-W-A-N-T-C-I-R-C-L-E-O-F-F-I-V-E."

"Who? What circle?"

"C-S-J-E-C." That stumped them for a while, until they saw it was an initial for everybody there: Charles, Seely, Julian, Elaine, Clyde.

"You can't go," Julian told Elaine.

"Why does he want us?" she said. "Why doesn't he want Keith? Ask him why he doesn't want Keith."

"Why," said Julian, as mouthpiece for the group, "do you not want Keith also?"

"H-E-A-L-R-E-A-D-Y-K-N-O-W-S-S-E-C-R-E-T-O-F-T-H-E-A-G-E-S." And they didn't have time for another question; the planchette was still on the move. "B-U-T-H-E-D-O-E-S-N-O-T-T-E-L-L-A-L-L." That oracle could, theoretically, have said anything, but nothing could have given it greater plausibility to that particular audience. I must have appeared to them, at that point, in an aura both of success and betrayal: I escaped, I deserted—either formulation suggests the other. Julian was going on.

"What about Rosmarie?" And this should be noted: the Genie of Old never answered any question about Rosmarie. She was, as it were, outside his jurisdiction. But over the next sessions—they were nightly and sometimes nightlong—he provided my family with a history, the last thing I thought we would ever have.

It started in Austria, the age not quite specific, with one Axis von Mueller. No details of his life—the name suffices. It provides, through otherwise vacant centuries, a line of identity. And it brings out of darkness the long-dead postmaster of Leeton, Missouri, who was our grandfather and whose name was Martin van Buren Mohler. One branch of the family, the Genie of Old reported, and they copied it down breathlessly, ended with Mad King Ludwig of Bavaria. And the other branch—which led by some path to Leeton, and on to this group of seekers in a ratty room in Champaign—the other branch "I-F-H-A-D-N-O-T-B-E-E-N-I-L-L-E-G-I-T-I-M-A-C-Y" would have climaxed in our generation. Charles and Julian *would have been* (not knowing exactly what they mean, I can only copy them out here) respectively, "E-M-P-E-R-O-R-O-F-B-O-T-H-T-H-E-A-M-E-R-I-C-A-S" and "C-H-I-L-D-C-O-N-Q-U-E-R-O-R-O-F-E-U-R-O-P-E."

I was much moved by these revelations, but it was not clear at all to me what I could or should do about them. It didn't seem very likely to me that Julian's soul would be absorbed by the Genie of Old. I was ready to bet on Julian.

In September 1970, I got back to Champaign. Julian had rented an old house on University Avenue where he and my mother lived, and out in front he had set up a fruit and vegetable market. University was, had been for years, the dividing line between white and black districts, the ghetto stretching west from the next parallel street. A black gang, calling themselves the Sons of Satan, decided the west side of University itself should have black businessmen only (at that point there was probably not one) and they began the liberation with volleys of gunfire, repeated sporadically over several months, sometimes from a moving car, sometimes from nearby rooftops. By the time I got there, it was a street—both sides, with a few exceptions—of vacant buildings. Julian's fruit stand, however, on the west side, was still there. My mother, who tended the stand most of the day, explained that the shooting drove away most of the customers, that the summer—the fruit season—being over, they had no prospects for the winter, that things were about ripe for the coming of the King in his glory. Tomatoes were still plentiful. The porch was loaded with watermelons. The front room of the house reeked with vegetable decay, but they lived in the back, mainly in one room, with several cats and many locks. She slept on the floor behind the TV, under some notion that that

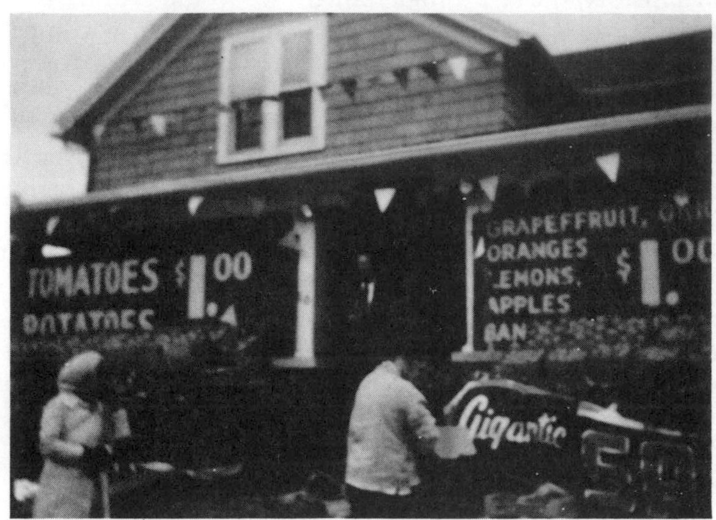

The fruit stand on University Avenue

was safer.

"Has there been more trouble?" I asked.

"No," she said, "not for a couple weeks." She was living out of a half dozen shopping bags. Pinned to the wall were several pages clipped from the *Voice of Healing,* showing faces of native evangelists, mostly Indian, those to whom she was sending offerings. "Most of our customers," she said, half to herself, "were colored people." She could find no easy explanation for all sorts of recent events, especially the sudden death of evangelist A. A. Allen in a San Francisco hotel room of—so the papers claimed—acute alcoholism. "Maybe he overworked," she decided, "and right at that moment the Devil tempted him to take a drink. Of course," she added, before I realized she was back to Julian, "they didn't like his campaigning." And I remembered how Charles and Julian were the local chairmen of the Wallace for President campaign, carried off in some dream of going in triumph to a career in Washington.

"Why don't you leave this place? It's silly, you know, to stay here."

"Oh," she said, "he won't leave. He's got that old gun." And indeed, leaning against a chair was a submachine gun. Through the worst of the raids—the police, by that time, avoided the whole area—he sat on the porch, firing back, while she lay inside, on the floor. Whenever I'm tempted to suppose that things are not completely hopeless, not entirely senseless, the attempt collapses if I bring that scene to mind: her praying behind the TV, and Julian fighting for his right to sell watermelons to the blacks.

We got together at Elaine's place—neither she nor Clyde would go near the fruit stand after dark. Rosmarie had not come west with me. Seely was off somewhere.

"Keith," Julian said, "have you seen anything recently on precognition?"

"Oh don't talk silly when we're all together," my mother said.

"No," I said.

"You'd better be thinking," Mother said to Julian, "about how you're going to spend eternity. Take that old cigar out of your mouth."

Charles said, "Shit."

"It's not lit," Julian said, which was true.

"He talks awful," Elaine told me, referring I suppose to Charles.

"This old world is going to rock and reel," my mother continued. "And it isn't going to be long now."

Charles scowled. He was looking skin and bones. "You've been saying that for as long as I can remember."

"You know it's true!" she shouted back. "The Devil's getting stronger. You ought to know as well as anybody." And that went on a while, but Charles was on the defensive. Because he as well as the others had come to believe in the Power—had in fact believed more completely than the others. He had seen, magnified in his mind's eye, a fortune proffered by the Genie of Old. And I may be wrong, but I cannot help feeling that if he was afraid for Julian's sanity, he would not, for all that, have withdrawn from the game for Julian's sake. But it was not, finally, Julian who had succumbed.

It was Seely. I never could quite get all the details, because everyone kept giving me explanations instead of information. "Her grandmother was a witch," my mother told me. They wouldn't talk about it among themselves; only when I was alone with one of them, it came out, compulsively, not really to me—more like lines of thought trying to unsnarl themselves. "She used to hear music before anyone died," Charles said; "she had sort-of comas." Those states, whatever they were, increased as the group met nightly to hear from the Genie of Old. "She isn't a very stable person," Elaine said. "She went into a screaming fit," Julian told

Wallace Workers' Cars Damaged by Fire, Paint

An auto owned by a co-chairman of the Urbana Wallace for President organization was set afire Thursday night, destroying the car's interior.

Another car owned by the Wallace organization's local secretary was reportedly spray-painted. Signs were also torn from the outside walls of the Urbana Wallace headquarters, Lincoln and University avenues.

Both cars were parked behind the headquarters at the time.

From the Champaign-Urbana Courier,
Friday, November 1, 1968

me—we were standing on University, between the tomatoes and the watermelons—"I had to keep a hold of her and Charles grabbed the Ouija board and tried to break it over a chair." "Well?" "Well, he couldn't break it. And she was screaming and kicking. And finally he ran out the back door and put it against a tree and stomped on it till it broke." "Did she stop then?" "No. Not until he got the gasoline on it and burnt it up. We were doing real well there for a while. I mean financially. She calmed down and was all right after that." I helped him move some overripe tomatoes out of the sun.

"I don't want to go to heaven," Julian said, "I want to go where Keith goes," and laughed loudly and went into the kitchen. My mother pointedly ignored him.

"He may come any time now," she said. Charles said something under his breath.

"It's just nice we can still all get together," Elaine said. "I always wonder if it won't maybe be the last time."

Late that night, when I was the only onc awakc, I called Rosmarie.

"How is it?" she said.

I said, "I hate evil."

From Film Noir
Jessica Hagedorn

I am now writing under weird pressure and there are days I really hate it. Expectations, according to my rodent rodeo observations, often = disappointments. Or else maybe one ends up writing simply to meet a deadline. Imposed by—you name it. Editors. Agents. Bill collectors. So I am trying not to fall into that abyss of second novelisms . . . or third.

I hear it gets worse.

I loved writing my first novel Dogeaters *because nobody gave a shit. There was so much reckless freedom in that feeling. To write when you have absolutely nothing to lose is to gain everything that matters as an artist. The willingness to take risks with content and language. And to write as if one were racing alone, racing alone with only one's self, against one's self, is an absolute thrill. And to know that one cannot afford to stop and look back—*delicious.

HERE'S WHAT I WANT TO SAY. Right before I gave up music, I was full of myself. The happiest I've ever been. Terrifying and permanently etched in my mind, those final concerts will always seem bigger than life. You slinking through the audience, decked out in emerald green lipstick and embroidered Turkish fez. Waving goodbye to us at the airport, as the band boards the jet that takes us on . . . a dream. Our first and last international tour. Straight to hell. My band as opening act for Sister Mercy's No Bullshit Satin Soul Revue. She is a living legend—a survivor of the chitlin' circuit—authentic, gritty, magnificent, temperamental. She calls her classic songs "ugly music," she calls herself "Godmother to James Brown." Hers is a fourteen-piece orchestra, complete with Sammy Davis, Jr. lookalike emcee and topless backup singers who call themselves "The Hoodoos." She only talks to the men in my band and marches past me as if I am invisible. I eat shit, I grovel like a white boy—I am so grateful to be on the same bill with her.

This tour is so nasty, you have to pay your own way. 120 degree heat and humidity. No shade. Parasites in the water. Boiled English food the only thing available. Where are we? I cry every day I'm there. "B. Goode! How could you be so bad?" Elvis and the boys needle our manager Brian mercilessly, in the last-ditch effort to keep our spirits up. I want to kill B. Goode, who responds by giving us daily pep talks on the importance of working, on work as an end in itself, and the prestige of opening for the legendary Sister Mercy, rumored to be the protégé and only female ex-lover of Little Richard. "Think of what you'll learn! Think of the riffs you can steal from the horn section!" Brian is hysterical and dehydrated, his pale face swollen with insect bites.

"Brian, what kind of shit have you got us into?" I wail in disgust. "They got bugs here so vicious they can bite your dick off!"

"Sister Mercy just as bad," Jamal says. Brian shrugs, helpless. We try to stay high enough so nothing matters. Ray shows up late for everything. Sometimes he doesn't show up at all. Elvis wanders off into the bush, looking for Ray. And you

in the dream, slinking down the Nile in your papyrus canoe. Walking a tightrope in your embroidered fez and gauze veil, the lipstick slash across your mouth a deliberately nasty, supernatural green. "I'll save you," you promise me, perfectly balanced and confident on your perch above the ravine. Nasty nasty nasty neon green.

And the only boa I ever wear is a constrictor around my neck, while Jamal whispers in panic, "Does the Congo still exist?" And Elvis responds with a sneer, "I can't keep up with history."

I am pregnant. I moonwalk and shuffle across the creaking, makeshift stage of the outdoor jungle arena. Searchlights blind my eyes. My mother suddenly appears, pushing my father onstage in his wheelchair. His hands are clasped in prayer, his tongue stuck out, ready for Holy Communion. We are in the Africa or Asia of my imagination; I'm ashamed I can't tell the difference. The foliage is familiar, it's easy to be fooled. My band is a flop. The natives are simply not interested in colored rock 'n' roll. A powerless concept to most of them.

They clamor for Madonna. They invoke Billy Idol. Something exotic, without gravity. They throw overripe bananas at me, and screeching spider monkeys at Sister Mercy, who stops in the middle of her fabulous rendition of "It's a Man's World" and stomps offstage. She returns a few seconds later, brandishing an Uzi. We aren't sure if it's a toy or for real, but no one wants to find out. You don't fuck with Sister Mercy; even this tough audience gets the message and simmers down.

I am pregnant. I wear a black Maidenform corset, gasping for breath. A lace boa constrictor is wrapped around my neck. To appease the restless crowd, sleazy B. Goode introduces me, with apparent desperation, as Madonna Demivida. "Straight from Motor City! You remember Motor City, don't you?" He's delirious with malaria, drunk from too much quinine. I stumble out, my hair hidden by a cheap blond wig from 14th Street. The booing begins all over again. Where are you? Where is Sister Mercy? Sister Mercy isn't there to protect me. She's backstage, fuming in the shadows. She wants no part of my sorry show. The mob curses us in English, threatening to throw us into the crocodile-infested river then laughing because it is all a joke. A village matriarch leaps up in my face. "You are not worth killing," she announces. She cracks a perfect brown egg on my forehead in a gesture of . . . blessing? Contempt? Again I am not sure. Government troops are forced to intervene. We are tried without a jury, dismissed and deported as SECOND-RATE WESTERN IMPERIALIST SO-CALLED ARTISTS before being shoved into a Russian army plane along with members of Sister Mercy's Satin Soul Revue.

We are flown out of the jungle in the middle of the night, back to the safety of Motown memory.

From Quite a Bit Longer Thing in Progress

David Foster Wallace

Parmenides has some stern words for people who discuss what doesn't yet exist. About all I can think of to say is I'm doing this long piece of fiction, and parts of it are a lot like this excerpt, and parts aren't like it at all.

For some reason while I was trying to think of what to say here that wouldn't be stupid or anti-Parmenidean I kept remembering this strange little story I heard in Sunday school when I was about the size of a fire hydrant. It takes place in China or Korea or someplace like that. It seems there was this old farmer outside a village in the hill country who worked his farm with only his son and his beloved horse. One day the horse, who is not only beloved but vital to the labor-intensive work on the farm, picks the lock on his corral or whatever and runs off into the hills. All the old farmer's friends come around to exclaim what bad luck this is. The farmer only shrugs and says "Good luck, bad luck, who knows?" A couple days later the beloved horse returns from the hills in the company of a whole priceless herd of wild horses, and the farmer's friends all come around to congratulate him on what good luck the horse's escape turned out to be. "Good luck, bad luck, who knows?" is all the farmer says in reply, shrugging. The farmer now strikes me as a bit Yiddish-sounding for an old Chinese farmer, but this is how I remember it. But so the farmer and his son set about breaking the wild horses, and one of the horses bucks the son off his back with such wild violence that the son breaks his leg. And here come the friends to commiserate with the farmer and curse the bad luck that had ever brought the wild horses onto his farm. The old farmer just shrugs and says "Good luck, bad luck, who knows?" A few days later the Imperial Sino-Korean Army or something like that comes marching through the village, conscripting every able-bodied male between like ten and sixty for cannon-fodder for some hideously bloody conflict that's apparently brewing, but when they see the son's broken leg, they let him off on some sort of feudal 4F, and instead of getting shanghaied the son stays on the farm with the old farmer. Good luck? Bad luck?

This is the sort of parabolic straw you cling to as you struggle with the issue of fun, as a writer. At the start, when you start out trying to write fiction, the whole endeavor's about fun. You don't expect anybody else to read it. You're writing almost wholly to get yourself off. It's terrific fun. Then, if you have good luck and people seem to like what you do, and you actually get to get paid for it, and you get to see your stuff professionally typeset and bound and blurbed and reviewed and even (once) being read on the AM subway by a pretty girl you don't even know, it seems to make it even more fun. For a while. Then things get confusing, frustrating, and scary. Now you feel like you're writing for other people, or at least you hope so. You're no longer writing just to get yourself off—which, since any kind of masturbation is lonely and hollow, is probably good. But what replaces the onanistic motive? You've found you very much enjoy having your writing liked by people, and you find you're extremely keen to have people like the new stuff you're doing. The motive of pure personal fun starts to get supplanted by the motive of being liked, of having pretty commuters you don't know like you and think you're a good writer. Onanism gives way to attempted seduction, as a motive. Attempted seduction is hard work, and its fun is offset by a terrible fear of rejection. Whatever "ego" means, your ego has now gotten into the game. Or maybe "vanity" is a better word. Because you notice that a good deal of your writing has now become basically showing off, trying to get people to think you're good. This is understandable. You have a great deal of yourself on the line, now, writing—your vanity is at stake. You discover a tricky thing about fiction writing: a certain amount of vanity is necessary to be able to do it at all, but anything more than that amount can be lethal. At this point 90+% of the stuff you're writing is motivated and informed by an overwhelming need to be liked. This results in shitty fiction. And the shitty work must get fed to the wastebasket, not because of any sort of artistic integrity, but simply because shitty work will make you disliked. At this point in the evolution of writerly fun, fun is hard to come by, because the very thing that's now motivating you to write is also motivating you to feed your writing to the wastebasket. This is a paradox and a kind of double bind, and it can keep you bound up mute for months and even years, during which you wail and gnash and rue your bad luck and wonder bitterly where all the fun of the thing went.

The smart thing to say, I think, is that the way out of this bind is to work your way somehow back to your original motivation, fun. And, if you can find your way back to the fun, you will find that the hideously unfortunate double bind of the late vain period turns out really to have been good luck for you. Because the fun you work back to has been transfigured by the unpleasantness of vanity and fear, an unpleasantness you're now so anxious to avoid that the fun you rediscover is a way fuller and more colorful kind of fun. It has something to do with Work as Play. Or with the discovery that disciplined fun is more fun than impulsive or hedonistic fun. Under fun's new administration, writing fiction becomes a way to go deep inside yourself and illuminate precisely the stuff you don't want to see or let anyone else see, which stuff turns out to be precisely the stuff all writers and readers share and respond to, inside. Fiction becomes a weird way to countenance yourself and tell the truth, instead of being a way to escape yourself or present yourself in a false way you think will be liked. This process is confusing and frustrating and scary, and also hard work, but it turns out to be the best fun there is.

The fact that you can now sustain the fun of writing only by confronting the very same unfun parts of yourself you'd first used writing to avoid or disguise is another paradox, but this one isn't a bind.

All this is completely smart and true, I think. The trouble is that one doesn't come to see this stuff by sitting in a chair blowing smoke rings and meditating his way toward epiphany. In my own poor case, I know that this fiction project, the third long piece I've ever done, really is going to get all the way done and typed and finished and mailed, but this is only because last year I finally ate the rat and decided to go ahead and take a $ advance from a publishing house for something that wasn't yet done. I'd always refused to do this before, not out of any sort of integrity but because I feared that if I took the $ up front and thus had to write something, the whole thing'd become work instead of fun.

So but I wish I could say I accepted this $ advance because I'd already meditated my way into some Zennish, contraria-sunt-complementa *understanding of hard work and great fun being not just coextensive but inseparable. But my real reasons were banal personal-life issues like wanting health insurance and being desperate to get out of metro Boston and being tired of dicking around with part-time jobs and freelance makework instead of doing what*

I really wanted to do but had gotten too vain and scared to do. Now the bind is I can't just feed the wastebasket, no matter how much I want to, because NYC guys in serious business suits have paid $ for something they're legally entitled to see 1/1/94, and there will be considerable unpleasantness if I don't fork something entire over to them on that date. End of story.

It occurs to me I should mention about this excerpt that nothing in here about Boston AA is supposed to represent anything objective or necessarily true. The paradox is that the people who really understand Alcoholics Anonymous are enjoined by AA's tradition of anonymity from making their real knowledge public. But we ignorants can go wild, if we want. It may be different elsewhere, but Boston AA has these "open" meetings where you don't have to be an AA member to go, or even to sit there with a notebook, and I've been to some of these, and I've had some head-crunching conversations with friends who are members. For anybody who's interested in any kind of genuine religious imperative at work in modern U.S. life, AA seems like a must-see. It costs at most a voluntary buck, and some of the proceedings I saw were clearly the best show in town.

ENNET HOUSE Drug and Alcohol Recovery Home is the sixth of seven exterior Units on the grounds of an Enfield Marine Public Health Hospital complex that, from the height of an ATHSCME 2100 industrial displacement fan or Enfield Tennis Academy's hilltop, resembles seven moons orbiting a dead planet. The hospital building itself, a VA facility of iron-colored brick and steep slate roofs, is closed and cordoned, bright pine boards nailed across every possible access and aperture, with really stern government signs about trespassing. Enfield Marine was built during either WWII or Korea, when there were ample casualties and much convalescence. About the only people who use the Enfield Marine complex in a VA-related way now seem to be wild-eyed old Vietnam veterans in fatigue jackets de-sleeved to make vests, or else drastically old Korea vets who are now senile or terminally alcoholic or both.

The Hospital building itself stripped of equipment and copper wire, defunct, Enfield Marine stays solvent by maintaining several smaller buildings on the complex's grounds—buildings the size of like prosperous homes, which used to house VA doctors and support staff—and leasing them to different state-related health agencies and services. Each building has a Unit number that increases with the Unit's distance from the defunct Hospital and with its proximity, along a rutted cement roadlet that extends back from the Hospital's parking lot, to a steep ravine that overlooks a particularly unpleasant part of Brighton, MA's Commonwealth Avenue and its Green Line train tracks.

Unit #1, right by the lot in the Hospital's afternoon shadow, is leased by some agency that seems to employ only guys who wear turtlenecks; the place counsels wild-eyed Vietnam vets for certain very-delayed stress disorders, and dispenses various pacifying medications. Unit #2, right next door, is a methadone clinic overseen by the same MA Division of Substance Abuse Services that licenses Ennet House. Customers for the services of Units #1 and #2 arrive around sunup and form long lines. The customers for Unit #1 tend to congregate in like-minded groups of three or four and gesture a lot and look wild-eyed and generally pissed off in some broad geopolitical way. The customers for the methadone clinic tend to arrive looking even angrier, as a rule, and their early-morning eyes tend to bulge and flutter like the eyes of the choked, but they do not congregate, rather stand or lean along #2's long walkway's railing, arms crossed, alone, brooding, solo acts, standoffish—50 or 60 people all managing to form a line on a narrow walkway waiting for the same small building to unlock its narrow front door and yet still managing to appear alone and standoffish is a strange sight, and if Don Gately had ever once seen a ballet he would, as an Ennet House resident, from his sunup smoking station on the fire escape outside the five-man bedroom upstairs, have seen the movements and postures necessary to maintain this isolation-in-union as balletic.

The other big difference between Units #1 and #2 is that the customers of #2 leave the building deeply changed, their eyes not only back in their heads but peaceful, if a bit glazed, but anyway in general just way better put-together than when they arrived, while #1's wild-eyed patrons tend to exit #1 looking even more stressed and historically aggrieved than when they went in.

When Don Gately was in the very early part of his Ennet House residency he almost got discharged for teaming up with a bad-news methedrine addict from New Bedford and sneaking out after curfew across the E.M.P.H.H. complex in the middle of the night to attach a big sign to the narrow front door of Unit #2's methadone clinic. The sign said CLOSED UNTIL FURTHER NOTICE BY ORDER COMMONWEALTH OF MASSACHUSETTS. The first staffer at the methadone clinic doesn't get there to open up until 8:00 AM, and yet it's been mentioned how #2's customers always begin to show up with twisting hands and bulging eyes at like dawn, to wait; and Gately and the speed freak from New Bedford had never seen anything like the psychic crises and near-riot among these semi-ex-junkies—pallid blade-slender chain-smoking homosexuals and bearded bruiser types in leather berets, women with mohawks and multiple sticks of gum in, upscale trust-fund-fritterers with shiny cars and computerized jewelry—who'd arrived, as they'd been doing like hyper-conditioned rats for years, many of them, arrived at sunup with their eyes protruding and with Kleenexes at their noses and scratching their arms and standing on first one foot and then the other, doing basically everything but truly congregating, wild for chemical relief, ready to stand in the cold exhaling steam for hours for that relief, who'd arrived with the sun and now seemed to be informed that the Commonwealth of MA was suddenly going to withdraw the prospect of that relief, until (and this is what really seemed to drive them right over the edge, out there in the lot) Further Notice. "Apeshit" has rarely enjoyed so literal a denotation. At the sound of the first windowpane breaking and the sight of a blown-out old whore trying to hit a leather-vested biker with an old pre-metric GRASS GROWS BY INCHES BUT IT DIES BY FEET sign from #2's clinic's pathetic front lawn, the methedrine addict began laughing so hard that she dropped the binoculars from the Ennet House upstairs fire escape where they were watching, at like 6:30 AM, and the binoculars fell and hit the roof of one of the Ennet House counselors' cars right below in the little roadlet, with a ringing clunk, just as he was pulling in, the counselor, his name was Calvin Thrust and he was four years sober and a former NYC porn actor who'd gone through the House and now took absolutely zero in terms of shit from any of the residents, and his pride and joy was his customized 'Vette, and the binoculars made rather a nasty dent, and plus they were the House Manager's amateur-ornithology binoculars and had been borrowed out of the back office without explicit permission, and the long fall and impact didn't do them a bit of good, to say the least, and Gately and the methedrine addict got pinched and put on Full House Restriction and very nearly kicked out. The addict from New Bedford picked up the aminating needle a couple weeks after that anyway and was discovered by a night staffer simultaneously playing air-guitar and polishing the lids of all the donated canned goods in the House pantry way after lights out, stark naked and sheened with meth-sweat, and after the formality of a urine test she was given the old administrative boot – over a quarter of incoming Ennet House residents get discharged for dirty urine within their first thirty days, and it's the same at all other Boston halfway houses – and the girl ended up back in New Bedford, and then within like three hours of hitting the streets got picked up by New Bedford's Finest on an old Default Warrant and sent to Framingham Women's for a 1-to-2 bit, and got found one morning in her bunk with a kitchen-rigged shiv protruding from her privates and another in her neck and a thoroughly eliminated personal map, and Gately's individual counselor Butchie Q. brought Gately the news and invited him to see the methedrine addict's demise as a clear case of There But For the Grace of God Goeth D.W. Gately.

Unit #3, across the roadlet from #2, is unoccupied but getting reconditioned for lease; it's not boarded up, and the Enfield Marine maintenance guys go in there a couple days a week with tools and power cords and make a godawful racket. Pat Montesian hasn't yet been able to find out what sort of group misfortune #3 will be devoted to servicing.

Unit #4, more or less equidistant from both the Hospital parking lot and the steep ravine, is a repository for Alzheimer's patients with VA pensions. #4's residents wear jammies 24/7, the diapers underneath giving them a lumpy and toddlerish aspect. The patients are frequently visible at #4's windows, in jammies, splayed and open-mouthed, sometimes shrieking, sometimes just mutely open-mouthed, splayed against the windows. They give everybody at Ennet House the howling fantods. One ancient retired Air Force nurse does nothing but scream "Help!" for hours at a time from a second-story window. Since the Ennet House residents are drilled in a Boston AA recovery program that places great emphasis on "Asking For Help," the retired shrieking Air Force nurse is the object of a certain grim amusement, sometimes. Not six weeks ago a huge stolen HELP WANTED sign was found attached to #4's siding right below the retired shrieking nurse's window, and #4's director was less than amused, and demanded that Pat Montesian determine and punish the Ennet House residents responsible, and Pat had delegated the investigation to Don Gately, and though Gately had a pretty good idea who the perps were he didn't have the heart to really press and kick ass over something like what he'd done himself, when new and cynical, and so the whole thing pretty much blew over.

Unit #5, kitty-corner across the little street from Ennet House, is for catatonics and various vegetablish, fetal-positioned mental patients subcontracted to a Commonwealth outreach agency by overcrowded LTI's. Unit #5 is referred to, for reasons Gately's never been able to pinpoint, as The Shed. It's understandably a pretty quiet place. But in nice weather, when its more portable inmates are carried out and placed in the front lawn to take the air, standing there propped-up and staring, they present a tableau it took Gately some time to get used to. A couple newer residents got discharged late in Gately's treatment for tossing firecrackers into the crowd of catatonics on the lawn to see if they could get them to jump around or display affect. On warm nights, one long-limbed bespectacled lady who seems more autistic than catatonic tends to wander out of The Shed wrapped in a bedsheet and lay her hands on the thin shiny bark of a silver maple in #5's lawn, stand there touching the tree until she's missed at bedcheck and retrieved; and since Gately graduated treatment and took the offer of a live-in Staffer's job at Ennet House he sometimes wakes up in his Staff cellar bedroom down by the payphone and tonic machine and looks out the sooty ground-level window by his bed and watches the catatonic touching the tree in her sheet and glasses, illuminated by Comm. Ave.'s neon or the weird sodium light that spills down from the snooty tennis prep school overhead on its hill, he'll watch her standing there and feel an odd chilled empathy he tries not to associate with watching his mother pass out on some piece of living-room chintz.

Unit #6, right up against the ravine on the end of the rutted road's east side, is Ennet House Drug and Alcohol Recovery Home, three stories of whitewashed New England brick with the brick showing in patches through the whitewash, a mansard roof that sheds green shingles, a scabrous fire escape at each upper window and a back door no resident is allowed to use and a front office around on the south side with huge protruding bay windows that yield a view of ravine-weeds and the unpleasant stretch of Commonwealth Ave. The front office is the director's office, and its bay windows, the House's single attractive feature, are kept spotless by whatever residents get Front Office Windows for their weekly chore. The mansard's lower slope encloses attics on both the male and female sides of the House. The attics are accessed from trap doors in the ceiling of the second floor and are filled to the beams with trash bags and trunks, the unclaimed possessions of residents who've up and vanished sometime during their term. The shrubbery all around Ennet House's first story looks explosive, ballooning in certain unpruned parts, and there are candy wrappers and styrofoam cups trapped throughout the shrubs' green levels, and gaudy homemade curtains billow from the second story's female side's bedroom windows, which are open what seems like all year round.

Unit #7 is on the west side of the streetlet's end, sunk in hill-shadow and teetering right on the edge of the eroding ravine that leads down to the Avenue. #7 is in bad shape, boarded up and unmaintained and deeply slumped at the red roof's middle as if shrugging its shoulders at some pointless indignity. For an Ennet House resident, entering Unit #7 (which can easily be entered through the detachable pine board over an old kitchen window) is cause for immediate administrative discharge, since Unit #7 is infamous for being the place where Ennet House residents who want to secretly relapse with substances sneak in and absorb substances and apply Visine and Clorets and then try to get back across the street in time for 11:30 curfew without getting pinched.

Behind Unit #7 begins far and away the biggest hill in Enfield, MA. The hillside is fenced, off-limits, densely wooded and without sanctioned path. But because a legit route involves walking north all the way up the rutted road through the parking lot, past the Hospital, down the steep curved driveway to Warren Street and all the way back south down Warren to Commonwealth, almost half of all Ennet House residents negotiate #7's back fence and climb the hillside each morning, short-cutting their way to minimum-wage temp jobs at like the Provident Nursing Home or Shuco-Mist Medical Pressure Systems, etc., over the hill up Comm., or custodial and kitchen jobs at the rich tennis school for blond gleaming tennis kids on what used to be the hilltop. Don Gately's been told that the school's maze of tennis courts lies now on what used to be the hill's hilltop before the Academy's burly cigar-chomping tennis-court-contractors shaved the curved top off and rolled the new top flat, the whole long loud process sending all sorts of damaging avalanche-type debris rolling down and all over Enfield Marine's Unit #7, something over which you can sure bet the

Enfield Marine VA administration litigated, successfully, years back; and but Gately doesn't know that ETA's balding of the hill is why #7 can still stand empty and unrepaired: Enfield Tennis Academy still has to pay full rent, every month, on what it almost buried.

•

Boston AA is like AA nowhere else on this planet. Just like AA everyplace else, Boston AA is divided into numerous individual AA groups, and each group has its group name like the Reality Group or the Allston Group or the Clean and Sober Group, and each group holds its regular meeting once a week. But almost all of Boston's groups' meetings are Speaker Meetings. That means that at the meetings there are recovering alcoholic speakers who stand up in front of everybody at an amplified podium and "share their experience, strength and hope."* And the singular thing is that these speakers are not members of the group that's holding the meeting, in Boston. The speakers at one certain group's weekly Speaker Meeting are always from some other certain Boston AA group. The people from the other group who are here at like your group speaking are here on something called a Commitment. Commitments are where some members of one group commit to hit the road and travel to another group's meeting to speak publicly from the podium. Then a bunch of people from the host group hit the opposite lane of the same road on some other night and go to the visiting group's meeting, to speak. Groups always trade Commitments: you come speak to us and we'll come speak to you. It can seem bizarre. You always go elsewhere to speak. You never speak publicly at your own group's weekly Speaker Meeting. At your own group's meeting you're a host; you just sit there and listen as hard as you can, and you make coffee in 60-cup urns and stack cups in ziggurats and sell raffle tickets and make sandwiches, and you empty ashtrays and scrub out urns and sweep floors when the other group's speakers are through. You never share your experience, strength and hope on stage behind a fiberboard podium with its cheap non-digital PA system's mike except in front of some other metro-Boston group that's hosting your Commitment. Every night in Boston, bumper-stickered cars full of totally sober people, wall-eyed from caffeine and trying to read illegibly scrawled

*Before groups' regular Speaker Meetings, there are often closed half-hour Beginner Discussion Meetings, where newcomers can share their inexperience, weakness and despair in a warm, supportive, private atmosphere.

directions by the dashboard's lights, crisscross the city, heading for the church basements or bingo halls or nursing-home cafeterias of other AA groups, to put on Commitments. Being an active member of a Boston AA group is probably a little bit like being a musician or an athlete, in terms of constant travel.

The White Flag Group of Enfield, MA, in metropolitan Boston, meets Tuesdays 8:00-9:30 PM in the cafeteria of the Provident Nursing Home on Hahneman Street, off Commonwealth Avenue a couple blocks west of Enfield Tennis Academy's flat-topped hill. Tonight the White Flag Group is hosting a Commitment from the Advanced Basics Group of Concord, a suburb of Boston. The Advanced Basics people have driven almost an hour to get here, plus there's always the problem of signless urban streets and directions given over the phone. On Friday night, a small horde of White Flaggers will drive out to Concord to put on a reciprocal Commitment for the Advanced Basics Group. Traveling long distances on signless streets trying to parse directions like "Take the second left off the rotary by the driveway to the chiropractor's" and getting lost and shooting your whole evening after a long day just to speak for like six minutes at a plywood podium is called "Getting Active With Your Group"; the speaking itself is known as "12th-Step Work" or "Giving It Away." Giving It Away is a cardinal Boston AA principle. The term's derived from an epigrammatic description of recovery in Boston AA: "You give it up to get it back to give it away." Sobriety in Boston is regarded as less a gift than a sort of cosmic loan. You can't pay the loan back, but you can pay it forward, by spreading the message that despite all appearances AA works, spreading this message to the next new guy who's tottered in to a meeting and is sitting in the back row unable to hold his cup of coffee. The only way to hang onto sobriety is to give it away, and even just 24 hours of sobriety is worth doing anything for, a sober day being nothing short of a daily miracle, if you've got the Disease like he's got the Disease, says the Advanced Basics member who's chairing this evening's Commitment, saying just a couple public words to the hall before he opens the meeting and retires to a stool next to the podium and calls his group's speakers by random lot. The chairperson says he didn't used to be able to go 24 lousy *minutes* without a nip, before he Came In. "Coming In" means admitting that your personal ass is kicked and tottering into Boston AA, ready to go to any lengths to stop the shit-storm. The Advanced Basics chairperson looks like a perfect cross between pictures of

Dick Cavett and Truman Capote—Gately's basement bedroom is plastered with cutout Scotch-taped photos of all sorts of esoteric celebrities past and present, it's a compulsive thing from his North Shore childhood—except the chairperson's also flamboyantly, gleamingly bald, and to top it off he's wearing a bright-black country-western shirt with baroque curlicues of white Nodie piping across the chest and shoulders, and a string tie, plus sharp-toed boots of some sort of weirdly imbricate reptile skin, and overall he's riveting to look at, grotesque in that riveting way that flaunts its grotesquerie. There are more cheap metal ashtrays and styrofoam cups in this broad hall than you'll see anywhere else ever on earth. Gately's sitting right up front in the first row, so close to the podium he can see the tailor's notch in the chairperson's outsized incisors, but he enjoys twisting around and watching everybody come in and mill around shaking water off their outerwear, trying to find empty seats. The Provident's cafeteria is packed by 8:00. This is the big established Tuesday meeting for AA's in Enfield and Allston and Brighton. Regulars come every week from Watertown and East Newton, too, often, unless they're out on Commitments with their own groups. The Provident cafeteria walls, painted an indecisive green, are tonight bedecked with portable felt banners emblazoned with AA slogans in Cub-Scoutish blue and gold. The slogans on them appear way too insipid even to mention what they are. "**One Day At A Time**," for one. The effete western-dressed guy concludes his opening exhortation, leads the opening Moment of Silence, reads the AA Preamble, pulls a random name out of the Crested Beaut cowboy hat he's holding, makes a quinty show of reading it, says he'd like to call Advanced Basics' first random speaker of the evening, and asks if his fellow group-member John L. is in the house, here, tonight.

John L. gets up to the podium and says "That is a question I did not used to be able to answer." This gets a laugh, and everybody's posture gets subtly more relaxed, because it's clear that John L. has some sober time in and isn't going to be one of those AA speakers who's so wracked with self-conscious nerves he makes the empathetic audience nervous too. Everybody in the audience is aiming for total empathy with the speaker; that way they'll be able to receive the AA message he's here to carry. Empathy, in Boston AA, is called "Identification."

Then John L. says his first name and what he is, and everybody calls Hello.

White Flag is one of the area AA meetings Ennet House requires its residents to attend. You have to be seen at a designated AA or NA meeting every single night of the week or out you go, discharged. A House Staff member has to accompany the residents when they go to the designated meetings, so they can be officially seen there. The residents' House counselors suggest that they sit right up at the front of the hall where they can see the pores in the speaker's nose and try to Identify instead of Compare. Again, "Identify" means empathize. Identifying, unless you've got a stake in Comparing, isn't very hard to do, here. Because if you sit up front and listen hard, all the speakers' stories of decline, fall and surrender are basically alike, and like your own: fun with the substance, then very gradually less fun, then significantly less fun because of like blackouts you suddenly come out of on the highway going 145 kph with companions you do not know, nights you awake from in unfamiliar bedding next to somebody who doesn't even resemble any known sort of mammal, three-day blackouts you come out of and have to buy a newspaper to even know what town you're in; yes gradually less and less actual fun but with some physical need for the substance, now, instead of the former voluntary fun, then at some point suddenly just very little fun at all combined with terrible daily hand-trembling need, then dread, anxiety, irrational phobias, dim siren-like memories of fun, trouble with assorted authorities, knee-buckling headaches, mild seizures and the litany of what Boston AA calls Losses—

"Then come the day I lost my job to drinking." Concord's John L. has a huge hanging gut and just no ass at all, the way some big older guys' asses seem to get sucked into their body and reappear out front as gut. Gately, in sobriety, does nightly sit-ups out of fear this'll all of a sudden happen to him, as 30 approaches. Gately is so huge no one sits behind him for several rows. John L. has the biggest bunch of keys Gately's ever seen. They're on one of those pull-outable-wire janitor's keychains that clips to a belt loop, and the speaker jangles them absently, unaware, his one tip of the hat to public nerves. He's also wearing gray janitor's pants. "Lost my damn job," he says. "I mean to say I still knew where it was and whatnot. I just went in as usual one day and there was some other fellow doing it," which gets another laugh.

—then more Losses, with the substance seeming like the only consolation against the pain of the mounting Losses, and of course you're in Denial about it being the substance that's causing the very Losses it's consoling you about—

—"Alcohol destroys *slowly* but *thoroughly*, is what a fellow said to me the first night I Come In, up in Concord, and that fellow ended up becoming my sponsor."

—then less mild seizures, DT's during attempts to taper off too fast, introduction to subjective bugs and rodents, then one more binge and more bugs; then eventually a terrible acknowledgment that some line has been undeniably crossed, and fist-at-the-sky, as-God-is-my-witness vows to buckle down and lick this thing for good, to quit for all time, then maybe a few white-knuckled days of initial success, then a slip, then more pledges, clock-watching, baroque self-regulations, repeated slips back into the substance's relief after like two days' abstinence, ghastly hangovers, head-flattening guilt and self-disgust, superstructures of additional self-regulations (e.g. not before 9:00 AM, not on a worknight, only when the moon is waxing, only in the company of Swedes) which also fail—

"When I was drunk I wanted to get sober and when I was sober I wanted to get drunk," John L. says; "I lived that way for years, and I submit to you that's not livin, it's death in life."

—then unbelievable psychic pain, fear of impending insanity (why can't I quit if I so want to quit, unless I'm insane?), appearances at hospital detoxes and rehabs, domestic strife, financial freefall, eventual domestic Losses—

"And then I lost my wife to drinking. I mean I still knew where she was and whatnot. I just went in one day and there was some other fellow doing it," at which there's not all that much laughter, lots of pained nods: it's often the same all over, in terms of domestic Losses.

—then vocational ultimatums, unemployability, financial ruin, pancreatitis, overwhelming guilt, bloody vomiting, cirrhotic neuralgia, incontinence, neuropathy, black depressions, searing pain with the substance affording increasingly brief periods of relief; then, finally, no relief available anywhere at all; finally it's impossible to get high enough to freeze what you feel like, being this way; and now you hate the substance, *hate* it, but you still find yourself unable to stop doing it, the substance, you find you finally want to stop more than anything on earth and it's no fun doing it anymore and you can't believe you ever liked doing it and but you *still* can't stop, it's like you're totally bats, it's like there's two yous; and when you'd sell your own dear Mum to stop and still, you find, can't stop, then the last layer of jolly friendly mask comes off your old friend the substance, it's midnight now and all masks come off, and you all of a sudden see the substance as it really is, for the first time you see the Disease as it really is, really has been all this time, you look in the mirror at midnight and see what owns you, what's become what you are—

"A fuckin livin death, I tell you it's not bein alive, by the end I was undead, not alive, and I tell you the idea of dyin was nothing compared to the idea of livin like that for another five or ten years and only *then* dyin," with audience heads nodding in rows like a windswept meadow; boy can they ever Identify. . . .

—and then you're in serious trouble, very serious trouble, and you know it, finally, deadly serious trouble, because this substance you thought was your one true friend, that you gave up all for, gladly, that for so long gave you relief from the pain of the Losses your love of that relief caused, your mother and lover and god and compadre, has finally removed its smily-face mask to reveal centerless eyes and a ravening maw, and canines down to here, it's the Face In The Floor, the grinning root-white face of your worst nightmares, and the face is your own face in the mirror, now, it's you, the substance has become you, and the puke-, drool- and substance-crusted T-shirt you've both worn for weeks now gets torn off and you stand there looking and in the root-white chest where your heart (given away to it) should be beating, in its exposed chest's center and centerless eyes is just a lightless hole, more teeth, and a beckoning taloned hand dangling something irresistible, and now you see you've been had, screwed royal, stripped and fucked and tossed to the side like some stuffed toy to lie in whatever posture you land in. You see now it's your enemy and your worst personal nightmare and the trouble it's gotten you into is undeniable and you *still* can't stop. Doing the substance now is like attending Black Mass but you still can't stop, even though the substance no longer gets you high. You are, as they say, Finished. You cannot get drunk and you cannot get sober; you cannot get high and you cannot get straight. You are behind bars; you are in a cage and can see only bars in every direction. You are in the kind of a hell of a mess that either ends lives or turns them around. You are at a fork in the road that Boston AA calls your "Bottom," though the term is misleading, because everybody here agrees it's more like someplace very high and unsupported: you're on the edge of something tall and leaning way out forward. . . .

If you listen for the similarities, all these speakers' substance-careers seem to terminate at the same cliff's edge. You are now Finished, as a substance user. It's the jumping-off place. You now have two choices. You can either eliminate your own map for keeps — blades are the best, or else pills, or there's always quietly sucking off the exhaust pipe of your repossessable car in the bank-owned garage of your familyless home. Something whimpery instead of banging. Better clean and quiet and (since your whole career's been one long futile flight from pain) painless. Though of the alcoholics and drug addicts who compose over 70 percent of a given year's suicides, some try to go out with a last great garish Balaclavan gesture: one longtime member of the White Flag Group is a prognathous lady named Louise B. who tried to take a map-eliminating dive off the old Hancock Building downtown in '81 but got caught in the gust of a rising thermal only six flights off the roof and blown cartwheeling back up and in through the smoked-glass window of an arbitrage firm's suite on the 34th floor, ending up sprawled prone on a high-gloss conference table with only lacerations and a compound of the collarbone and an experience of willed self-annihilation and external intervention that has left her rabidly Christian — rabidly, as in foam — so that she's comparatively ignored and avoided, though her AA story, being just like everybody else's but more spectacular, has become metro-Boston AA myth. But so when you get to this jumping-off place at the Finish of your substance career you can either take your own Brody — at age 60, or 32, or 17 — or you can get out the very beginning of the Yellow Pages and make a blubbering 2:00 AM phone call and admit to a gentle grandparentish voice that you're in trouble, deadly serious trouble, and the voice will try to soothe you into hanging on until a couple hours go by and two pleasant, earnest, weirdly calm guys in conservative attire appear smiling at your door sometime before dawn and speak quietly to you for hours and leave you not remembering anything from what they said except the sense that they used to be eerily like you, just where you are, utterly fucked, and but now somehow aren't anymore, fucked like you, at least they didn't seem like they were, unless the whole thing's some incredibly involved scam, this AA thing, and so but anyway you sit there on what's left of your furniture in the lavender dawn light and realize that by now you literally have no other choice besides trying this AA thing or else eliminating your map, so you spend the day killing every last bit of every substance you've got in one last joyless bitter farewell binge and resolve, the next day, to go ahead and swallow your pride and maybe your common sense too and try these meetings of this "Program" that at best is probably just Unitarian happy horseshit and at worst is a cover for some glazed and canny cult-type thing where they'll keep you sober by making you spend 20 hours a day selling cellophane cones of artifical flowers on the median strips of heavy-flow roads. And what defines this cliffish nexus of exactly two total choices, this miserable road-fork Boston AA calls your "Bottom," is that at this point you feel like maybe selling flowers on median strips might not be so bad, not compared to what you've got going, personally, at this juncture. And this, at root, is what unites Boston AA: it turns out that this same resigned, miserable, brainwash-and-exploit-me-if-that's-what-it-takes-type desperation was the jumping-off place for just about every AA you meet, once you've actually gotten it up to stop darting in and out of the big meetings and start walking up with your wet hand out and trying to actually personally meet some Boston AA's. As the one particular tough old guy or lady you're always particularly scared of and drawn to says, nobody ever Comes In because things were going really well and they just wanted to round out their PM social calendar. Everybody, but *everybody* Comes In dead-eyed and puke-white and with their face hanging down around their knees and with a well-thumbed firearm-and-ordnance-mail-order catalogue kept safe and available at home, map-wise, for when this last desperate resort of hugs and clichés turns out to be just happy horseshit, for you. You are not unique, they'll say: this initial hopelessness unites every soul in this broad cold salad-bar'd hall. They are like Hindenburg survivors. Every meeting is a reunion, once you've been in for a while.

And then the palsied newcomers who totter in desperate and miserable enough to hang in and keep coming and start feebly to scratch beneath the unlikely insipid surface of the thing, Don Gately's found, then get united by a second common experience. The shocking discovery that the thing actually does seem to work. Does keep you straight. It's improbable and shocking. When Gately finally snapped to the fact, one day about four months into his Ennet House residency, that quite a few days seemed to have gone by without his playing with the usual idea of slipping over to Unit #7 and getting loaded in some non-uremic way the courts couldn't prove, that several days had gone by without his even *thinking* of oral narcotics or a tightly rolled duBois or a cold foamer on a hot day . . . when he realized that the various substances he didn't used to be able to go a day without absorbing hadn't even like *occurred* to him in almost a week, Gately hadn't felt so much grateful or joyful as just plain shocked. The idea that AA might actually somehow *work* unnerved him. He suspected some sort of trap. Some new sort of trap. At this stage he and the other Ennet residents who were still there and starting to snap to the fact that AA might work began to sit around together late at night going bats together because it seemed to be impossible to figure out just *how* AA worked. It did, yes, tentatively seem maybe actually to be working, but Gately couldn't for the life of him figure out how just sitting on hemorrhoid-hostile folding chairs every night looking at nosepores and listening could work. Nobody's ever been able to figure AA out, is another binding commonality. And the folks with serious time in AA are infuriating about questions starting with How. You ask the scary old guys How AA Works and they smile their chilly smiles and say Just Fine. It just works, is all; end of story. The newcomers who abandon common sense and resolve to hang in and keep coming and then find their cages all of a sudden open, mysteriously, after a while, share this sense of deep shock and possible trap; about newer Boston AA's with like six months clean you can see this look of glazed suspicion instead of beatific glee,* an expression like that of bug-eyed natives confronted with indoor plumbing. And so this unites them, nervously, this tentative assemblage of possible glimmers of something like hope, this grudging move toward maybe acknowledging that this unromantic, unhip, clichéd AA thing — so unlikely and unpromising, so much the inverse of what they'd come too much to love — might really be able to keep the lover's toothy maw at bay. The process is the neat reverse of what brought you down and In here: substances start out being so magically great, so much the interior jigsaw's missing piece, that at the start you just know, deep in your gut, that they'll never let you down; you just know it. But they do. And then this goofy slapdash anarchic system of low-rent gatherings and corny slogans and saccharine grins and hideous coffee is so lame you just know there's no way it could ever possibly work except for the utterest morons . . . and then Gately seems to find out AA turns out to be the very loyal friend you thought you'd had and then lost, when you Came In. And so you hang in and stay

*See, for instance, photos of people released after long periods in concentration camps; do they look "happy"?

sober and straight; and out of sheer hand-burned-on-hot-stove terror you heed the improbable-sounding warnings not to stop pounding out the nightly meetings, even after the substance cravings have left and you feel like you've got a grip on the thing at last and can now go it alone, you still don't try to go it alone, you heed the improbable warnings because by now you have no faith in your own sense of what's really improbable and what isn't, since AA seems, improbably enough, to be working, and with no faith in your own senses you're confused, flummoxed, and when people with AA time strongly advise you to keep coming you nod robotically and keep coming, and you sweep floors and scrub out ashtrays and fill stained steel urns with hideous coffee, and you keep getting ritually down on your big knees every morning and night asking for help from a sky that still seems a burnished shield against all who would ask aid of it — how can you pray to a "God" you believe only morons believe in, still? — but the old guys say it doesn't yet matter what you believe or don't believe, Just Do It they say, and like a shock-trained organism without any kind of independent human will you do exactly like you're told, you keep coming and coming, nightly, and now you take pains not to get booted out of the squalid halfway house you'd at first tried so hard to get discharged from, you hang in and hang in, meeting after meeting, warm day after cold day . . . ; and not only does the urge to get high stay more or less away, but more general life-quality-type things — just as improbably promised, at first, when you'd Come In — things seem to get progressively somehow better, inside, for a while, then worse, then even better, then for a while worse in a way that's still somehow better, realer, you feel weirdly unblinded, which is good, even though a lot of the things you now see about yourself and how you've lived are horrible to have to see — and by this time the whole thing is so improbable and unparsable that you're so flummoxed you're convinced you're maybe brain-damaged, still, at this point, from all the years of substances, and you figure you'd better hang in in this Boston AA where older guys who seem to be less damaged — or at least less flummoxed by their damage — will tell you in terse simple imperative clauses exactly what to do, and where and when to do it (though never How or Why); and at this point you've started to have an almost classic sort of Blind Faith in the older guys, a Blind Faith in them born not of zealotry or even of belief but just of a chilled conviction that you have no faith whatsoever left in yourself,* and now if the older guys say Jump you ask them to hold their hand at the desired height, and now they've got you, and you're free.

Another Advanced Basics Group speaker, whose first name Gately loses in the crowd's big Hello but whose last initial is E., an even bigger guy than John L., a green-card Irishman in a skallycap and a Sinn Fein sweatshirt, with a belly like a swinging sack of meal and a thoroughly visible ass to back it up, is sharing his hope's experience by listing the gifts that have followed his decision to Come In and put the plug in the jug and the cap on the Dexedrine bottle and stop driving long-haul truck routes in unbroken 96-hour metal-pedaled states of chemical psychosis. The rewards of his abstinence, he stresses, have been more than just spiritual. Only in Boston AA can you hear a 50-year-old immigrant wax lyrical about his first solid bowel movement in adult life.

"'d been a confarmed bowl-splatterer for yars b'yond contin'. 'd been barred from t'facilities at sartin troock stops. T'wallpaper in de loo a t'ome hoong in t'ese carled sheets froom t'wall, ay till yo. But now woon dey . . . ay'll remaember't'always. T'were a wake to t'day ofter ay stewed oop for me ninety-dey chip. Ay were tray moents sobber. Ay were thar on t'throne a't'ome, yo new. No't'put too fain a poin t'on it, ay prodooced as er uzhal and . . . and ay war soo amazed as to no't'belaven' me yairs. T'was a soned so wonefamiliar at t'first ay tought ay'd droped me wallet in t'loo, do yo new. Ay tought ay'd droped me wallet in t'loo as Good is me wetness. So doan ay bend twixt m'knays and'ad a luke in t'dim o't'loo, and codn't belave me'yize. So gud paple ay do then ay drope to m'knays by t'loo an't'ad a rail luke. A loaver's luke, d'yo new. And friends t'were loavely past me pur poewers t'say. T'were a *tard* in t'loo. A *rail tard.* T'were farm an' teppered an' aiver so jaintly aitched. T'luked . . . *conestroocted* instaid've sprayed. T'luked as ay fel't'in me 'eart Good 'imself maint a tard t'luke. Me friends, this tard'o'mine practically had a *poolse.* Ay sted doan own m'knays an tanked me Har Par, which ay choose t'call me Har Par Good, an' ay been tankin me Har Par own m'knays aiver sin, marnin and natetime an in t'loo s'well, aiver sin." The man's red-leather face radiant throughout. Gately and the other White Flaggers fall about, laugh from the gut, a turd that practically had a pulse, an ode to a

*A conviction common to all who hang in with AA, after a while, and abstracted in the cliché slogan "My Best Thinking Got Me Here."

solid dump; but the lightless eyes of certain palsied back-row newcomers widen with a very private identification and possible hope, hardly daring to imagine. . . . A certain Message has been Carried.

Gately's biggest asset as an Ennet House live-in Staffer – besides the size thing, which is not to be discounted when order has to be maintained in a place where guys come in fresh from detox still in withdrawal with their eyes rolling like cattle and an earring in their eyelid and a tattoo that says BORN TO BE UNPLEASANT – besides the fact that his upper arms are the size of pieces of meat you rarely see unfrozen, his big plus is he has this ability to convey his own experience about at first hating AA to new House residents who hate AA and resent being forced to go and sit up in nose-pore-range and listen to such limply improbable clichéd drivel night after night. Limp AA looks, at first, and actually limp it sometimes really is, Gately tells the new residents, and he says no way he'd expect them to believe on just his say-so that the thing'll work if they're miserable and desperate enough to hang in against common sense for a while. But he says he'll clue them in on a truly great thing about AA: *they can't kick you out.* You're In if you say you're In. Nobody can get kicked out, not for any reason. Which means you can say *anything* in here. Talk about solid turds all you want. The molecular integrity of shit is small potatoes. Gately says he defies the new Ennet residents to try and shock the patient smiles off these Boston AA's' faces. Can't be done, he says. These folks have literally heard it all. Impotence. Priapism. Onanism. Projectile-incontinence. Autocastration. Elaborate paranoid delusions, the grandiosest megalomania, Communism, fringe-Birchism, National-Socialist-Bundtism, psychotic breaks, sodomy, bestiality, daughter-diddling, exposures at every conceivable level of indecency. Coprophilia and -phagia. Four-year White Flagger Glenn K.'s personally chosen Higher Power is *Satan,* for fuck's sake. Granted, nobody in White Flag much likes Glenn K., and the thing with the hooded cape and makeup and the candelabrum he carries around draws mutters, but Glenn K. is a member for exactly as long as he cares to hang in.

So say anything you want, Gately invites them. Go to the Beginner Meeting at 7:30 and raise your shaky mitt and tell the unlacquered truth. Free-associate. Run with it. Gately this morning, just after required AM meditation, Gately was telling the angry little educated new guy Ewell, with the hypertensive flush and little white beard, telling him how he, Gately, had perked up considerably at 30 days clean when he found he could raise his big mitt in Beginner Meetings and say publicly just how much he hates this limp AA drivel about gratitude and humility and miracles and how he hates it and thinks it's horseshit and hates the AA's and how they all seem like limp smug moronic self-satisfied shit-eating pricks with their lobotomized smiles and goopy sentiment and how he wishes them all violent technicolor harm in the worst way, new Gately sitting their spraying vitriol, wet-lipped and red-eared, *trying* to get kicked out, purposely *trying* to outrage the AA's into giving him the boot so he could quick-march back to Ennet House and tell crippled Pat Montesian and his counselor Butchie Q. how he'd been given the boot at AA, how they'd pleaded for honest sharing of innermost feelings and OK he'd honestly shared his deepest feelings on the matter of *them* and the grinning hypocrites had shaken their fists and told him to screw . . . and but so in the meetings the poison would leap and spurt from him, and how but he found out all the veteran White Flaggers would do as a group when he vocally wished them harm was nod furiously in empathetic Identification and shout with maddening cheer "Keep Coming!" and one or two Flaggers with medium amounts of sober time would run up to him after the meeting and say how it was so good to hear him share and *boy* could they ever Identify with the deeply honest feelings he'd shared and how he'd done them the service of giving them the gift of a real "Remember-When"-type experience because they could now remember feeling just exactly the same way as Gately, when they first Came In, only they confess to not then having the spine to honestly share it with the group, and so in a bizarre improbable twist they'd leave Gately ending up standing there feeling like some sort of AA hero, a prodigy of vitriolic spine, both frustrated and elated, and before they bid him orevwar and told him to come back they'd make sure to give him their phone numbers on the back of their little raffle tickets, phone numbers Gately wouldn't dream of actually calling up (to say *what,* for chrissakes?) but which he found he rather liked having in his wallet, to just carry around, just in case of who knew what; and then plus maybe one of these old Enfield-native White Flag guys with geologic amounts of sober time in AA and a twisted ruined old body and clear bright-white eyes would hobble sideways like a crab slowly up to Gately after a meeting in which he'd spewed vitriol and reach way up to clap him on his big sweaty shoulder and say in their fremitic smoker's croak that well you at least seem like a ballsy little bastard, all full of piss and vinegar and whatnot, and that just maybe you'll be OK, Don G., just maybe, just Keep Coming, and, if you'd care for a spot of advice from somebody who likely spilled more booze in his day than you've even consumed in yours, you might try to just simply sit down at meetings and relax and take the cotton out of your ears and put it in your mouth and shut the fuck up and just listen, for the first time perhaps in your life really *listen*, and maybe you'll end up OK; and they don't offer their phone numbers, not the really old guys, Gately knows he'd have to eat his pride raw and actually *request* the numbers of the old ruined grim calm longtimers in White Flag, "The Crocodiles" the less senior White Flaggers call them, because the old twisted guys all tend to sit clustered together with hideous turdlike cigars in one corner of the Provident cafeteria under a 16x20 framed glossy of crocodiles or alligators sunning themselves on some verdant riverbank somewhere, with the maybe-joke legend OLD-TIMERS CORNER somebody had magisculed across the bottom of the photo, and these old guys cluster together under it, rotating their green cigars in their misshapen fingers and discussing completely mysterious long-sober matters out of the sides of their mouths. Gately sort of fears these old AA men with their varicose noses and flannel shirts and white crewcuts and brown teeth and coolly amused looks of appraisal, feels like a kind of low-rank tribal knucklehead in the presence of stone-faced chieftains who rule by some unspoken shamanistic fiat,* and so of course he hates them, the Crocodiles, for making him feel like he fears them, but he oddly also ends up looking forward a little to sitting in the same big nursing-home cafeteria with them and facing the same direction they face, every Tuesday, and a little later finds he even enjoys riding at 30 kph tops in their perfectly maintained 25-year-old sedans when he starts going along on White Flag Commitments to other Boston AA groups. He eventually heeds a terse suggestion and starts going out and telling his grisly personal story publicly from the podium with other members of White Flag, the group he finally officially joined. This is what you do if you're new and have what's called The Gift of Desperation and are willing to go to any excruciating lengths to stay straight, you officially join a group and put your name and sobriety date down on the group secretary's official roster, and you make it your business to start to get to know other

*None of these are Gately's terms.

members of the group on a personal basis, and you carry their numbers talismanically in your wallet; and, most important, you get Active With Your Group, which here in Gately's Boston AA "Active" means not just sweeping the footprinty floor after the Lord's Prayer and making coffee and emptying ashtrays of gasper-butts and ghastly spit-wet cigar ends but also showing up regularly at specified PM times at the White Flag Group's regular haunt, the Elit (the final e's neon's ballast's out) Diner in Enfield Center, showing up and pounding down tooth-loosening amounts of coffee and then getting in well-maintained Crocodilian sedans whose suspensions' springs Gately's mass makes sag and getting driven, wall-eyed with caffeine and cigar fumes and general public-speaking angst, to like Lowell's Joy of Living Group or Charlestown's Plug In The Jug Group or Bridgewater State Detox or Concord Honor Farm with these guys, and except for one or two other pale wall-eyed newcomers with The Gift of utter Desperation it's mostly Crocodiles with geologic sober time in these cars, it's mostly the guys that've stayed sober in White Flag for decades who still go on every single booked Commitment, they go every time, dependable as death, even when the Celtics are on spontaneous cartridge, they hit the old Commitment trail, they remain rabidly Active With Their Group; and the Crocodiles in the car invite Gately to see the coincidence of long-term contented sobriety and rabidly tireless AA activity as not a coincidence at all. The Crocodiles up front look into the rearview mirror and narrow their baggy bright-white eyes at Gately in the sagging back seat with the other new guys, and the Crocodiles say they can't even begin to say how many new guys they've seen Come In and then get sucked back Out There, Come In to AA for a while and hang in and put together a little sober time and have things start to get better, head-wise and life-quality-wise, and after a while the new guys get cocky, they decide they've gotten *"well,"* and they get really busy at the new job sobriety's allowed them to get, or maybe they buy season Celtics tickets, or they rediscover pussy and start chasing pussy (these withered gnarled totally post-sexual old guys actually say "pussy"), but one way or another these poor cocky clueless new bastards start gradually drifting away from rabid Activity In The Group, and then away from their group itself, and then little by little gradually drift away from any AA meetings at all, and then, without the protection of meetings or a group, in time—oh there's always plenty of time, the Disease is fiendishly patient—how in time they forget what it was like, the ones that've cockily drifted, they forget who and what they are, they forget about the Disease, until like one day they're at like maybe a Celtics-Sixers game, and the Garden's hot, and they think what could just one cold foamer hurt, after all this sober time, now that they've gotten *well.* Just one cold one. What could it hurt. And after that one it's like they'd never stopped, if they've got the Disease. And how in a month or six months or a year they have to Come *Back* In, back to the Boston AA halls and their old group, tottering, DTing, with their faces hanging down around their knees all over again, or maybe it's five or ten years before they can get it up to get back in, beaten to shit again, or else their system isn't ready for the recurred abuse again after some sober time and they die Out There—the Crocodiles are always talking in hushed, 'Nam-like tones about Out There—or else, worse, maybe they kill somebody in a blackout and spend the rest of their lives in MCI-Walpole drinking raisin jack fermented in the seatless toilet and trying to recall what they did to get in there, Out There; or else, worst of all, these cocky new guys drift back Out There and have nothing sufficiently horrible to Finish them happen at all, just go back to drinking 24/7/365, to not-living, behind bars, undead, back in the Disease's cage all over again. The Crocodiles talk about how they can't count the number of guys that've Come In for a while and drifted away and gone back Out There and died, or not gotten to die. They even point some of these guys out—gaunt gray spectral men reeling on sidewalks with all that they own in a trashbag—as the White Flaggers drive slowly by in their well-maintained cars. Old emphysemic Bobby Hurst in particular likes to slow his LeSabre down at a corner in front of some wobbling loose-faced homeless guy who'd once been in AA and drifted cockily out and roll down his window and yell "Live it up!"

Of course—the Crocodiles dig at each other with their knobby elbows and laugh—they say when they tell Gately to either hang in AA and get rabidly Active or else die in misery, it's only a *suggestion.* They howl and choke and slap their knees at this. It's your classic in-type joke. There are, by ratified tradition, no "musts" in Boston AA. No doctrine or dogma or rules. They can't kick you out. You don't have to do what they say. Do exactly as you please—if you still trust what seems to please you. The Crocodiles roar and wheeze and pound on the dash and bob in the front seat in abject mirth.

Boston AA's take on itself is that it's a benign anarchy, that any order to the thing is a function of "Miracle." No regs, no musts, only love and support and the occasional humble suggestion born of shared experience. A non-authoritarian, dogma-free movement. Normally a gifted cynic, with a keen bullshit-antenna, Gately needed over a year to pinpoint the ways in which he feels like Boston AA really is actually sub rosa dogmatic. You're not supposed to pick up any sort of altering substance, of course; that goes without saying; but the Fellowship's official line is that if you do slip or drift or fuck up or forget and go Out There for a night and absorb a substance and get all your Disease's triggers pulled again they want to know they not only invite but urge you to come on back to meetings as quickly as possible. They're pretty sincere about this, since a lot of new people slip and slide a bit, total-abstinence-wise, in the beginning. Nobody's supposed to judge you or snub you for slipping. Everybody's here to help. Everybody knows that the returning slippee has punished himself enough just being Out There, and that it takes incredible desperation and humility to eat your pride and wobble back In and put the substance down again after you've fucked up the first time and the substance is calling to you all over again. There's the sort of sincere compassion about fucking up that empathy makes possible, although some of the AA's will nod smugly when they find out the slippee didn't take some of the basic suggestions. Even newcomers who can't even start to quit yet and show up with suspicious flask-sized bulges in their coat pockets and list progressively to starboard as the meeting progresses are urged to keep coming, hang in, stay, as long as they're not too disruptive. Actual drooling inebriates are discouraged from driving themselves home after the Lord's Prayer, but nobody's going to wrestle your keys away. Boston AA stresses the autonomy of the individual member. Please say and do whatever you wish. Of course there are about a dozen basic suggestions,* and of course people who cockily decide they don't wish to abide by the basic suggestions are constantly going back Out There and then wobbling back in with their faces down around their knees and confessing from the podium that they didn't take the suggestions and have paid full price for their willful arrogance and have learned

*E.g., in Boston, join group, get Active, get phone numbers, get sponsor, call sponsor daily, call other AA's daily, shlep to meetings daily, pray like a fiend for a daily reprieve from Disease, practice rigorous personal honesty, don't kid self that you can still hang out in bars playing darts and just drinking seltzer, etc.

the hard way and but now they're back, by God, and this time they're going to follow the suggestions to the bloody *letter*, just see if they don't. Gately's sponsor Bobby Hurst, the Crocodile that Gately finally got up the juice to ask to be his sponsor, compares the totally optional basic suggestions in Boston AA to, say for instance, if you're going to jump out of an airplane, we "suggest" you wear a parachute. But of course you do what you want. Then he starts laughing until he's coughing so bad he has to sit down.

The bitch of the thing is you have to *want* to do it. If you don't *want* to do as you're told—I mean as it's suggested you do—it means that your own personal will is still in control, and Butchie Q. over at Ennet House never tires of pointing out that your personal will is the web your Disease sits and spins in, still. The will you call your own ceased to be yours as of who knows how many substance-drenched years ago. It's now shot through with the spidered fibrosis of your Disease. Butchie Q. favors entomologic analogies. You have to starve the spider. You have to surrender your will. This is why most people will only Come In and hang in after their own will has just about killed them. You have to want to surrender your will to people who know how to starve the spider. You have to want to take the suggestions, want to abide by the traditions of anonymity, humility, surrender to the group conscience. If you don't obey, nobody will kick you out. They won't have to. You'll end up kicking *yourself* out, if you steer by your own sick will. This is maybe why just about everybody in the White Flag Group tries so hard to be so disgustingly humble, kind, helpful, tactful, cheerful, non-judgmental, tidy, energetic, sanguine, modest, generous, fair, orderly, patient, tolerant, attentive and truthful. It isn't like the group makes them do it. It's more like that the only people who end up able to hang for serious time in AA are the ones who willingly try to be these things. This is why, to the cynical newcomer or surly Ennet House resident, serious AA's look like these weird combinations of Gandhi and Mr. Rogers with tattoos and enlarged livers and no teeth who used to beat wives and diddle daughters and now rhapsodize about their bowel movements. It's all optional; do it or die.

Then but there *is* a kind of coercion in Boston AA. But what kind? It's not any kind of coercion Don Gately's ever seen. And Gately's been on both sides of plenty of coercive-type situations.

Like e.g. Gately puzzled for quite some time about why these AA meetings where nobody kept order seemed so orderly. No interrupting, fisticuffery, no heckled invectives, no poisonous gossip or beefs over the tray's last Oreo. Where was the hard-ass sergeant at arms, some enforcer of these principles they guaranteed would save your ass? Why the fuck don't they have a sergeant at arms if the stakes are as high as they say? Pat Montesian and Butchie Quinones and Bobby Hurst the Crocodile wouldn't answer Gately's questions about where's the enforcement. They just all smiled coy smiles and said to Keep Coming, an apothegm Gately found just as trite as "Easy Does It!" or "Live and Let Live!"

How do trite things get to be trite? Why is the truth usually not just un- but anti-dramatic? Is God a dull date? Does destiny dress off the rack? Because every one of the seminal little mini-epiphanies you have in early AA are dull and polyesterishly banal, Gately admits to residents. He'll tell how, as a resident, right after that one Harvard Square heavy-metal punk, this guy whose name was Bernard but insisted on being called Plasmatron-7, right after old Plasmatron-7 drank nine bottles of Nyquil in the men's upstairs head and pitched forward face-first into his instant spuds at supper and got discharged on the spot, and got fireman-carried by Calvin Thrust right out to Comm. Ave's Green Line T-stop, and Gately got moved up from the newest guys' five-man room to take Plasmatron-7's old bunk in the less-new guys' three-man room, Gately had an epiphanic AA-related nocturnal dream he'll be the first to admit was banally trite. In the dream Gately and row after row of totally average and non-unique U.S. citizens were kneeling on their knees on polyester cushions in a crummy low-rent church basement. The basement was your average low-rent church basement—colored chalkdust and exposed pipes and cans of food-bank food and stacks of old defoliated hymnals, and long folding tables smeared with nursery-school fingerpaints and colored chalk—except for the basement walls of this dream-church's basement walls were of like thin clean clear glass. So they were transparent, he says. Everybody was kneeling on these cheap but comfortable cushions, it wasn't all that uncomfortable to be on your knees, except it was weird because nobody seemed to have any clear idea why they were all on their knees, and there was like no tier-boss or sergeant-at-arms-type figure around coercing them into kneeling, and yet there was this sense of some compelling unspoken reason why they were all kneeling. It was one of those dream things where it didn't make sense but did. And but then some lady over to Gately's left got off her knees and all of a sudden stood up, just like to stretch, and the minute she stood up she was all of a sudden yanked backward with terrible force and sucked out through one of the clear glass walls of the basement, and Gately had winced to get ready for the sound of serious glass, but the glass wall didn't shatter so much as just let the cartwheeling lady sort of melt right through, and healed back over where she'd melted through, and she was gone. Her cushion and then Gately notices a couple other polyester cushions in some of the rows here and there sat there empty, so some rows as he looked down them lengthwise looked like combs missing teeth. It was then, as he was looking around, that Gately in his dream looked slowly up overhead at the ceiling's exposed pipes and could now all of a sudden see, rotating slow and silent through the basement a meter above the different-shaped and -colored heads of the kneeling assembly, he could see a long plain hooked stick, like the crook of a giant shepherd, like the hook that appears from stage-left and drags bad acts out of tomato-range, moving slowly above them in French-curled circles, nice and easy, almost demurely, as if quietly scanning; and when a mild-faced guy in a cardigan happened to stand up and was hooked by the hooked stick and pulled ass-over-teakettle out through the soundless glass membrane Gately turned his big head as far as he could without leaving the cushion and could see, now, just outside the wall's clean pane, trolling with the big stick, an extraordinarily snappily-dressed and authoritative figure manipulating the giant shepherd's crook with one hand and coolly examining the nails of his other hand from behind a mask that was simply the plain yellow smily-face circle that accompanied invitations to have a nice day. The figure was so impressive and trustworthy and casually self-assured as to be both soothing and compelling. The authoritative figure radiated good cheer and abundant charm and limitless patience. It manipulated the big stick in the coolly purposeful way of the sort of angler who you know isn't going to throw back anything he catches. The slow silent stick with the hook he held was what kept them all kneeling below the baroque little circumferences of its movement overhead.

One of Ennet House's Live-In Staffers' rotating PM jobs is to be awake and on-call in the front office all night for Dream Duty—people in early recovery from substances often get hit with real horror-show dreams, or else traumatically seductive substance dreams, and sometimes trite but important epiphanic dreams, and the Staffer on Dream Duty is required to be up doing paperwork or sit-ups or staring out the broad bay window in the front office downstairs, ready to make coffee and listen to the residents' dreams and offer the odd practical upbeat Boston-AA-type insight into possible implications for the dreamer's progress in recovery—but Gately had no need to clomp downstairs for a Staffer's feedback on this one, since it was so powerfully, tritely obvious. It had come clear to Gately that Boston AA had the planet's most remorselessly hard-ass and efficient sergeant at arms. Gately lay there, overhanging all four sides of his bunk, his broad square forehead wrinkled and beaded with revelation. Boston AA's sergeant at arms stood *outside* the orderly meeting halls, in that much-invoked Out There where exciting clubs full of good cheer throbbed gaily below lit signs with neon bottles endlessly pouring. AA's patient enforcer was always and everywhere Out There: it stood casually checking its cuticles in the astringent fluorescence of pharmacies that took forged Talwin scrips for a hefty surcharge, in the onionlight through paper shades in the furnished rooms of strung-out nurses who financed their own cages' maintenance with stolen pharmaceutical samples, in the isopropyl reek of the storefront offices of stooped old chain-smoking MD's whose scrip-pads were always out and who needed only to hear "pain" and see cash. In the home of a snot-strangled Canadian VIP and the office of an implacable Revere A.D.A. whose wife has opted for dentures at 35. AA's disciplinarian looked damn good and smelled even better and dressed to impress and his blank black-on-yellow smile never faltered as he sincerely urged you to have a nice day. Just one more last nice day. Just one cold one. For Auld Lang, just one, what could it hurt, after all this time. . . .

And that was the first night that cynical Gately willingly took the basic suggestion to get down on his big knees by his undersized Ennet House bunk and ask for help from something he still didn't believe in, ask for his own sick spidered will to be taken from him and fumigated and squished. He asked for the willingness to voluntarily become his own sergeant at arms.

And mentally, at least, newcomer resident Gately could relax a bit after that trite night's dream, because it at least seemed like he'd at last figured out that there *was* enforcement in Boston AA, good old coercive compulsion, albeit a very odd kind that wasn't compulsion but a sort of anti-compulsion, the enforcer at once external to the halls where AA met and also deeply internal to the Diseased personal will of everybody who was trying to hang in there . . . he got that far in the epiphany's analysis and then found he was able to Let It Go because it made his big head hurt so.

But and plus in Boston AA there is, unfortunately, dogma, too, it turns out; and some of it is both dated and smug. And there's an off-putting jargon in the Fellowship, a psychobabbly dialect that's damn near impossible to follow at first, says Ken Erdedy, the college-boy ad exec semi-new at Ennet House, complaining to Gately at the White Flag meeting's raffle break. Boston AA meetings are unusually long, an hour and a half instead of the national hour, but here they also have this formal break at about 45 minutes where everybody can grab a sandwich or Oreo and their sixth cup of coffee and stand around and chat, and bond, where people can pull their sponsors aside and confide some trite insight or emotional snafu that the sponsor can swiftly, privately validate but also place in the larger imperative context of the primary need not to absorb a substance today, just today, no matter what happens. While everybody's bonding and interfacing in a bizarre system of catch-phrases, there's also the raffle, another Boston idiosyncrasy: the newest of the White Flag newcomers trying to Get Active in Group Service wobble around with rattan baskets and packs of tickets, one for a buck and three for a fin, and the winner eventually gets announced from the podium and everyone hisses and shouts "Fix!" and laughs, and the winner wins a Big Book or an *As Bill Sees It* or a *Came To Believe,* which if he's got some sober time in and already owns all the AA literature from winning previous raffles he'll stand up and publicly offer it to any newcomer who wants it, which means any newcomer with enough humble desperation to come up to him and ask for it and risk being given a phone number to carry around in his wallet.

At the White Flag raffle break Gately usually stands around chain-smoking with the Ennet House residents, so that he's casually available to answer questions and empathize with complaints. He usually waits til after the meeting to do his own complaining to Bobby Hurst, with whom Gately now shares the important duty of "breaking down the hall," sweeping floors and emptying ashtrays and wiping down the long cafeteria tables. Gately rather likes Ken Erdedy, who came into the House about a month ago from some cushy Belmont rehab. Erdedy's an upscale guy, what Gately's late mother would have called a yuppie, an account executive at Viney and Veals Advertising downtown his intake form said, and though he's about Gately's age he's so softly good-looking in that soft mannequinish way Harvard and Tufts schoolboys have, and looks so smooth and groomed all the time even in jeans and a plain cotton sweater, that Gately thinks of him as much younger, totally ungrizzled, and refers to him mentally as "kid." Erdedy's in the House mainly for marijuana addiction, which Gately has a hard time identifying with anybody getting in enough trouble with weed to leave his job and condo to bunk in a room full of tattooed guys who smoke in their sleep, and to work like pumping gas (Erdedy just started his nine-month humility job at the Merit station down by North Harvard St. in Allston) for 32 minimum-wage hours a week. But it's not Gately's place to say what's bad enough to make somebody Come In and what isn't, not for anybody else but himself, and the shapely but big-time troubled new girl Kate Gompert—who mostly just stays in her bed in the five-woman room when she isn't at meetings, and is on a Suicidality Contract with Pat, and isn't getting the usual pressure to get a humility job, and gets to get some sort of scrip-meds out of the meds locker, every morning—Kate Gompert's counselor Danielle S. reported at the last Staff Meeting that Kate had finally opened up and told her she'd mostly Come In for weed, too, and not the lightweight prescription tranks she'd listed on her intake form. Gately used to treat weed like tobacco. He wasn't like some other narcotics addicts who smoked weed when they couldn't get anything else; he always smoked weed and could always get something else and simply smoked weed while he did whatever else he could get. Gately doesn't miss weed much. The shocker-type AA Miracle is he doesn't much miss the Demerol, either, today.

A hard November wind is spattering goopy sleet against the broad windows all around the hall. The Provident Nursing Home cafeteria is lit by a checkerboard array of oversized institutional bulbs overhead, a few of which are always dicky and give off fluttery strobes. The fluttering bulbs are why Pat Montesian and all the other area epileptic AA's never go to White Flag, opting for the Freeway Group over in Brookline or the candyass Lake Street meeting up in west Newton on Tuesday nights. The White Flag hall is so brightly lit up all Gately can see out any of the windows is a kind of shiny drooling black against everybody's pale reflection.

"Miracle"'s one of the Boston AA terms Erdedy and the brand-new veiled girl resident standing over him complain they find hard to stomach, as in "We're All Miracles Here" and "Don't Leave Five Minutes Before The Miracle Happens" and "To Stay Sober For 24

Hours Is A Miracle."

Except the veiled new girl, Joelle V., says she finds even "Miracle" preferable to the constant talk about "the Grace of God," which reminds her of wherever she grew up, where she's indicated places of worship were often aluminum trailers or fiberboard shacks and churchgoers played with copperheads in the services to honor something about serpents and tongues.

Gately's also observed how Erdedy also has that Tufts-Harvard way of speaking without seeming to move his lower jaw.

"It's as if it's its own country or something," Erdedy complains, legs crossed in maybe a bit of a faggy schoolboy way, looking around at the raffle break, sitting in Gately's generous shadow. "The first time I ever talked, over at the St. E's meeting on Wednesday, somebody comes up after the Lord's Prayer and says 'Good to hear you, I could really ID with that bottom you were sharing about, the isolating, the can't-and-can't, it's the greenest I've felt in months, hearing you.' And then gives me this raffle ticket with his phone number that I didn't ask for and says I'm right where I'm supposed to be, which I have to say I found a bit patronizing."

The best noise Gately produces is his laugh, which booms and reassures, and a certain haunted hardness goes out of his face when he laughs. Like most huge men, Gately has kind of a high hoarse speaking voice; his larynx sounds compressed. "I still hate that right-where-you're-supposed-to-be thing," he says, laughing. He likes that Erdedy, sitting, looks right up at him and cocks his head slightly to let Gately know he's got his full attention. Gately doesn't know that this is a requisite for a white-collar job where you have to show you're attending fully to clients who are paying major sums and get to expect an overt display of full attention. Gately is still not yet a good judge of anything about upscale people except where they tend to hide their valuables.

Boston AA is intensely social. The raffle break goes on and on. An intoxicated street-guy with a venulated nose and missing incisors and electrician's tape wrapped around his shoes is trying to sing "Volare" up at the empty podium microphone. He is gently, cheerfully induced offstage by a Crocodile with a sandwich and an arm around the shoulders. There's a certain pathos to the Crocodile's kindness, his clean flannel arm around the weatherstained shoulders, which pathos Gately feels and likes being able to feel it, while he says "But at least the 'Good to hear you' I quit minding. It's just what they say when somebody's got done speaking. They can't say like 'Good job' or 'You spoke well,' cause it can't be anybody's place here to judge if anybody else did good or bad or whatnot. You see what I'm saying, there, Tiny?"

Tiny Ewell, in a blue suit and laser chronometer and tiny shoes whose shine you could read by, is sharing a dirty aluminum ashtray with Nell Gunther, who has a glass eye which she amuses herself by usually wearing so the pupil and iris face in and the dead white and tiny manufacturer's specifications of the back of the eye face out. Both of them are pretending to study the blond false wood of the tabletop, and Ewell makes a bit of a hostile show of not looking up or responding to Gately or entering into the conversation in any way, which is his choice and on him alone, so Gately lets it go. Wade McDade has a Walkman going, which is technically OK at the raffle break, although it's not a real good idea. Chandler Foss is flossing his teeth and pretending to throw the used floss at Jennifer Belbin. Most of the Ennet House residents are mingling satisfactorily. The couple of residents that are black are mingling with other blacks.* Peter Diehl and Doony Glynn are amusing themselves telling homosexual jokes to Morris Hanley, who sits smoothing his hair with his fingertips, pretending to not even acknowledge, his left hand still bandaged. Alfonso Parias-Carbo is standing with three Allston Group guys, smiling broadly and nodding, not understanding a word anybody says. Bruce Green has gone downstairs to the men's head and amused Gately by asking his permission first. Gately told him to go knock himself out. Green has good big arms and no gut, even after all the substances, and Gately suspects he might have played some ball at some point. Kate Gompert is totally by herself at a non-smoking table over by a window, ignoring her pale reflection and making little cardboard tents out of her raffle tickets and moving them around. Clenette Henderson clutches another black girl and laughs and says "Girl!" several times. Emil Minty is clutching his head. Geoff Day in his black turtleneck and blazer keeps lurking on the fringes of various groups of people, pretending he's part of the conversations. No immediate sign of Joe Desmond or Charlotte Treat. Randy Lenz, in his cognito white mustache and sideburns, is doubtless at the pay phone in the northeast corner of the Provident lobby downstairs: Lenz spends nearly unacceptable amounts of time either on a phone

*Gately's blue-collar North Shore term for blacks is "niggers," which is still all he knows.

or trying to get in position to use a phone. "Cause what I like," Gately says to Erdedy (Erdedy really is listening, even though there's a compellingly cheap young woman in a brief white skirt and absurd black mesh stockings sitting with her legs nicely crossed—one-strap low-spike black Ferragamos, too—at the periphery of his vision, and the woman is with a large man, which makes her even more compelling; and also the veiled new girl's breasts and hips' clefs are compelling and distracting, next to him, even in a long baggy loose blue sweater that matches the embroidered selvage around her veil), "What I think I like is how 'It was good to hear you' ends up, like, saying two separate things together." Gately's also saying this to Joelle, who it's weird but you can tell she's looking at you, even through the linen veil—there's maybe half a dozen or so other veiled people in the White Flag hall tonight; a decent percentage of people in the 11-Step Union of the Hideously and Improbably Deformed are also in 12-Step fellowships for other issues besides hideous deformity. Most of the room's veiled AA's are women, though there is this one male veiled U.H.I.D. guy that's an active White Flagger, a guy who years ago nodded out on a stuffed acrylic couch with a bottle of Remy and a lit Tiparillo; the guy now wears U.H.I.D. veils and a whole spectrum of silk turtlenecks and assorted hats and classy lambskin driving gloves. Gately's had the U.H.I.D.-and-veil philosophy explained to him in passing a couple times but still doesn't much get it, it seems like a gesture of shame and concealment, still, to him, the veil. Pat Montesian had said there's been a few other U.H.I.D.'s who'd gone through Ennet House prior to the Year of Dairy Products From the American Heartland, which is when new resident Gately came wobbling in, but Joelle ver Nooy, who Gately feels he has zero handle on yet as a person or how serious she is about putting down substances and Coming In to really get straight, this Joelle is the first veiled resident Gately's had under him, as a Staffer. This Joelle girl, that wasn't even on the two-month Waiting List for intake, got in overnight under some private arrangement with somebody on the House's Board of Directors, upscale Enfield guys into charity and directing. There'd been no intake interview with Pat at the House; the girl just showed up two days ago right after supper. She'd been up at Brigham and Women's for five days after some sort of horrific OD-type situation said to have included both defib paddles and priests. She'd had real luggage and this like Chinese portable dressing-screen thing with clouds and pop-eyed dragons that even folded lengthwise took both Green and Parias-Carbo to lug upstairs. There's been no talk of a humility job for her, and Pat's counseling the girl personally. Pat's got some sort of privately directed arrangement with the girl; Gately's already seen enough private-type arrangements between certain Staffers and residents to feel like it's maybe kind of a character defect of Ennet House. A girl from the Brookline Young People's Group over in a cheerleader skirt and slut stockings is ignoring all the ashtrays and putting her gasper out on the bare tabletop two rows over as she laughs like a seal at something an acned guy in a long camelhair car coat he hasn't taken off and sockless leather dance shoes Gately's never seen at a meeting before says. And he's got his hand on hers as she grinds the gasper out. Something like putting a cigarette out against the wood-grain plastic tabletop, which Gately can already see the ragged black burn-divot that's formed, it's something the rankness of which would never have struck him one way or the other, before, until Gately took on half the break-down-the-hall-and-wipe-down-the-tables job at Bobby Hurst's suggestion, and now he feels sort of proprietary about the Provident's tabletops. But it's not like he can go over and take anybody else's inventory and tell them how to behave. He settles for imagining the girl pinwheeling through the air toward a glass wall.

"When they say it it sort of means like what you said was good for them, it helped them out somehow," he says, "but plus now also I like saying it myself because if you think about it it also means it was good to be *able* to hear you. To really hear." He's trying subtly to alternate and look at Erdedy and Joelle both, like he's addressing them both. It's not something he's good at. His head's too big to be subtle with. "Because I remember for like the first sixty days or so I couldn't hear shit. I didn't hear nothing. I'd just sit there and compare, I'd go to myself, like, 'I never rolled a car,' 'I never lost a wife,' 'I never bled from the rectum.' Butchie'd tell me to just keep coming for a while and sooner or later I'd start to be able to both listen and hear. He said it's hard to really hear. But he wouldn't say what was the difference between hearing and listening, which pissed me off. But after a while I started to really *hear.* It turns out—and this is just for me, maybe—but it turned out *hearing* the speaker means like all of a sudden hearing how fucking similar the way he felt and the way I felt were, Out There, at the Bottom, before we each Came In. Instead of just sitting here resenting being here and thinking how he bled from the ass and I didn't and how that means I'm not as bad as him yet and I can still be Out There."

One of the tricks to being of real service to newcomers is not to lecture or give advice but to only talk about your own personal experience and what you were told and what you found out personally, and to do it in a casual but positive and encouraging way. Plus you're supposed to try and identify with the newcomer's feelings as much as possible. Bobby Hurst says this is one of the ways guys with just a year or two sober can be most helpful: being able to sincerely ID with the newly Sick and Suffering. Bobby Hurst told Gately as they were wiping down tables that if a Crocodile with decades of sober AA time can still sincerely emphathize and identify with a whacked-out bug-eyed Disease-ridden newcomer then there's something deeply fucked up about that Crocodile's recovery. The Crocodiles, decades sober, live in a totally different spiritual galaxy, inside. One longtimer describes it as he has a whole new unique interior spiritual castle, now, to live in. One of Boston AA's more dogmatic promises is that the person you brought in here will change radically as you progress in recovery from the Disease. You either Grow or Go, is the relevant slogan here. Gately uses the end of one gasper to light another; lighters aren't in his budget. He says "For me, I think that's part of this Miracle they always talk about. Really being able to hear somebody all of a sudden. It's an experience. It took some time. I had to hang in for a while, but it's a real fucking experience. That might sound like bullshit. It sounded like bullshit to me when somebody said it to me. But it's the first time that line about But For the Grace of God stopped sounding like some kind of Moonie bullshit everybody says like a robot, and now I started IDing with what it really meant. Just a little, at first. It takes time," he says. "That ugly four-letter word 'Time.' TIME: Things I Must Experience. TIME: Things I Must Earn."

Erdedy says "TIME: Tortures I Might Enjoy."

Gately laughs. "FEAR: Fuck Everything And Run. FEAR: False Evidence Appearing Real. FEAR: Forgetting Everything's All Right. There's shitloads of them."

Part of this new Joelle girl's pull for Ken Erdedy isn't just the sexual thing of her body, which he finds made way sexier by the way the overlarge blue coffee-stained sweater tried to downplay the body thing without being so hubristic as to try to hide it—sloppy sexiness pulls Erdedy in like a well-groomed moth to a lit window—but it's also the veil, wondering what horrific contrast to the body's allure lies swollen or askew under that veil; it gives the pull a perverse sideways slant that makes it even more distracting, and so Erdedy cocks his head a little more up at Gately and narrows his eyes to make his listening-look terribly intense. He doesn't know that there's an abstract distance in the look that makes it seem like he's studying a real bitch of a 7-iron on the 10th rough or something; the look doesn't communicate what he thinks his audience wants it to.

The raffle break is winding down as everybody starts to want his own ashtray. Two more big urns of coffee emerge from the kitchen door over by the literature table. Joelle ver Nooy now says something very strange. It's a very strange little moment, right at the end of the raffle break, and Gately later finds it impossible to describe it in his Log entry for the PM shift. It is the first time he realizes that Joelle's voice—crisp and oddly empty, her accent just barely southern and with a strange Arkansan lapse in the pronunciation of all apicals except *s*—is familiar in a faraway way that both makes it familiar and yet lets Gately be sure he's never once met her before, Out There. She inclines the plane of her blue-bordered veil briefly toward the floor's tile (very bad tile, scab-colored, nauseous, worst thing about the big room by far), brings it back up level (unlike Erdedy she's standing, and in flats is nearly Gately's height) and says that she's finding it especially hard to take when these earnest ravaged folks at the lectern say they're "Here But For the Grace of God," except that's not the strange thing she says, because when Gately nods hard and starts to interject about "It was the same for—" and wants to launch into a fairly standard Boston AA agnostic-soothing riff about the "God" in the slogan being just shorthand for a totally subjective and up-to-you "Higher Power" and AA being merely spiritual instead of dogmatically religious, a sort of benign anarchy of subjective spirit, Joelle cuts off his interjection and says that but that *her* trouble with it is that "But For the Grace of God" is a subjunctive, a counter-factual, she says, and can make sense only when introducing a conditional clause, like e.g. "But For the Grace of God I *would* have died on Molly Notkin's bathroom floor," so that an indicative transposition like "I'm here But For the Grace of God" is, she says, literally senseless, and regardless of whether she *hears* it or not it's meaningless, and that the foamy enthusiasm with which these folks can say what in fact means nothing at all makes her want to put her head in a RadaRange at the thought that substances have brought her to the sort of pass where this is the sort of language she has to have Blind Faith in. Gately looks at a rectangular blue-selvaged expanse of clean linen whose gentle rises barely allude to any features below, he looks at her and has no idea whether she's serious or not, or whacked, or trying like Dr. Geoff Day to erect Denial-type fortifications with some kind of intellectualish showing off, and he doesn't know what to say in reply, he has absolutely nothing in his huge square head to identify with her with or latch onto or say in encourging reply, and for an instant the Provident cafeteria seems pin-drop silent, and his own heart grips him like an infant rattling the bars of its playpen, and he feels a greasy wave of an old and almost unfamiliar panic, and for a second it seems inevitable that at some point in his life he's going to get high again and be back in the cage all over again, because for a second the blank white veil leveled at him seems a screen on which might well be projected a casual and impressive black and yellow smily-face, grinning, and he feels all the muscles in his own face loosen and descend kneeward; and the moment hangs there, distended, until the White Flag raffle coordinator for November, Glenn K., glides up to the podium mike in his scarlet velour caparison and make-up and candelabrum with candles the same color as the floor tile and uses the plastic gavel to formally end the break and bring things back to whatever passes here for order, for the raffle drawing. The Watertown guy with middle-level sober time who wins the Big Book publicly offers it to any newcomer that wants it, and Gately is pleased to see Bruce Green raise a big hand, and decides he'll just turn it over and ask Bobby H. for feedback on subjunctives and countersexuals, and the infant leaves its playpen alone inside him, and the rivets of the long table his seat's attached to make a brief distressed noise as he sits and settles in for the second half of the meeting, asking silently for help to listen to the very best of his limited ability.

•

An oiled guru sits in yogic full lotus in Spandex and tank top. He's maybe forty. He's in full lotus on top of the towel dispenser just above the shoulder-pull station in the weight room of the Enfield Tennis Academy, Enfield, MA. Saucers of muscle protrude from him and run together so that he looks almost crustacean. His head gleams, his hair jet black and extravagantly combed. His smile could sell things. Nobody knows where he comes from or why he's allowed to stay, but he's always in there, sitting yogic about a meter off the rubberized floor of the weight room. His tank top says TRANSCEND in silkscreen; on the back it's got DEUS PROVIDEBIT in day-glo orange. It's always the same tank top. Sometimes the color of the Spandex leggings changes. He lives off the sweat of others. Literally. The fluids and salts and fatty acids. He's like a beloved nut. He's an ETA institution. You do like maybe three sets of benches, some leg extensions, inclined abs, crunches, work up a good shellac of sweat; then, if you let him lick your arms and forehead, he'll pass on to you some little nugget of fitness-guru wisdom. His big one for a long time was: "And the Lord said: Let not the weight thou wouldst pull to thyself exceed thine own weight." His advice on conditioning and injury prevention tends to be pretty solid, is the consensus. His tongue is little and rough but feels good, like a kitty's. It isn't like a faggy or sexual thing. Some of the girls let him, too. He's harmless as they come. He supposedly went way back with Dr. Incandenza, the Academy's founder, in the past. Some of the newer kids think he's a creep and want him out of there. What kind of guru wears Spandex and lives off others' perspiration? they complain. God only knows what he does in there when the weight room's closed at night, they say. Sometimes the newer kids who won't let him near them come in and set the poundage on the shoulder-pull at a weight greater than their own weight. He just sits there and smiles and doesn't say anything. They squat, then, and try to pull the bar down, but the overweighted shoulder-pull becomes a chin-up. Up they go toward the bar they're trying to pull down. Everyone should get at least one good look at the eyes of a man who finds himself rising toward what he wants to pull down to himself. And I like how the guru on the towel dispenser doesn't laugh at them, or even shake his head sagely on its big brown neck. He just smiles, hiding his tongue. He's like a baby. Everything he sees down there hits him and sinks without bubbles. He just sits there. I want to be like that. Able to just sit quiet and pull life toward me, one forehead at a time. His name is supposedly Lyle.

•

But it's funny what they'll find funny, AA's at Boston meetings, listening. The next Advanced Basics guy summoned by their western-wear chairman to speak is dreadfully, transparently unfunny: painfully new but pretending to be at ease, to be an old hand, desperate to amuse and impress them. The guy's got the sort of professional background where he's used to trying to impress gatherings of persons. He's dying to be liked up there. He's performing. The White Flag crowd can see all this. Even the idiots among them see right through the guy. This is not a regular audience. A Boston AA is very sensitive to the presence of ego. When the new guy introduces himself and makes an ironic gesture and says "I'm told I've been given the Gift of Desperation. I'm looking for the exchange window," it's so clearly unspontaneous, calculatedly rehearsed—plus commits the subtle but cardinal message-offense of appearing to deprecate the Program rather than the Self—that just a few polite titters resound, and people shift in their seats with a slight but signal discomfort. The worst punishment Gately's seen inflicted on a Commitment speaker is when the host crowd gets embarrassed for him. Speakers who are accustomed to figuring out what an audience wants to hear and then supplying it find out quickly that this particular audience does not want to be supplied with what someone else thinks it wants. It's another conundrum Gately finally ran out of cerebral steam on. Part of finally getting comfortable in Boston AA is just finally running out of amines in terms of trying to figure stuff like this out. Because it literally makes no sense. Close to two hundred people all punishing somebody by getting embarrassed for him, killing him by empathetically dying right there with him, for him, up there at the podium. The applause when this guy's done has the relieved feel of a fist unclenching, and their cries of "Keep Coming!" are so sincere it's almost painful.

But then in equally paradoxical contrast have a look at the next Advanced Basics guy—also painfully new, this poor bastard completely and openly nerve-wracked, wobbling his way up to the front, his face shiny with sweat and his talk full of blank cunctations and disassociated leaps—as the guy speaks with terrible abashed chagrin about trying to hang on to his job Out There as his AM hangovers became more and more debilitating until he finally got so shaky and aphasiac he just couldn't bear to even face the customers who'd come knocking on his Department's door—he was, from 8:00 to 4:00, the Complaint Department of Finlon's Department Store—

—"What I did finally, Jesus I don't know where I got such a stupid idea from, I brought this hammer in from home and brought it in and kept it right there under my desk, on the floor, and when somebody knocked at the door I'd just . . . I'd sort of like *dive* onto the floor and crawl under the desk and grab up the hammer, and I'd start in to pounding on the leg of the desk, real hard-like, whacketa whacketa, like I was fixing something down there. And if they opened the door finally and came in anyhow or came in to bitch about me not opening the door I'd just stay out of sight under there pounding away like hell and I'd yell out I was going to be a moment, just a moment, emergency repairs, be with them momentarily. I guess you can guess how all that pounding felt, you know, under there, what with the big head I had every morning. I'd hide under there and pound and pound with the hammer till they finally gave up and went away, I'd watch from under the desk and tell when they finally went away, from I could see their feet from under the desk."

—And about how the hiding-under-the-desk-and-pounding thing worked, incredibly enough, for almost the whole last year of his drinking, which ended around this past Labor Day, when one vindictive complainant finally figured out where in Finlon's to go to complain about the Complaint Dept.—the White Flaggers all fell about, they were totally pleased and amused, the Crocodiles removed their cigars and roared and wheezed and stomped both feet on the floor and showed scary teeth, everyone roaring with Identification and pleasure. This even though, as the speaker's confusion at their delight openly betrays, the story wasn't meant to be one bit funny: it was just the truth.

Gately's found it's got to be the truth, is the thing. He's trying hard to really hear the speakers—he's stayed in the habit he'd developed as an Ennet resident of sitting right up where he could see dentition and pores, with zero obstructions or heads between him and the podium, so the speaker fills his whole vision, which makes it easier to really hear—trying to concentrate on receiving the Message instead of brooding on that odd old dark moment of aphasiac terror with this veiled intellectual-type girl who was probably just in some sort of complex Denial, or on whatever doubtlessly grim place he feels like he knows that smooth echoless slightly southern voice from. The thing is it has to be the truth to really go over, here. It can't be a calculated crowd pleaser, and it has to be the truth unslanted, unfortified. And maximally unironic. An ironist in a Boston AA meeting is a witch in church. Irony-free zone. Same with sly disingenuous manipulative pseudo-sincerity. Sincerity with an ulterior motive is something these tough ravaged people know and fear, all of them trained to remember the coyly sincere, ironic, self-presenting fortifications they'd had to construct in order to carry on Out There, under the ceaseless neon bottle.

This doesn't mean you can't pay empty or hypocritical lip service, however. Paradoxically enough. The desperate, newly active White Flaggers are always encouraged to invoke and pay empty lip-service to slogans they don't yet understand or believe—e.g. "Easy Does It!" and "Turn It Over!" and "One Day At a Time!" It's called "Fake It Til You Make It," itself an oft-invoked slogan. Everybody on a Commitment who gets up publicly to speak starts out saying he's an alcoholic, says it whether he believes he is yet or not; then everybody up there says how Grateful he is to be sober today and how great it is to be Active and out on a Commitment with his Group, even if he's not grateful or pleased about it at all. You're encouraged to keep saying stuff like this until you start to believe it, just like if you ask somebody with serious sober time how long you'll have to keep shlepping to all these goddamn meetings he'll smile that infuriating smile and tell you just until you start to *want* to go to all these goddamn meetings. There are some definite cultish, brainwashy elements to the AA Program (the term "Program" itself resonates darkly, for those who fear getting brainwashed), and Gately tries to be candid with his residents re this issue. But he also shrugs and tells them that by the end of his oral-narcotics and burglary careers he'd sort of decided the old brain needed a good scrub and soak anyway. He says he pretty much held his brain out and told Pat Montesian and Butchie Quinones to wash away. But he tells his residents he's thinking now that the Program might be more like deprogramming than actual washing, considering the psychic job the Disease had done on them all. Gately's most marked progress in turning his life around in sobriety, besides the fact that he no longer drives off into the night with other people's merchandise, is that he tries to be just about as verbally honest as possible at almost all times, now, without too much calculating about how a listener's going to feel about what he says. This is harder than it sounds. But so that's why on Commitments, sweating at the podium as only a large man can sweat, his thing is that he always says he's Lucky to be sober today, instead of that he's Grateful today, because he admits that the former is always true, every day, even though a lot of the time he still doesn't feel Grateful, more like shocked that this thing seems to work, plus a lot of the time also ashamed and depressed about how he's spent almost half his life, and scared he might be permanently brain-damaged or retarded from substances, plus also usually without any sort of clue about where he's headed in sobriety or what he's supposed to be doing or about really anything at all except that he's not at all keen to be back Out There behind any bars, again, in a hurry. Bobby Hurst likes to punch Gately's shoulder and tell him he's right where he's supposed to be.

So but also know that causal attribution, like irony, is death, speaking-on-Commitments-wise. At a Boston AA podium, *never* try to sound like you're trying to explain your Disease in terms of what caused it in you. Etiology is out. A sure way to make the audience uncomfortable for you. The White Flaggers will actually get pale with tension if you start trying to blame your addiction on some cause or other. Cf. their discomfort when the skinny hard-faced Advanced Basics girl who gets up to speak next to last posits that she was an eight-bag-a-day dope fiend *because* at sixteen she'd had to become a stripper and semi-whore at the infamous Naked I Club out on Route 1 (a number of male eyes in the audience flash with sudden recognition, and despite all willed restraint automatically do that crawly north-to-south thing down her body, and Gately can see every ashtray on the table shake from the force of Joelle V.'s shudder), and then but that she'd had to become a stripper at sixteen *because* she'd had to run away from her foster home in Saugus, MA, and that she'd had to run away from home *because* . . . —here at least some of the room's discomfort is from the fact that the audience can tell the etiology is going to get head-clutchingly prolix and involved; this girl has not yet learned to Keep It Simple— . . . because, well, to begin with, she'd been adopted, and the foster parents also had their own biological daughter, and the biological daughter had, from birth, been totally paralyzed and retarded and catatonic, and the foster mother in the household was—as Joelle V. put it later to Gately—crazy as a Fucking Mud-Bug, and was in total Denial about her biological daughter being a vegetable, and not only insisted on treating the invertebrate biological daughter like a valid member of the chordate phylum but also insisted that the father and the adopted daughter also treat It as normal and undamaged, making the adopted daughter share a bedroom with It, bring It along to slumber parties (the speaker uses the term "It" for the invertebrate sister, and also to tell the truth uses the phrase "drag It along" rather than "bring It along," which Gately wisely screens out), and even to school with her, and softball practice, and the hairdresser's, and Campfire Girls, etc., where at whatever place she'd dragged It along to It would lie in a heap, drooling and incontinent under exquisite mother-bought fashions specially altered for atrophy and top-shelf Lancôme cosmetics that looked just *lurid* on It, and with only the whites of Its eyes showing, with fluid dribbling from Its mouth and elsewhere, and making unspeakable gurgly noises, completely pale and moist and stagnant; and then, when the adopted daughter now speaking turned 15, the rabidly Catholic whacko foster mother even announced that OK now that the adopted daughter was 15 she could go out on dates, but only as long as It got to come along too, in other words that the only dates the 15-year-old adopted daughter could go out on were double dates with It and whatever sub-mammalian escort the speaker could root up for It; and how this sort of stuff went on and on; and how the nightmarishness of Its continual pale soggy ubiquitousness in her young life would alone be more than sufficient to cause and explain the speaker's later drug addiction, she feels, but that also it so happened that the foster family's quiet smiling patriarch, who worked 9:00 to 9:00 as a claims processor for Aetna, it turned out that the cheerful smiling foster father actually made the whacko foster mother look like a Doric column of stability by comparison, because there turned out to be things about the biological daughter's utter paralytic pliability and catatonic inability to make anything except unspeakable gurgly noises that the smiling father found greatly to a certain very sick advantage the speaker says she has trouble openly discussing, still, even at 31 months sober in AA, being as yet still retroactively Wounded and Hurting from it; but so in sum that she'd been ultimately forced to run away from the adoptive foster Saugus home and so become a Naked-I stripper and so become a raging dope fiend not, as in so many ununique cases, because *she* had been incestuously diddled, but because she'd been abusively forced to share a bedroom with a drooling invertebrate who by 14 was *Itself* getting incestuously diddled on a nightly basis by a smiling biological claims processor of a father who—the speaker pauses to summon courage—who apparently liked to pretend It was Raquel Welch, the former celluloid sex goddess of the father's glandular heyday, and he even called It "*RAQUEL!*" in moments of incestuous extremity; and how, the New England summer the speaker turned 15 and had to start dragging It along on double dates and then having to make sure to drag It back home again by 11:00 so It had plenty of time to be incestuously diddled, that summer the smiling quiet foster father even bought, had found somewhere, a cheesy rubber Raquel Welch full-head pull-on *mask,* with hair, and would now nightly come in in the dark and lift Its limp soft head up and struggle and lug to get the mask on and the relevant holes aligned for air, and then would diddle his way to extremity and cry out *"RAQUEL!,"* and then but he would just clamber out and off and leave the dark bedroom smiling and sated and lots of times leave the mask still *on* It, he'd forget, or not care, just as he seemed oblivious (But For the Grace of God, in a way) to the fetally curled skinny form of the adopted daughter lying perfectly still in the next bed, in the dark, pretending to sleep, silent, shell-breathing, with her hard skinny wounded pre-addiction face turned to the wall, in the room's next bed, her bed, the one without the collapsible crib-like hospital railings along the sides. . . . The audience is clutching its collective head, by this time only partly in empathy, as the speaker specifies how she was de facto emotionally all but like *forced* to flee and strip and swan-dive into the dark spiritual anesthesia of active drug addiction in a dysfunctional attempt to psychologically deal with one particular seminally scarring night of abject horror, the indescribable horror of the way It, the biological daughter, had looked up at her, the speaker, one particular final time on this one particular one of the frequent occasions the speaker had to get out of bed after the father had left and come and gone and tiptoe over to Its bed and lean over the cold metal hospital railing and remove the rubber Raquel Welch mask and replace it in a bedside drawer under some back issues of *Ramparts* and *Commonweal,* after carefully closing Its splayed legs and pulling down Its variously-stained designer nightie, all of which she made sure to do when the father didn't bother to, at night, so that the whacko foster mother wouldn't come in in the AM and find It in a rubber Raquel Welch mask with Its nightie hiked up and Its legs agape and put two and two together and get all kinds of deep Denial shattered about why the foster father always went around the foster house with a silent creepy smile, and flip out and make the invertebrate catatonic's father stop diddling It—because, the speaker figured, if the foster father had to stop diddling It it didn't exactly take Sally Jessy Raphael M.S.W. to figure out who was then probably going to get promoted to the role of Raquel, over in the next bed. The silent smiling claims-processor father never once acknowledged the adopted daughter's little post-incestuous tidyings-up. It's the kind of sick unspoken complicity characteristic of wildly dysfunctional families, confides the speaker, who's also proud she says to be a member of a splinter 12-Step Fellowship, an Adult-Child-type thing called Wounded, Hurting, Inadequately-Nurtured but Ever-Recovering Survivors. But so she says it was this one particular night soon after she'd turned 16, after the father had come and gone and uncaringly just left Its mask on again, and over to Its bedside the speaker had to creep in the dark, to tidy up, and but this time it turned out there was a problem with the Raquel Welch mask's long auburn horsehair tresses having gotten twisted and knotted into the semi-living strands of Its own elaborately overmoussed coiffure, and the adopted daughter had to activate the perimeter of lights on Its bedside table's many-bulbed vanity mirror to see to try to get the Raquel Welch wig untangled, and when she finally got the mask off, with the vanity mirror still blazing away, the speaker says how she was forced to gaze for the first time on Its lit-up paralytic post-diddle face, and how the expression thereon was most assuredly quite enough to force anybody with an operant limbic system* to leg it right out of her dysfunctional foster family's home, nay and the whole community of Saugus, MA, now homeless and scarred and forced by dark psychic forces straight to Route 1's infamous gauntlet of neon-lit depravity and addiction, to try and forget, rasa the tabula, wipe the memory totally out, numb it with opiates. Voice trembling, she accepts the chairperson's proffered bandanna-hankie and blows her nose one nostril at a time and says she can almost see It all over again: Its expression: in the vanity's lights only Its eyes' whites showed, and while Its utter catatonia and paralysis prevented the contraction of Its luridly rouged face's circumoral muscles into any conventional human facial-type expression, nevertheless some hideously mobile and expressive layer in the moist regions below real people's expressive facial layer, some slow-twitch layer unique to It had blindly contracted, somehow, to gather the blank soft cheese of Its face into the sort of pinched gasping look of neurologic concentration that marks a carnal bliss beyond smiles or sighs. Its face looked post-coital sort of the way you'd imagine the vacuole and optica of a protozoan looking post-coital after it's shuddered and shot its mono-cellular load into the cold waters of some really old sea. Its facial expression was, in a word, the speaker says, unspeakably,

*The speaker doesn't use the terms "thereon," "most assuredly," or "operant limbic system," though she really had said "chordate phylum."

unforgettably ghastly and horrid and scarring. It was also the exact same expression as the facial expression on the stone-robed lady's face in this one untitled photo of some Catholic statue that hung (the photo) in the dysfunctional household's parlor right above the little teak table where the dysfunctional foster mother kept her beads and Hours and lay breviary, this photo of a statue of a woman whose stone robes were half hiked up and wrinkled in the most godawfully sensually prurient way, the woman reclined against uncut rock, her robes hiked and one stone foot hanging off the rock as her legs hung parted, with a grinning little totally psychotic-looking cherub-type angel standing on the lady's open thighs and pointing a bare arrow at where the stone robe hid her cold tit, the woman's face upturned and cocked and pinched into that exact same shuddering-protozoan look beyond pleasured or pained. The whacko foster mom knelt daily to that photo, in a beaded and worshipful posture, and also required daily that It be hoisted by the adopted daughter from Its never-mentioned wheelchair and held under Its arms and lowered so as to approximate the same knelt devotion to the photo, and while It gurgled and Its head lolled the speaker had gazed at the photo with a nameless revulsion each morning as she held Its dead slumped weight and tried to keep Its chin off Its chest, and now was being forced into seeing by mirror-light the exact same expression on the face of a catatonic who'd just been incestuously diddled, an expression at once reverent and greedy on a face connected by dead hair to the slack and flapping rubber visage of an old sex goddess's empty face. And to make a long story short (the speaker says, not trying to be funny as far as the Flaggers can see), the traumatically scarred adopted girl had legged it from the bedroom and foster house into the brooding North Shore teen-runaway night, and had stripped and semi-whored and IV-injected her way all the way to that standard two-option addicted cliff-edge, hoping only to Forget. That's what caused it, she says; that's what she's trying to recover from, a day at a time, and she's sure grateful to be here with her Group today, sober and courageously remembering, and newcomers should definitely Keep Coming. . . . As she's telling what she sees as etiological truth, though the monologue seems sincere and unaffected and at least a B+ on the overall AA-story lucidity scale, faces in the hall are averted and heads clutched and postures uneasily shifted in empathetic distress at the look-what-happened-to-poor-me invitation implicit in the tale, the talk's tone of self-pity itself less offensive (even though plenty of these White Flaggers, Gately knows, had personal childhoods that made this girl's look like a day at Six Flags) than the subcurrent of explanation, an appeal to exterior *cause* that can slide, in the addictive mind, so insidiously into *excuse* that any causal attribution is in Boston AA feared, shunned, punished by empathic distress. The *Why* of the Disease is a labyrinth it is strongly suggested all AA's boycott, inhabited as the maze is by the twin minotaurs of *Why me?* and *Why not?*, Self-Pity and Denial, two of the smily-faced sergeant at arms' more fearsome aides de camp. The Boston AA "In Here" that protects against a return to "Out There" is not about explaining what caused your Disease. It's about a goofily simple practical recipe for how to remember you've got the Disease day by day and how to treat the Disease day by day, how to keep the seductive ghost of a bliss long absconded from baiting you and hooking you and pulling you back Out and eating your heart raw and (if you're lucky) eliminating your map for good. So no whys or wherefores allowed. In other words check your head at the door. Though it can't be conventionally enforced, this, Boston AA's real root axiom, is almost classically authoritarian, maybe even proto-Fascist. Some ironist who decamped back Out There and left his effects to be bagged and tossed by Staff into the Ennet House attic had, all the way back in the Year of the Tucks Medicated Pad, permanently engraved his tribute to AA's real prime directive with a rosewood-handled boot knife in the plastic seat of the five-man men's room's commode:

Do not ask WHY
If you dont want to DIE
Do like your TOLD
If you want to get OLD*

•

NYC's Liberty Island's gigantic Lady has the sun for a crown and holds what looks like a gigantic photo album under one iron arm, and the other arm holds aloft a product. The product is changed each 1 Jan. by brave men with pitons and cranes.

•

But it's not like Boston AA recoils from the idea of *responsibility*, though. Cause: no; responsibility: yes. It seems like it all depends on which way the arrow of presumed responsibility points. The hard-faced adopted stripper had pointed the arrow away from herself;

*Sic.

she'd presented herself as the object of an outside cause. Now the arrow comes back around as tonight's meeting's last and maybe best Advanced Basics speaker, another newcomer, a round pink girl with no eyelashes at all and a 'base-head's ruined teeth, gets up there and speaks in an r-less South Boston brogue about being pregnant at 20 and smoking 'base cocaine like a fiend all through her pregnancy, even though she knew it was bad for the baby and wanted desperately to quit. She tells about having her water break and contractions start late one night in her welfare hotel room when she was right in the middle of an eight-ball she'd had to spend the evening turning unbelievably sordid and degrading tricks to pay for; she did what she had to do to get high, she says, even while pregnant, she says; and she says even when the pain of the contractions got to be too bad to bear she'd been unable to tear herself away from the 'base-pipe to go to the free clinic to deliver, and how she'd sat on the floor of the welfare hotel room and free-based her way all through labor (that new Joelle girl's veil billowing in and out with her breath, Gately sees, just like it also was during the last speaker's description of the statue's orgasm in the catatonic's dysfunctional Catholic mother's devotional photo); and how she'd finally delivered of a stillborn infant right there alone on her side like a cow on the rug of her room, all the time throughout still compulsively loading up the glass pipe and smoking, and how the emerged infant was tiny and withered and the color of strong tea, and dead, and also had no face, had in utero developed no eyes or nostrils and just a little lipless hyphen of a mouth, and its limbs were malformed, and there had been some sort of translucent reptilian webbing between its digits; the speaker's mouth is a quivering arch of woe, her baby had been poisoned before it could grow a face or make any personal choices, it would have soon died of substance-withdrawal in the free clinic's Pyrex incubator if it had emerged alive anyway, she could tell, she'd been on such a bad 'base-binge all that pregnant year; and but so eventually the eight-ball was consumed and then the screen and steel-wool ball in the pipe itself smoked and the cloth prep-filter smoked to ash and then of course likely-looking pieces of lint had been plucked off the rug and also smoked, and the girl finally passed out, still umbilically linked to the dead infant; and how when she came to again in unsparing noonlight the next day and saw what still clung by a withered cord to her empty insides she got introduced to the real business-end of the arrow of responsibility, and as she gazed in daylight at the withered faceless stillborn baby she was so overcome with grief and self-loathing that she erected a fortification of complete and black Denial, like total Denial. She held and swaddled the dead thing just as if it were alive instead of dead, and she began to carry it around with her wherever she went, just as she imagined devoted mothers carry their babies with them everywhere they go, the faceless infant's corpse completely veiled and hidden in a little pink blanket the addicted expectant mother'd let herself buy at Woolworth's at seven months, and she also kept the cord's connection intact until her end of the cord finally fell out of her and dangled, and smelled, and she carried the dead infant everywhere, even when turning sordid tricks, because she knew single motherhood or not she still needed to get high and still had to do what she had to do, to get high, so she carried the blanket-wrapped infant in her arms as she walked the streets in her velvet fuchsia minipants and spike heels, turning tricks, until there began to be strong evidence, as she circled her block—it was August—let's just say compelling evidence that the infant in the stained cocoon of blanket in her arms was not a biologically viable infant, and passersby on the South Boston streets began to reel away white-faced as the girl passed by, stretch-marked and brown-toothed and lashless (lashes lost in a substance-accident; fire hazard and dental dysplasia go with the free-base territory) and also just hauntedly calm-looking, oblivious to the olfactory havoc she was wreaking in the sweltering streets, and but her August's trick-business soon fell off sharply, understandably, and eventually word that there was a serious infant-and-Denial problem here got around the streets, and her fellow Southie 'base-heads and street-friends came to her with gentle r-less remonstrances and scented hankies and gently prying hands and tried to reason her out of her Denial, but she ignored them all, she guarded her infant from all harm and kept it clutched to her—it was by now sort of stuck to her and would have been hard to separate from her by hand anyway—and she'd walk the streets shunned and trickless and broke and in early-stage substance withdrawal, with the remains of the dead infant's tummy's cord dangling out from an unclosable fold in the now ominously ballooned and crusty Woolworth's blanket: talk about Denial: this girl was in some major-league Denial; and but finally a pale and reeling beat-cop phoned a hysterical olfactory alert in to the Commonwealth's infamous Department of Social Services—Gately sees alcoholic moms all over the hall cross themselves and shudder at the mere mention of D.S.S., every addicted parent's worst nightmare, D.S.S., they of the several different abstruse legal definitions of Neglect and the tungsten-tipped battering ram for triple-locked apartment doors; in a dark window Gately sees one reflected mom sitting over with the Brighton AA's that has her two little girls with her in the meeting and now at the D.S.S. reference clutches them reflexively to her bosom, one head per bosom, as one of the girls struggles and dips her knees in the little curtsies of impending potty—but so now D.S.S. was on the case, and a platoon of blandly efficient Wellesley-alum D.S.S. field personnel with clipboards and scary black Chanel women's businesswear were now on the prowl in the streets for the addicted speaker and her late faceless infant; and but finally around this time, during last year's awful late-August heat wave, evidence that the infant had a serious bio-viability problem started presenting itself so forcefully that even the Denial-ridden addict in the mother could not ignore or dismiss it—evidence that the speaker's reticence about describing (save to say that it involved an insect-attraction problem) makes things all the worse for the empathetic White Flaggers, since it engages the dark imaginations all substance-abusers share in surplus—and so but the mother says how she finally broke down, emotionally and olfactorily, from the overwhelming evidence, on the cement playground outside her own late mother's abandoned Project building off the L Street Beach in Southie, and a D.S.S. field team closed in for the pinch, and she and her infant got pinched, and special D.S.S. spray-solvents had to be sent for and utilized in order to detach the Woolworth baby-blanket from her maternal bosom, and the blanket's contents were more or less reassembled and were interred in a D.S.S. coffin the speaker recalls as being the size of a makeup case, and the speaker was medically informed by somebody with a clipboard from D.S.S. that the infant had been involuntarily toxified to death somewhere along in its development toward becoming a boy, and the mother spent the next four months on the locked ward of Metropolitan State Hospital in Waltham, MA, catatonic with guilt and cocaine-withdrawal and searing self-hatred; and how when she finally got discharged from Met State with her first SSI-Mental-Disability check she found she had no taste for chunks or powders, she wanted only tall smooth bottles whose labels spoke of Proof, and she drank and drank and believed in her heart she would never stop or swallow the truth, but finally she got to where she had to, she says, swallow it, the truth; how she quickly drank her way to the old two-option welfare-hotel window-ledge and made a blubbering 2:00 AM phone call, and then so here she is, apologizing for going on so long, trying to tell the truth she hopes someday to swallow and transcend, inside. When she concludes by asking them to pray for her it almost doesn't sound corny. Gately tries not to think. Here is no *cause* or *excuse*. It is simply what happened. This final speaker is truly new, ready: all defenses have been burned away. Smooth-skinned and steadily pinker, her eyes squeezed tight, she looks like *she's* the one that's the infant. The host White Flaggers pay this burnt public husk of a newcomer the ultimate Boston AA compliment: they have to consciously try to remember even to blink as they watch her, listening. IDing without effort. There's no judgment. It's clear she's been punished enough. And it was basically the same all over, after all, Out There. And the fact that it was so good to hear her, so good that even Tiny Ewell and Kate Gompert and the rest of the worst of them all sat still and listened without blinking, looking not just at the speaker's face but into it, helps force Gately to remember all over again what a tragic adventure this is, that none of them signed up for.

From Foreign Parts

Janice Galloway

Shortly after I started writing the novel this is a piece of, I stopped.

I do that sometimes when I'm writing.

I stop and wonder what it is I'm doing.

This is never useful: it only destroys confidence and uses up precious TIME *that could be used to some better purpose.*

Nonetheless, I did it. I stopped and wondered.

I wondered why I was writing something set in France with two main female characters who spoke little of the language of that country. I wondered why I had put the two women in a situation where they would have little or no chance to overhear conversations or meet new people and would have only themselves to fall back on. And I wondered why I was focusing on those two women: both terse, seldom saying what they feel, often thinking at cross purposes AND *traveling in their own sealed chamber on the wrong side of the road. I worried I was setting myself up for difficulties.*

And so I was.

The trouble is YOU CAN'T TELL YOURSELF WHAT TO WRITE ABOUT. *You don't drive the material: the material drives you. It doesn't work any other way. Deliberate tinkering with the politics or the nature of characters which have arisen naturally out of the subconscious is not only a dishonest but a redundant exercise. Worse, a self-important avoidance tactic.*

Still, avoiding like hell, engaged in useless wondering about irrelevant things, I was stuck with Rona and Cassie doing nothing for a year and a half. Now I did do other things in that year and a half, not the least of which was to have a baby. This was good for a lot of obvious reasons and surprisingly good for unexpected others as well. Because having a baby who has no grasp whatever of the concept of sleep forces the head to clear itself of anything other than ESSENTIALS. *When I finally (fitfully) got back to my desk, what wanted to be written was free to surface in its own way; multiple isolations, unspoken feelings, restrictions and all. It was only by not wondering, by not putting self-consciousness* first, I realized what it was for.

It's hardly contentious to say that a significant number of contemporary Scottish novels are more notable for their preoccupation with what is not said rather than what is said; with the struggle to express emotion and find a sense of self-worth and, more importantly, a voice: what Gavin Wallace calls "the twisted, broken heart of the Scottish novel's grim fascination with damaged identity."

This, of course, has much to do with Scotland's history as a colonized nation, our lack of real political clout and neglect by successive Westminster governments and the repressive and very real psychological damage wrought by centuries of contempt for our accent, syntax and expression. In the fine, time-served tradition of colonized people, we have been eager to internalize the contempt and pass it on to our children. In my own time, teachers and parents have passed on their own sense of linguistic inferiority via a number of well-worn maxims familiar to anyone from a Scottish background: "It's not aye, it's yes"; "You won't get far with an accent like that," and so on ad nauseam. I remember a child in my primary school class being belted (i.e., hit over the hands with a leather strap wielded from shoulder height) for refusing to say isn't instead of isny to a teacher who chose to regard the refusal as "cheek." My mother, a paragon of internalized contempt, condemned the accent she spoke in as "common" and often affected a Yorkshire accent when answering the phone – presumably in order to be thought better of at first hearing. Note that even in this class-ridden country, it was not the class connotations of her accent she found most embarrassing but its Scottishness. She knew, as I did, our way of speaking was unworthy and unworthwhile; that our language was a not-language, something best hidden or apologized for. This quite literal repression of the Scottish voice has no small connection with the notoriously awkward business (for the Scottish writer) of trusting her own mouth. So with any and all disempowered, artificially silenced groups. For the woman writer from a working-class or workaday Scottish background, the sense of loss of voice is trebly familiar.

Now, while a loss of trust that what one has to say will be listened to for emotional truth is not good for developing a strong sense of cultural confidence, it is good for some other things. Learning, for example, to be fluent in several registers whilst knowing your own is no less a central reality than anyone else's. Learning, for example, that new ways of rendering emotional truth, breaking stereotype *and disregarding the limitations of the conventional academic canon are essential if you are to write honestly. Learning, for example, that the only way forward is to actively choose to write outside the "rules," to talk with our own truths as the center – not because, as the self-promoting literary canon would have us believe, we canny talk right but precisely because we* can.

Rona and Cassie, stuck in the middle of a foreign place with slim chance of making themselves comprehensible and only each other to fall back on, were not anything to wonder about at all. They were no more and no less than home ground: complexly simple products of Scottish female experience. Terra, in the end, entirely firma.

SIX MINUTES TO.

They'd be stopping soon at some café or other. They would have to go in and order. Cassie had seen Belle de Nuit at the GFT. Cyrano de Bergerac and Trop Belle pour Toi. She had read The Second Sex and Huis Clos. JE VEUX meant I insist. She could remember Asterix cartoon books DE QUOI NOURRISIEZ-VOUS VOTRE CHIEN and nothing else. L'enfer c'est les autres.

They'd manage.
They always managed when they had to.

> NORMANDY is an agricultural region, full of farms and meadowland, orchards and rich green pasture which produces the excellent dairy produce for which the region is justly famous. Normandy is a place to explore and take time over, full of echoes of the Viking past and peasant or fishing present. Merchants, pilgrims and sightseers have come in their hundreds since the 11th Century.

Historic Rouen, beautiful cathedral, headdresses, the charm of old marketplaces, orchards, pancakes, apple wine. There were three lines about the war.

> The north provides many beautiful cemeteries devoted to the memory of the Great War dead of several countries. Lovingly tended by the French and often full of summer

blooms, they are well worth a visit.

She flipped back.

NORMANDY farms meadowland pasture Viking peasant fishing pilgrims headdresses charm pancakes.

It was right enough. Three lines.

The adjoining map was raddled with crosses, great blocks of landscape given over to the same pattern. They were here, driving a trench through all that crucifixion. Out the window, there were just yards of FLAT. It was flatter than Holland for godsakes. FLAT FOR MILES. But there was no mention of how it got that way, the shelling and reshelling over the same bare yards in some instances, the earth puréed under countless thousands of army boot soles then flooded with mud that would have dried out like plaster. Sealed and level. It looked like all the life had been tramped out of it, like it was nothing at all. Never mind. At least it left the locals with cemeteries worth a visit. That would be a great comfort. Cassie looked up from the page.

This book's desperate Rona. Cassie shook her head and tried to look grimly amused.

Rona was driving away, oblivious, the flatness stretching out through the glass behind her driving arm.

I hope you didn't pay for it.

Nah Rona said. Library. What's it say?

Nothing.

Oh.

It says we should try the apple pancakes and visit a cemetery.

Hmm.

Rona was not cooperating. She was not picking up the irony.

Och just it says as good as nothing you know? Three lines about the fucking war. All those men ploughed under the fields out there. See. They're dead flat.

Rona said nothing.

It's flat because of the war.

Rona said nothing.

The war. They bombed it all to hell.

Rona did nothing.

Just the books says nothing much about it but when you think about it jesus eh? Imagine what happened out there. You can't really it's too awful. All those gullible souls coming all this way and realizing too late and getting shot to hell and knowing it was for no reason eh? You think you should be able to feel it, the place should be charged with some kind of static that makes you know what happened. Terrible. Look at it for godsakes. Bombed to hell.

Rona squinted quick out her side window. Look she said. Cows.

Cassie looked at her. Rona didn't often chat when she was driving and it would have been good to encourage her. Cows though. It wasn't anything you could respond to but maybe that wasn't the point. She couldn't have heard a word of anything Cassie had said. Then again maybe it was too early in the morning. Cows. There was something typical about it though she couldn't think what. Cows. Rona's hands were holding the wheel tight. Her knuckles pale. It would be the other side of the road thing, all the concentrating that was doing it while Cassie sat here doing damn all, imagining she was thinking deep thoughts. Rona was busy doing something, something Cassie could not begin to imagine. Right and left were not explicable. They were just because kind of things: you either knew them or you didn't and Cassie didn't. Rona knew left and right, port and starboard and the points of the compass. It was probable she also knew how to put enemy horses off the scent, how to get out of a spiked man trap and what sort of rodents were edible. Rona was that sort. A survivor. Cassie looked over at the kind of hands survivors had then back at her own. Liked fileted fish on the jean legs. Unable to drive. Unteachable now probably. She was only the passenger, being hurtled over strange terrain down an unknowable side of the road, not able to work out if it was the right one. It was dizzying really. Astonishing. The total because ignorant trust that Rona knew what the hell she was doing, a necessary taking for granted she would keep going and not plough them into a tree. Rona could drive for miles sometimes and not even seem to be awake, the way she drove to the office in the mornings and said O we're here when she was turning into the carpark like it was a surprise. But she had to be. It wasn't possible that people careered about on the road, not registering anything or even being conscious maybe, avoiding death by sheer luck. It was unthinkable. Cassie sneaked a look at Rona to check. Unexpectedly, she was looking back.

See? Cows.

Cassie looked out where she had pointed and saw an empty field. Rona snorted, both hands back in place.

Didn't look in time. Too bad. Anyway, she said, I'm dying for a coffee. Look for signs to somewhere.

Cassie shut the book. It was just as well Rona was giving her something to do. The book wasn't going to be good for her.

A big wooden crate with petrol pumps came up fast on the near-side. It looked too awful even to think about stopping for. Cassie stared hard out of the side window in the opposite direction. At the side of the road, a lone woman was trying to thumb a lift. You could watch her approach, come level, retreat. From behind, her whole back and a foot above her head was consumed by backpack. She didn't as much as turn to see if they had slowed. Cassie watched the reflection of the woman in the vanity mirror over the passenger seat eyeshade. It was so flat you could see her grow smaller for miles.

> This is one of the Cortina. We got the MoT just the day we were due to be going somewhere. Edinburgh, I think. Edinburgh. Anyhow we'd been working on it flat out. I got to fill dents in the bodywork then sand them down. When you felt the sanded places afterwards, stroking to see if the edges were smooth through the chalky powder it was warm: warm, hard smoothness that made your fingers feel like sparklers. It took a whole weekend to respray with two guys from work, handkerchiefs over their mouths. All they took was two cans of Newcastle Brown but they let me sit and watch for a while, didn't say much. Man's work. Tom went out for a drink with them after and I poured cold tea down the sink before I went to bed. I knew not to wait up. Next day he was late home. He came in pink and sweating to say he'd just taken Billy and Eddie for a drive and she went like a wet dream. I should have seen her, out along the shore road doing the ton. She went like a fuck. A bent garage gave us the MoT just in time for his scheduled fortnight.
>
> It was you know. It was definitely Edinburgh. Because here's one of Tom outside the otter house. There isn't any otter because they wouldn't come out. I used to have snaps of the whole thing: the zoo, Castle, Arthur's Seat, C&A

> and Bargain Books. The zoo was the best. He's got one of me throwing sandwiches at penguins. I've always liked animals.

Something dunted. The windows were full of rising dust. Cassie closed her mouth and blinked. Sleeping with her mouth open again. Outside, Rona chapped the passenger window and looked up at the sky open-eyed. Her mouth freshly scented with mint. Cheery as hell.

Inside the place seemed to have no idea it was supposed to be morning. Bulbs were on somewhere, not helping much. Four men in T-shirts with paunches over the belt bands and spaghetti stains on the fronts of their T-shirts hung about in front of the counter. A dull hissing noise that might have been a radio came and went out of the murk where the gantry must have been. Either that or it was giant flies. Cassie hoped it was a radio. Nobody said anything either to each other or the two women who had just come in. It wasn't just from outside then: it looked bloody awful inside as well, full of tables still with chairs stacked on top. And these men with stomachs. Cassie tried not to look over and failed. The stains on the T-shirts quivered when they breathed in. This was short change. Frenchmen were supposed to be suave.

Rona was stumping off, probably scouting for a toilet. One of the men scrutinized her back as she walked past. Cassie sat down. There was a novel in her back pocket. It was always good to carry a novel or a notebook when you went into somewhere strange in case you needed to look self-contained. She brought it out and looked at the cover. Thérèse Raquin. Zola in translation. It seemed unlikely the men would be able to make out the title in this light though, or even if they did, come over and open conversation about the bloody thing. Assuming she spoke French. Good French as well. They would think she was an idiot. Worse. An English female idiot. They always thought you were English. It was usually possible to last out though, she had done it before. And every time you forgot how hellish it was, this confrontation with alienness: that it felt so awful you said you would never do it again. Cassie footered with the book, feeling mildly sick till she heard Rona coming back, bumping into a table.

Did you order?

Cassie tried to look as though she thought the idea was outlandish. Outrageous even.

Rona sighed then went to the counter. She walked right between the men who were waiting. The man behind the counter didn't even look up though he must have known perfectly well she was there. The bastard needed a shave.

Frenchmen were supposed to be suave.

They were supposed to have close-shaved clean chins and have those mesomorphic outlines, suggestion of muscle rippling through the polo shirt sleeves, neat little crocodile effect belts and pleated trousers, cleverly coiffed with side-partings and a flop of dark hair over the one eye. Lopsided grins. Yves St. Laurent or Chanel uncurling from manly necks, discreet watches braceleting biteable wrists. But there were only these four men with stains and a man needing a shave.

Frenchmen were supposed to be suave.

Turks were sex-crazed. They followed you about, muttering filth.

Scots were dour but could fuck all night.

Rona's voice, half an octave higher than usual, asked for coffees in wounded French. Cassie watched cracks on the facing wall and dirt along the picture rail, the cocooned gray corpse of something a spider would come back for later wavering on a thin wire. There had to be stalls somewhere. You got them in France: roadside stalls with fruit. They could get apples, a melon mibby, they could buy stuff to eat there and not have to do this again. But Rona arrived triumphant with two tiny cups. Flushed. Cassie knew they would drink the coffee, warding off the impending tip question and whether they would leave one, how much. Foreign countries jesus. Eight o five. An interminable two weeks of this to come. They drank coffee quick and in silence. When Rona started untangling the 500F note from the purse, getting the harmless smile ready, Cassie picked up her Zola.

The sun. She had forgotten how bright it had been. She walked to the car, knowing it was shut. It was getting worse, this thing. This inability to speak or be at ease somewhere strange. Surely to god she wasn't always like this, this whatever it was. Surely it would only be a matter of time before

before what?

before

something else. She had not always been like this. Only here—what the hell time was it—only here an hour and fifteen minutes and something like regret was cranking up already. It was a record. No it wasn't. The time they went to Denmark she had phoned up the night before and said You don't need to go with me if you don't want in the premenstrual voice—the time they went to Denmark, THAT was the record. First days were always the same. Maybe she had always been like this only not noticed it so much. Maybe a lot of things. The windscreen had dead things stuck to it, a light coating of sticky filth. It was a mess already, a mess and locked. Rona had both sets. Rona always did. But soon she would come and open up the doors. They would get into the car and get moving again, maybe listen to some music. That's what they would do. They would listen to it and feel

Cassie didn't know what they would feel but it might be better. Through the window, she could see the personal stereo, under the travel kettle and two bags of polythene bags Rona brought to put dirty washing in. The personal stereo but no tapes. But it would be a matter of minutes, seconds even before Rona was there unlocking then starting the car, the thrill of a tire dunting off the gravel and onto the road thank god for tarmac and the Romans the road the road moving again and no stops to worry about for a while. Only the one coffee so no need to worry about stopping for toilets. She would put on the headphones even with no tape and listen to the hiss of the empty reels turning, stare out at the sky. Everything was fine so long as they were moving. Keeping going along the road.

This is one of a wolverine. Edinburgh Zoo.

I am rolling on the grass with coke spraying out my mouth

like a water sprinkler because I'm laughing so much but I can't remember what about. Tom looks sideways and looks away. He doesn't like the loss of dignity on my part, this unladylike foaming at the mouth. He says Cassie you laugh like a drain. From under a tree and walking slow to help my composure I watch him run all the way down the hill to the Monkey House then run even faster back out holding his nose. Sometimes he wants to make me laugh: other times it's an embarrassment. The secret to keeping it good is to be restrained: nothing to excess. Nothing too noisy. He holds me when I laugh this time, pleased. Further down the hill is a bear in a concrete box, pacing along a naked parapet and back again, hypnotizing itself. A man in a deerstalker stands watching it for a while before he takes a paper bag from his pocket and throws what looked like chunks of fruit cake through the bars. Twice. The bear doesn't even blink but the swaying intensifies. I know if I get depressed I would ruin the day out so I stop looking. It's only a bear, he says, it doesn't know any different. It's ok.

We take the car with its bent MoT and try to find the castle but I get us lost. No good with directions. In the end he takes the map off me and throws it into the back and we guess. When we get there, he wants to spend forever looking at the guns and halberds, bloody great swords. One of them is pitted along the edge and taller than me. One has serrated teeth, stained brown. The spikes on the maces are blunt as park railings, long as fingers. I tell him I need some fresh air, just a wee walk outside and leave him in there, rapt in front of a glass case of rapiers. We were eighteen. Eighteen. You know bloody nothing then do you? Nothing a-bloody-tall.

Flat fields and the bombsite remains. Cows and rabbits and flat fields, Normandy butter brewing inside those fourfold bovine guts from the green bit over the top of the flatness. Apple trees. Flat wasteland that had greened over again, things trying to recover from the bombed-to-hellness it had once been. In the distance,

Cassie made out things like huge fingertips poking over the tops of the whitewashed wall. Cassie read out the sign.

Canadian Cemetery. Jesus eh?

Rona looked keen but said nothing.

You never think of Canadians in the First World War. All that way. You never think of Canadians at all I suppose.

Cassie looked back at the stone tips. Nameless obelisks to bits of strewn Canadian. Then the flatness came back, the cows and the trees dredging up sap from the ground to make cider and that brandy stuff. Calvados. An Australian cemetery on the other side. Canadians and Australians for godsake, stuck out here in this flatness and being processed into Calvados by the apple trees. Cassie stared at the turned earth of the nearside field. Australians to christ. Sucked dry by tree roots. Just before she shut her eyes, she saw it again.

BRICOLAGE.

Look. Cassie didn't point. She didn't even open her eyes. She knew, lying back, she knew Rona would be occupied doing something else. That even if she said anything it wouldn't be an answer. She said Look again for luck and heard Rona blowing her nose. Invisible.

From The River of Olives

Paul Gervais

It isn't often that I wish to have been left behind in the pages of a book I've just read, but when it happens, the writing that provokes such feelings is likely to be autobiographical fiction.

Recently, I read West with the Night *by Beryl Markham, and when I put it down, and the dream she wove for me had ended, I looked up and saw, framed by the window of my study in Massa Macinaia, the Tuscan view I see every day, the matched pair of cypress trees, the Apuan Alps beyond, white the year round with marble dust, and it all looked so much less wonderful to me than the Kenyan landscape I'd just walked through with its teeming secrets and its flowering of indigenous human life. My world seemed pretty ordinary compared to Beryl Markham's, and I worried that it was too late to do anything about it. It was a feeling akin to the one I got when my mother told me, after I'd said I wanted to be a child star, that soon I'd no longer be a child, and that Hollywood was three thousand miles away.*

How fortunate Beryl Markham was to have grown up a character in an enchanted tale, in the kind of place that hands a book to an author on a silver platter. Just as Kenya had to exist, West with the Night *had to be written, and its readership was out there long before Beryl Markham decided to tell her story in print. How lucky can a writer get?*

What makes someone a writer is the life he leads, but of course that life doesn't have to be exotic to be special. What's important is how deeply the author feels; with deep feelings, he can paint a richly inhabited landscape using only the materials at hand. Sometimes I've been left in that very state of loss, described above, by books that have taken me no farther than the familiar American living room where the TV set is on, and the dog snores.

I revere those writers who manage to pull characters and situations out of their imaginations and have them, somehow, ring fully true, authors who can write a book set in Uruguay, say, without ever having been there. Whenever I try to "make it all up" the results don't convince me, and if I'm not moved and touched, somehow, by what I write, how can I expect the reader to think of my novel or story as, at best, anything more than a piece of decent craftsmanship?

But maybe this has to do with my particular tastes in literature, which seem to run toward those novels in which the author is always right there just beyond the reach of my perception – like an unanswered question, like the man or woman I want to know, but, fortunately, will never know – as Proust was always there in his remembrances, goading me with his personal mysteries, with all he withheld, through his work's many volumes. Those novels that have touched me deeply are many and varied, but they all have one thing in common: an ever-present author who's held me captive with his intimacy, and who has, thank heavens, left me in a state of suspended wonder by his holding back. It might seem strange that in longing to know the author's own story I prefer to get his novelistic version, full of lies and lacunae. But, paradoxically, it's in these very lies and lacunae that a reader uncovers the truth.

I'm much less fond of autobiography and memoir than of what is commonly called autobiographical fiction – a term that some reviewers use dismissively, I'm afraid. In autobiography and memoir, the author pins himself down (especially with his poses and his inevitable stretched truths), and soon the reader, like a butterfly collector suddenly grown bored with his hobby, files the sample away with a hundred dead others that have given up their final secrets. In autobiographical fiction, belief is the reader's option, and disbelief can draw you further and further into that realm of mystery where it is only doubt that can't be captured.

A lot of books have worn the qualifying words "a Memoir" on their dust jackets instead of, more appropriately to my mind, "a Novel." At the risk of seeming afflicted with mal d'Africa, *as the Italians call it, I'll admit to being especially fond of* Out of Africa. *I think of it not as memoir but as fiction in which the author is present in all of the characters and events portrayed.*

How engaging I find this romantic premise of leaving one's homeland to begin afresh in a strikingly foreign country, doing so with no other motive in mind but the desire for adventure, for a life beyond the conventional one assigned us by circumstances out of our control.

I've always known, of course, that one day I'd write a novel about my leaving America for Italy where, in 1981, I bought an olive farm and a five-hundred-year-old, rundown manor house. Isak Dinesen waited until she'd moved back to her own country of Denmark before composing her wistful opening lines, "I had a farm in Africa, at the foot of the Ngong Hills." I, on the other hand, wrote the pages that follow this introduction with my second life, my adventure, still in progress.

A recent, difficult experience, which my novel will fictitiously recount, severed some of my roots to this land, and in so doing gave me a fresh look at all I've gained and lost here. One day, I gazed out the window of my study in Massa Macinaia, and realized that my life was extraordinary after all, and that this was only in part owing to the varieties of trees I saw framed there or the quality of light that gave them dimension. Suddenly, I felt ready to write my book about Tuscany, and my tribute to certain loved ones who have harvested its fruits with me. Without having to physically leave Italy and my farm, I managed to gain distance and perspective on the past eleven years of my life, and with it a broadened view of this landscape that is still around me, brilliant, admittedly, and edifying, a green theater for the staging of my novelized personal drama which I ask the reader to offset with his own. My novel is called The River of Olives, *and though it is fiction in every sense of the word, I can't help but be present, in its pages.*

THOUGH IT WAS Glenn's idea to buy a big manor house with lots of land, moving to Italy was Peter's.

When Peter was seventeen he had a premonition and he guarded it guiltily like a dollar he'd found in the street. It came upon him at the Catholic church he attended with his parents, an enormous Gothic structure built at the turn of the century. There was a recessed area next to the sidewalk where you could see, in a chiseled helix of sunlight, a section of the building's foundation. The gray cut stones and the sturdy iron grille had a hold on Peter that felt eternal. It was what he imagined France to be like: a strong place, masterfully worked and strangely melancholy, that shored up one's resolve somehow. One morning, after Mass, Peter looked down into this light well and understood that he was meant to live in Europe.

When he was younger, he wanted to live in New York City, but this was a common dream made of the weak stuff of yearning and not a vision. He wanted a Greenwich Village apartment like the one in *Bell, Book and Candle.* He liked the way it was decorated when Kim Novak was still a witch, before she went straight and painted the walls pale yellow. He dreamed of having an irresistible influence, as did the character she played in the movie, upon the salient events of his city life.

On the living room floor of the Chelmsford farmhouse he grew up in, he would spread out the real estate section of the Sunday paper and imagine himself set up in a New York summer sublet. He wanted to be the preteen nonconformist in Washington Square wearing hand-made sandals, his shirttails untucked. He dreamed of spending his afternoons reading plays at the Lincoln Center library, of befriending a young intellectual there who would familiarize him with the card catalogue systems. She would have long, Semitic black hair and she would carry her books in a wicker basket mounted on the handlebars of her bicycle.

In one of Peter's recent dreams of living in Italy—a dream that was far more detailed than any presage—he and Glenn had an apartment like Jill Clayburgh's in Bertolucci's *Luna.* It was in Rome and it had a ground-floor terrace. Beyond the statues, the flowering shrubs and the fragment of an aqueduct that served as a garden wall, market stands teemed with shoppers who pressed their ochre thumbs into fresh peaches. Peter and Glenn were the Anglo aesthetes who emerged now and then to uncover treasures like archaeologists, to hold history in their acquisitive hands and brush away the dust of obscurity.

When Glenn was a child in Boston, his parents dreamed of country life, and they shared these dreams with their four children. The horses, right there. Birds, right there in the feeder. The thermometer in the kitchen window. The garden, the clean air, the silence.

Glenn's parents are his mentors, his role models. Peter envies this unlikely relationship with a latent suspicion. But sometimes Peter wonders if Glenn isn't emulating his parents a bit too faithfully by having to have an important house in the country with lots of land all around. The sixty-acre estate his parents eventually bought on the Massachusetts coast includes an island. Their serpentine driveway is one mile long. Most of their property is virgin woods, and when Peter and Glenn are visiting there, Glenn is constantly asking Peter to reaffirm his appreciation of the land's natural beauty. "Isn't it wonderful?" he says, again and again, and Peter, doubting that Glenn will ever be convinced that he appreciates it as much as Glenn does, has to keep saying, "Yes it is, Glenn, it's wonderful. I mean it, I really do."

While they were waiting for their California house to sell, Glenn would look over Peter's shoulder at the photographs they'd taken of Mutigliano, their future home. Even though Glenn was sure that Peter loved the landscape depicted there as much as Glenn did, he couldn't help saying, "Isn't it wonderful, Peter?"

Perhaps it looks different because the shutters are closed, Peter thinks, and because it's standing in the shadow of a cloud pausing over Monte Serra along its inland course. The last time they saw their villa, Irma Hughey, the former owner, was still living in it; the shutters were open that day, and the late afternoon sun unified the myriad hues of its faded, rose facade.

And the garden didn't look at all like this then. The lawn was freshly mown, and there weren't all these weeds in the rectangular rose beds by the driveway. Peter can't hide his disappointment as he gets out of Marcello's and Joost's Deux Cheveaux and walks across the muddy parking area strewn with crumbling shards of terra-cotta. He remembers this place as it was last September, fields blooming afresh with the full commission of May, wine grapes darkening on the vines, fig trees laden with bursting fruit that quickly fell prey to multitudes of song birds. It all had Peter convinced that he wanted this villa as much as Glenn did.

What Peter finds now, however, is a disintegrating farmhouse set in a wintry, abandoned garden, and it makes him think, with ironic longing, of the house in California he gladly left behind just a few months ago. It functioned perfectly for Glenn and Peter since they built it to their own specifications. Its only problem was where it was.

Sesto, the farmer, appears in his doorway at the top of a narrow, steep staircase. There is a green oilcloth umbrella hanging from the iron and glass shelter over his head. It is lunchtime and he's chewing and smiling as he buttons his hunting jacket and skips down the steps to welcome his new Padroni.

Peter and Glenn shake Sesto's hand. It is hard with stratified calluses and covered with small cuts at various stages of healing. Sesto is a good-looking man with a handsome figure. Irma Hughey once referred to him as "my dearest Sesto." Another time she said,

"I would trust him with my body and soul." Peter thought, With her soul? Glenn remembers overcoming his early doubt about Sesto; he seemed, at first, disinterested and hard—it's his weathered face that gave Glenn this mistaken idea.

Sesto lives in one third of the main house with his wife and two children: a teenage girl, and a five-year-old boy. When Peter and Glenn first looked at the property, six months ago, they hadn't understood that this was where the farmer and his family lived; they thought he lived in one of the two ancillary cottages which stood near the main house as if in waiting. They didn't understand until Sesto, showing them the upstairs of the villa, pointed across a wide, unfinished space where the grain had once been stored and said, "Beyond that door is my part." In Glenn's eyes the house grew suddenly smaller, diminished as much by its lack of privacy as by all that square footage that wouldn't be available to Peter and him. It's a house divided onto itself, Glenn realized, wondering what exactly that might mean to them if they indeed bought it. Joost and Marcello had said, "But you want them, these contadini; they're doing *everything* for you." Peter wasn't sure he wanted to live with someone who did everything for him. He was only thirty-five years old, and he still enjoyed doing most things for himself.

Marcello and Joost greet Sesto now and they exchange a few remarks that are incomprehensible to the new owners of the house, who clap their gloved hands to warm them. The words Marcello says out loud seem to have very little to do with those Peter has studied on paper, and this fills him with an immediate sense of defeat; it's all going to be much harder than he thought.

"La vedo deluso," Sesto says, looking at Peter. "C'é qualcosa que non va?"

"He says you look disappointed," Joost says.

"Oh no," Peter says, forcing a smile. "Just tired after a long flight."

Sesto carries their baggage to the front door and everyone follows. Even through two-foot-thick walls they can hear the furnace in the cellar; it rumbles, then clicks and goes silent. They can smell the vegetables Sesto's wife is frying in her kitchen whose window looks out onto the garden.

Sesto puts down one bag. He opens the front door, then takes the key out of the lock and, without the slightest hint of ceremony, places it in the outstretched palm of Peter's hand. Old-fashioned and huge, this key makes Peter think of the ones in childhood storybooks that are just as likely to unlock coffers of gold as admit the holder to a chamber of horrors.

In the entrance hall, Glenn rushes to open the shutters, and a small measure of comfort comes in with the light. At last, he says to himself, looking out at the view whose transporting powers he could never have forgotten. The Apuan Alps are covered with snow; the lamb-shaped clouds butting them are agile and playful.

Peter feels reassured watching Glenn take possession of this house for which they spent much more money than they had. He goes to one of the radiators, and in a fearless, proprietary way, puts his hand on it; it isn't cold, but you could hardly say it's warm.

Looking at Peter as he speaks, Sesto explains something Peter doesn't quite get. Marcello translates, "There is almost no gasolio in the tank. He says that by tomorrow it will be finished." His words get vaporized in the icy cold room whose marble chip floor is covered with tiny cupolas of dew.

"What do you mean?" Glenn says.

Marcello laughs. "The tank is empty," he says.

"You mean she didn't leave us any oil for the furnace?" Glenn says, angrily. "Not even a lousy week's worth? What'd she do, siphon it off and take it to England with her?"

"The Signora Hughey moved out of the house a month early," Sesto explains, "so that she would not have to buy more oil than she would use herself. The Signora Hughey turned off the heat, then went to stay with a friend in Tofori until her business was done and she could leave."

Peter and Glenn look at each other questioningly. Their scarves are pulled tightly to their necks. They are determined not to let this business about the oil upset them more than it should.

In rough Italian, Peter asks Sesto how much it costs to fill the tank.

"One and one half million," Sesto says.

"That's more than a thousand dollars," says Glenn. It's a thousand dollars they hadn't planned on spending their first day in Italy.

"Welcome to villa life," Marcello says, as if to imply that the next surprise will surely be worse than the last.

Peter decides to change the subject to pleasantries. He tells Sesto, "Signora Hughey wrote to say that the wine is very good this year." Irma Hughey's husband, who died last spring, built the vineyard and improved the cantina where a small quantity of wine is made.

Peter and Glenn have tasted it only once. They sat out on the front balcony with Irma Hughey the day they agreed to buy the property, and she poured them each a sample glass of it to sip as they watched the sun go down behind the Apuans. Peter was pleased by its light, fresh taste. Irma Hughey insisted that what they really needed were martinis, however, and left her glass of wine untouched as she rushed off to fetch the ice, vodka and vermouth.

"Yes," says Sesto. "Eighty-one was a very good year." He smacks his lips together gently as if tasting it even now. He turns to Marcello and explains something quickly. Peter doesn't understand, but notes a shade of regret in his voice, in his gestures.

"But there is no wine left," Joost translates. "The signora sold it all before she went away."

"Sold it?" Peter says. "Sold it to who?"

"To him," Joost says, pointing to Sesto, who casts his gaze to the floor, embarrassed to be caught in the middle of this.

"But she said she'd leave it for us," Glenn says.

"She didn't," says Marcello, smiling. He seems to find these problems amusing. "You obviously don't know the English," he says.

Glenn opens more windows as they walk, together, through a series of empty rooms. When he unlatches the shutters and leans out to spread them apart, the white walls brighten. Electric wires twist out of crumbly holes where sconces had hung. There are black tongues of soot over the electric outlets. The paintings Irma Hughey shipped off to England have left behind their faint shadows.

Leaning against the wall is a stack of doors. The one on top wears a sticker with a hand-written code number beneath the printed logo of a moving company. "What's all this?" Glenn asks, looking at a door jamb where the male parts of its hinges stick straight up, longingly.

"The Signora Hughey wanted to take these doors to England with her," Sesto explains. His face doesn't reveal how he feels about this. "But the movers would not let her take them. They told the signora that this is unheard of, and so she left them there for you."

"How kind of her," Glenn says. With his arms spread wide he picks up one of the doors and goes to hang it in the closest door jamb. Sesto rushes to give him a hand aligning the upper hinge as Peter sees to the bottom one. Peter doubts that it's the right door for this jamb, but miraculously, it is. With a gentle push, the door swings silently, then the latch bolt clicks precisely, into place.

The three of them step back to admire their good work. It is the first job they have done together, the first of many they will do throughout the years Peter and Glenn will live here, and they look at each other now and smile, understanding that they share a dream for this place, assured that working together in this way, they will make that dream come true.

From Defoe

Leslie Scalapino

The genesis of Defoe was war, the mounting fear and inner resistance preceding the bombing of Iraq, intertwined with memories "leaking out" from the Vietnam War period, and then from all periods of one's/my subjective field – as if that is a visual field that is opened and at the same time narrowed to its sky horizon (as the entire rim of the actual sky) as concentration.

So that the night and all actual dreams, whatever was occurring then, about the day, are in it – and the rim of that (form) actual horizon is held and eliminated, as concentration.

Insofar as I noticed myself trying to change or avert reality by the writing, I had to realize that such a motive is fantasy and childish.

Rather, the writing should be pushed to be itself only by concentration – in which is one's fear, anger, etc.

One has to be fragile to be without protection in this reality.

Also to push "it" to where even weariness causes it (no difference between weariness and the horizon and writing) to collapse on itself where it's still, visibly flapping.

I wanted to get the writing to the point of being that still.

> A memory as just a thin disc, as it is seen that way. there is no event. Warm, the birds stirring and flying. I had a memory of being on an empty street in San Diego nearby the ocean, just that. that as a disc because it became so stagnant it seemed it was going to collapse, and be still. it flapped. my mind had become so tired its resistance was going. The mind being weary as clarifying in itself.

Defoe is in two parts, "Part I: Waking Life" and "Part II: Defoe." Among the streams of sort of pop plots in "Waking Life": the (other) who is the main figure, in love with James Dean, is at one point on a desert which is exploding with fires in which the henna man, a drug dealer, wrapped in a cocoon is carried by starving boys.

Images arise as the way of undercutting the image: because they do not resemble themselves or war. So these images float out, as the bulb of the sun does, eliminated on the rim (which vastly expands):

> *One just sees from one's social group perspective say and then the huge bright day is dilated flapping with that; so it's involuntarily let go as it's large and while hitting the recesses in front of one in the present, remains there shuttering.*

The section printed here is from "Part II: Defoe." In this section, a character emerges, a woman named Defoe. The form of the writing is to be utter simplicity so that while personality emerges its movements arise and are seen from not having self-confidence.

The text has to make the social life be brought to only going on as the effect of (perceiving without self-confidence) or after that.

One has to stop doing the social actions. At all.

Plot is so simple in Part II that it has nothing to do with reflecting social or private psyche, which it is. It can't generate it.

Positions of erotica occur in the text, which are love then. In those exact minute motions; these have a rhythm of presentation in the text that is in spurts and not planned. When it is subject to only its movement, it has no other reflection. It isn't social perception; or rather, is it only then. What's that?

One time, she sees the couple in the BMW floating up the street, where she's crossing at the crosswalk.

they're waving smiling. bow to that.

She has no goal.

The newspaperman is sitting at his desk with his feet up. The newspeople flaccid are around creating some commotion which is empty.

Our leader just visited a country. He fainted onto the floor under the table first barfing in the lap of their premier which was censored on screens at first.

The reflection of it comes on their screen now in the office. Carried by security men from the room, he flexed his arm muscle to show he was strong.

Going to a taxi, the taxi is out in the traffic. The driver behind the dash speaking, it is forward.

A man is going up the street, the stalled traffic floating behind him.

It is shortened legs and thin elongated body as if a powerful trunk.

that's a thin sinewed trunk.

that is covered.

His hair is slicked back, floating face with blond hair above it in which the lidded eyes are slightly open calm.

they are nearly closed. colorless eyes in a flaccid yet thin face.

his lips open a slit.

that moves with the colorless eyes.

the yellowed teeth in the white slit lie. the stream of stalled traffic where the man is going by quickly.

The long stream doesn't move. He goes in and out amidst the cars to the other side.

The narrowed eyes look at him in the sunlight. The man is on the city council; he's come out of a building.

he's corrupt. a weevil. which one is. the lidded eyes look up the street. floating as if trotting, the shortened legs on the thin elongated body go toward him.

there's no space.

the buildings move upward so there isn't. they're there.

she isn't there

the sinewed trunk is twisting around yet passing the pedestrians.

He comes up to him. There's no connection or contact. between them.

He's floating in the pond the carcass of the shortened legs.

Had been seeing the men.

Then is floating on its side.

There are so many siphoning the city. They may have wanted to improve things to keep it going for a while for themselves, but they're dumb.

They can't figure out how to improve things—though figuring out after and before is irrelevant—so they are simply taking everything and get out.

The elongated trunk floating is not dumb. in front of the traffic, there is no connection. There is no way to have realistic apprehension.

he isn't dumb, from being empty. jeering flaccid at the dead. he doesn't think it. I'm not seeing him.

there is no center in that the leader has allowed them to take and facilitated it.

the real figure is completely awful.

the man with stumps for arms has no goal therefore.

he is not himself and so he is peaceful. he does not have to be himself.

that's what they say. so he's restored. has forgotten.

We don't have to be responsible to a leader therefore.

I haven't read the paper for days.

Returned to being childish, we can read all the time.

To remove this from its former authority, what could be harder than that? This is very hard to do.

in their compartments, for outside one can't see anything.

Rather, they can see from memory, a man floats up the street and goes into a drug store.

Walking, one goes into a shoe store. To clean the shoes costs some.

People are sitting in a coffee shop but one didn't notice as it's a light day.

They go by but really are back there not retained. One's sitting. or standing.

On Ashby Avenue at College.

One's looking in a jewelry store window, for the rings.

The sky and grass crush
in the white light
I have to work
or I will be crushed
in myself

The cop with his face seeming to be taut is lying back in his chair with his feet up on the desk.

He holds a cup. He sips coffee. the sip is bitter.

The old won't make that motion.

When he was running.

We have a value as to what's unadulterated.

I am placing reverberations on them. infusing them in minor reverberations.

That is to see it with no confidence.

Then there won't be them there.

Defoe sees the man in the garden. She's walking on the path. It's a light sky in which there's no breath.
The halcyon air is still.
Birds fly by.

As the light sky is still, there is no backwash. The birds fly in it.
She walks on the path.
Cattle turn in a circle which is a mill.

From far away, the man with stumps for arms runs.
the light submerges the entire countryside.

The real occurrence demystifies itself. It is not seen. This is doing both. in the same time. which is what it is.
it hasn't time because that is irrelevant.

so there is no space for contemplation of it.

I walk under the rumpled purple clouds
when I am on the street.
Lightning flecks through them.

doing the same thing as it, doesn't matter. there's no imitating of the occurrence.
it represses contemplating. which is not at the same time.

he's in a light obscuring. Birds fly up.
though it's in her eyes, she goes on.

The man is standing out, with his part extended.
She's dropped, and with her hand moves his part.

Flattened on the long part. the hardened part is in her.
lying on him that's stretched out. She comes.

One time, lying on him on the long hardened part, he comes. as she's lying forward, propped on the arms.

She's flattened and then on them, swimming on the arms.

It's past him. who's coming. his hardened part is in her still and she's flattened on her own arms.

then she's on them, moving.

Birds fly by in front of her.

The man stands out. His back is to her and he doesn't see her. From the side it is apparent that his part is extended up.

Approaching his back she gets on the part, when the sky is light. Then it's evening.

Lying in bed
Vast beds of clouds arise with rain pouring from them.
The rain is hitting in waves
The swat that's the sheet of rain
is beside her who's inside.

He will have mortal
flesh that will molder.
that can't be

It is not at the same time. One is free.
Not blaming oneself for protecting to find oneself, it's free inside.

One time, she hurries to the garden. The man is leaving through a door in the wall at the back from her.

She sees him in the evening air.

his part is not in her.

The long extended part not up in her, she sees him ahead on the path one evening.

She follows quietly watching him.

His part is hardened and standing up in his middle. He hasn't put it in her.

She is not on the long hardened part, seeing him lying out one evening.

Had been flattened on him on it but not with it in her. He's lying face up.

The sky is above him.

he does not put the part in her.

The part is standing up in the man's middle.
Getting on it, then it isn't in her, hard slips out.

He's lying on her flattened. breathing. His hardened part up in her, he comes on her.
Then he leaves.

There's a glimpse of the man standing in the garden with his long part extended. (seen further on as if memory)
he puts it in her.

A bird flies up.

She sees the man out once.
He puts his part in her.
Comes as he's standing and removes it.
Then he leaves.

Though she can't see them, she's walking, cattle are braying ahead in the air above.
In the white light, they're moving.

There's cows' voices bleating. there isn't anything. She can't see them.
their bleating troubled voices rise and beneath theirs is yapping. A dog may be driving them.
There is simply the yellow mounds of hills. She never sees the troubled cattle on the rise ahead.

The air crushes them.
They're floating in it.

There's nothing that can be placed in this.
The stick falls in it.

Our leader barfing in their country.
The stick falls in it. One wades in it.

Defoe gets into her car: There's a stream of ants where the door closes and opens, going forward into a hole.
She just thinks Damn. ants. But later, driving elsewhere far

away, she sees them again trailing to the hole along the threshold. Someone asks her did the ants look the same?

She was walking not contemplating and thought of falling down and wham is going to laugh when beside some whom she knows. It may be because it's not acceptable.

But he's cruel. from being mindless. true.
She's by some people and begins laughing as if falling down out, one time.
So I'm frightened of falling on the floor as flaccid flesh.

A spokesman who's a countryman of the people with whom she had the thought of being their houseboy when she was driving in the BMW, says we're illiterate.

That's why we fail.
Only a man who can't tell the meaning of a green light from a red is given that designation.
There's an uproar and our government says not so many are illiterate as they say.

I was out milling in a crowd where there was nowhere to sit. A woman nude and smeared with dirt was in a cart being dragged there.
I was trying not to cry.

The back with the disc is in excruciating pain. It is fragile but that is what one is trying to see.
it is (the stick) falling where there is nothing that enables it to be reflected.
Why did we think that is nothing?

The crowd was alongside the cart and milling around.
One did not seem to be speaking to themself there.

So they're in a conditional circumstance
which is conception.
There's no memory of the present.

Then, there's their furniture being carried out and placed on the sidewalk, when they're evicted from their housing. It's not that they weren't skilled, but their job has disappeared because the whole system along the way has collapsed.

The very wealthy can remain that way based on nothing.

A man decides to try to fix a car as a job, who can't repair. That's not his ability.

But there's nothing else to do. It's a shining day with the flocks of tiny birds in the light.

Defoe is out that day. She sees the man having taken the entrails of the car out.

There's a food line on this one corner where it always is.

Maybe one can't see the difference between red and green lights.

The officials themselves who have created this category don't know what literacy is apparently.

for other civilizations have ended before this one.

Defoe once worked in a cigarette factory.

People are curled along the street.

The entrails of the car unfolded on the ground, the man hovers working on it very hard. He's trying to figure it out.

He is slow to understand, to assimilate, though darting back on it continually.

Maybe figuring out doesn't work, which is in him. So some other is lying on the walk opening a tin.

Under the sky, he's opening the tin slowly with a fork which is what's there.

This is not a criticism.

It's seeing how they hadn't thought of something, before.

From The Tent of Orange Mist
P*aul* W*est*

You begin to recognize what it is that runs through everything you do, what continues even at your most distracted: The Novel. *You write it to figure out what the darned thing is, and the result is a self-defining enigma. As soon as you've come up with your definition, have added it to the sum of novelness –* summa fabulissima *– the notion of the novel has changed. So you never know what you're doing, not quite; but you do know that you constantly entertain the yearning to peer long and deep, getting down what it feels like to be all sorts and conditions of humans, not committed to any formula for the novel, but to the energies that shake it into being: the lunge, the saunter, the squint, the eavesdrop, the auscultation, the booby trap. Perhaps the novel is like plastic explosive, taking safely any shape you give it, but sensitive to spark.*

What are you doing? I often wonder that as I accumulate pages, and I answer myself that I am writing prose on the occasion of a field full of folk. The novel is an amplified story, yes, but also a percussive meditation, a dithyramb about how it feels to be somebody, a contingency sample of the All. The novel is a camel dragged through the eye of a needle, a toboggan made of words sent careening over the brow of a hill to see what happens to it, a stent fixed into a blood vessel to catch cruising embolisms. I can think of any number of metaphors that satisfy me for half a minute. The novelist is someone who makes a pantomime out of the conversation the mind has with itself. The result is a deponent verb: active in meaning, but passive in form. The reader sits as still as the novelist or composer, unless the novelist be reading aloud, which I suspect the novelist of our 1990s should perhaps not be doing. Perhaps the novel is following twelve-tone music, abstract expressionism; after all, you cannot expect intelligent prose-lovers to watch TV ad nauseam. *What can you do when an editor in a well-known publishing house declares, as one did in 1991, "I can't stand prose more complex than somebody just saying Hi." The novel is what is new in fiction, what the old novel is evolving into. All I know is that such extremes as we find in Greek tragedy belong in the novel, perhaps to keep mundane and humdrum circumstances company, but scything through them as life scythes through us, dropping us once we have served our genetic purpose. Art cuts across that process, giving us something to justify ourselves by while being treated as mere vessels and conduits by the life force. The novel is no more dedicated to the planet than prose style is to endangered species. The novel is artificial, corresponds to nothing, and, if it has anything to say after all, says it to defy the Creator, saying, "You never thought of that, did you, Kyrie?"*

About the novel there is something hubristic, arrogant; trumpeting imagination, praying to prose. Your novel-ist sits in a brightly lit room full of old newspapers, turning the read into something other. It can be accidental. Wholly dependent on you, like the light bulbs Russian readers have to carry to unlit libraries. Hey Prousto, we say: we/she are manqués manqués. We come from Detroitus. The novelist going out for a morning walk is terrifying: in one hand he/she grasps the leash-ends of a dozen small model planes whose petrol engines snarl and buzz as the noses leap up and down, yelping like huskies, eager to burst away in different directions. The novelist holds them at bay on their leashes, dreaming up new paragraphs while affronted neighbors gather. The novelist takes a trouvaille and makes a big production of it. Example: hanging on my wall, a souvenir de Paris, a TWA Expedite Baggage label, says the following, in copperplate ballpoint: "il ne sait pas ce qu'il manque"—he doesn't know what's missing. *I never lock my bag. Hence the comment. I can never find the key. The French crack is a profound remark, whether it means "he doesn't know what he's lost" or "he doesn't know what else he could have." I could make a novel out of that, and one day probably will. Not far from this house lives a literato with a condom collection; my plumber told me about it, and I wonder what on earth you do with such a thing. Extrapolation of such a trouvaille would be a delight. Am I giving anything away? No, my version would never be yours. Blood arrives on the stickum of an envelope's flap, and I guess at the cut lip, the sudden sound that prompted the flinch in the licker. Off we go again, speculating. A lovely Italianate girl at a nearby airport has billiard table legs; today, as I pass by her counter, I see she has both wrists in plaster casts. Are her legs dragging her downward, on steps, say? Not much, it's a beginning, anyway, and the seething commotion of disparate phenomena begins to come together in a magic carpet whose weave is tangential. I keep by me, usually written on hotel paper, hundreds of little observations, ringed in ink, and I glue the sheets together as if making a sail, sometimes having a dozen of them joined side to side. When I use an item I scribble through it, and in reaching it I eye scores of others. Here, on this homemade cloth of gold, I shuffle microcosms, wondering which of them are novels, which of them four-word phrases, which of them inexhaustible objects of contemplation, as for instance "celibate gusto," which I sometimes use as a teaching example. The phrase just came to me one day, hopped up on to the page to be used. And it was. One day soon a sentence will begin "No stranger to Cleveland and the Midwest," once I have the rest of it. I keep wanting to write about the peanut fart you get when you open those silver-foil bags the airlines give you: bulging they come, vented they sag. We novelists put the world together, as the old symbolists used to do. Sumballein means "throw together," either a thing and its word, or a human and its deity.*

Is fonseca a dry fountain? Was Nakshidid an ornament of the heart? Whose legs move in the air while he/she contemplates a headstone? Someone sees even in the face of joy a quivering, a quavering, a desire not to die, and so feels incurably sorry for everybody.

Some ideas for novels lie hidden for years, twitched into action by a newspaper story or a song sung on radio. The novel I think I am going to call The Tent of Orange Mist *came to life when I read that certain Korean women, of ripe years, were filing suit against the Japanese government for forcing them into prostitution in World War Two. The creation of brothels full of such women, the Japanese argued, would deter their troops from raping local women during the rape of Asia. Historians place the number of such women at 100,000 to 200,000. The Japanese chief cabinet secretary said his government had ruled out hearings at which the first group of Korean women could testify – such hearings might violate the privacy of other victims. The striking fact in all this was the price list: one yen for a Chinese woman, one and a half for a Korean woman, two for a Japanese woman.*

So this is another historical impersonation, the type of novel I thought I had abandoned, after several exercises in the mode. Clearly it has not abandoned me. It has been more than interesting to investigate Japanese sexual practices, some of which appear in the novel. The Tent in the title is the brothel's name. In my first draft, I used the city of Nanking, infamously raped in 1937, but change it here to Shanghai (also raped and plundered) for the sake of the double entendre, the allegorical touch. This novel belongs, I think, with Rat Man of Paris*, being about civilians being taken prisoners of war without any of the rights traditionally assigned to POWs. The book's epigraph draws attention to this. I should add that writing this book has lured me into the subtleties and sorceries of the Chinese and Japanese languages, from which maze I may never emerge, at least no longer speaking English.*

> "I refer you to the Geneva Treaty, and I quote: 'Combatants who are captured are entitled to that protection which their own state isn't able to afford them. Their lives, ceasing to be *jura publica*, under the dominion of belligerency, have become *jura universalia* when seen from one point of view and *jura provata* when seen from another. Thus by a double portal they re-enter the sphere of normal relations. Though separated for the time being from any political community, they once more belong to humanity and to themselves. And, as of their lives, so of their liberties; it is of their combatant liberty alone that belligerency can dispose.' So you see, your Honor, you can't try us in a civil court."
>
> —Captain Greenbaum, *The Purple Heart* (1944)

SHE HAD BEEN REARED to arrive at preferences through common sense and delicacy of soul; so she kept with her, after not too long a pondering, the sight of wealthy scholars gathered together in—what else?—a garden, poring over antiquities, arranged two-dimensionally on top of one another on the visual plane, with floating tables, gazebos and platforms, as in the Ming dynasty painting by Qiu Ying: *Eighteen Scholars Ascend to the Ying Zhou Isle of Immortality*. That was what she had been ready for: the movement upward of measured, orderly life toward a constellation of benign crags. Time and again she had perused that painting in her mind's eye, having seen it only once, but prepared on the strength of it to believe in levitation, float and soar. To be impelled upward by brush was not so raw a fate, she thought, grazing a teahouse roof on our way, making temporary contact with an ascending unbewildered horse. From that to soldiers who, with saved-up fury, bayoneted the furniture, made water in lazy yellow arcs onto the rugs and spat against the walls, leaving a signature of green wet oysters. That the uplifting, gentle side of life was so far from the berserk inroads of soldiery upset her no end: you went from one to the other in no time at all, unable to reconcile the two, wishing you had been trained for this kind of clash. She had always adored the image of a table prepared with dishes and linens, little beds of cast iron in which food slept until tenderly roasted. Out of the soft earth, trees' roots came curling up to be caressed or just eyed, destined to sink down again but not until fully appreciated as veins and conduits, sunless propellers. She loved all this, as glimpsed by Qiu Ying: not so much a foretaste of heaven, or indeed the Ying Zhou Isle of Immortality, as natural vitality and civilized ease fused, then orchestrated into a sensible program of living. She was a sane girl back then, she thought, and looked forward to a sane world.

Was this why, dear reader, she did something so reckless, after the Japanese colonel draped a thin rug over her where she lay on a couch after he had finished initiating her into the twentieth century? Instead of speaking, at which she was adept, she got up, stumbling, and looked for her inkstick: a replica. Then, with yet another replica, feeling she was dipping her brush into darkest midnight, she painted in that magical modicum of animal glue and pine soot a message as ancient as her writing tools themselves: "I give myself to you," and completed it as the poetry it was:

> To be treated like jade.
> To place me among gold and
> grain would be to insult me.

That was all. Caviar to the colonel, who deciphered it feebly anyway, although, to give him credit, he did remember and utter something distant and unverifiable about plum blossom, between which and the fruit from a horse's anus he no longer knew the difference, being that censurable species, the man of taste turned savage without quite losing the formulas in which he used to take pride, on which he prided himself, Hayashi the ruptured connoisseur, eyebrows like brushes, mouth a bulbous taupe domino marred by cold sores in several different conditions. He saw that she had communicated something to him, to her own satisfaction at least, and swallowed the rebuke, wishing he were not a man but a freshly painted trellis. No organs at all. No innards. No rank. No crime.

No fool until recently, he knew enough of China to wish himself on the way back to his homeland. China was too vast for any narrow nation to seize. A not quite erased portion of his schooling had acquainted him with just such personages and images as, like a temperate sibilant spring, flowed through the mind of Scald Ibis. The emperor Kangxi, long-nailed and at the squat, his look one of forbearing disbelief, sat at his studies, ever reading Confucius. The painter in Kong Shangren's play *The Peach Blossom Fan* still opportunistically worked the stains on the fan into the overall pattern by working a few leaves and twigs around them. He always would, an eternal fixer. And in their hundreds, candidates for scholarly degrees fretted the hours away, awaiting their exam results in the time of the Ming dynasty, milling about and fussing in ornate halls of learning that smelled of celery and scented smoke. Even their horses looked anxious. It was against this classy backdrop that Hayashi and his men had savaged Scald Ibis's home, not to mention her body. She felt she had been desecrated in the presence of China's greatness in its entirety, whereas Hayashi was aware of echoes only, foreign fixations, uncomprehended tropes. An outsider, but a backslider also, letting his men go on the rampage to calm them down for military use later on.

But what happened in Shanghai that day was not altogether systematic. The soldiery had expected an easy win after fighting for months and taking heavy losses. Fed up, weary, flummoxed and hungry, they saw a city denuded of its menfolk, a city full of victims, so they ran riot, making of themselves a huge, bloody punctuation mark. Nothing and no one protected anyone, though Scald Ibis in later years rebuked herself for (as she saw it) thinking some highfalutin combination of ancient classics would interpose itself between the marauders and herself: a screen, a shield. Yet perhaps not so blameworthy after all — so long as what she remembered numbed her mind, anaesthetizing it with actual aesthetics. This was a quaint reciprocity, could she have recognized it; she had survived only because desirable, usable, helpless and more or less the plaything of Hayashi, for whom she was easy meat. Now he wanted to start all over again and appear before her, a genial apparition in fresh-laundered white tunic with pearl appendages and golden aiguillettes. He wanted to bow, to click heels like a

German, to disembowel himself in front of her; but he was no paragon of mercy and heroism, though brave enough in his way, and he knew enough about unbearable premises to shove onward and exploit the atrocity as best he could.

"And so?" he almost yelled.

She did not respond, though she opened her eyes.

"What did you mean? Speak to me."

Her eyes closed. Her stomach rumbled.

"Why *write* to me?"

Her indifference told him she had not written to him, but to herself, to Emperor Kangxi, the Ming dynasty, any Japanese horse's ass save himself. Blood had crusted all over her. She sounded as if she were choking. Her hair was an oiled tuft. Only her hands seemed likely to survive, making the merest twitches as if the act of writing had worn them out, or away.

"And so?" he whispered.

"No," she murmured, declining grammatical links with what he said. That was all he got: not even a sneer, a curl of her broken lip, a glob of spit. She was waiting to die, to melt away, half suspecting the junior officers he had dismissed would soon be back, ready to start on her again as a woman of the world new-made. What, she wondered, were all the officers doing together? Had they been in hiding? Was this hiding? Perhaps they were not officers at all. But she was right. Their mothers would have barbered them like hogs for this, and chopped off their lips.

Marginal things plucked at her mind and soothed her. Where had the Japanese come from? One minute they were not there, and then they were. Had they driven here? Or had they marched? Why were the officers together? Did they expect to turn the house into a command post? They did. Would they use their revolvers as well as their swords? Why did the Japanese love swords? What were the Japanese doing in China? Could they not invade ancient history instead, in vain stabbing the past in the eye? Now she began to realize her family was no longer there. Something dreadful had begun and ended without her, but she still could not sit up and peer. Where had the other officers gone? Who was this older man, whose rank or station she did not at the time know? Had he really violated her? Was that what violation was? She had heard the word from other girls, siting it in her imagination next to gods, the past and Confucius. She had never known such pain, like a silver acid wafting through the inmost recesses of her slight body. It would never happen again, she was sure of that. Whatever she possessed that drove these men to such frenzies, it would be gone for good now, no longer a delicacy, a magic, a meat.

Reading poetry, she had marveled at how layers of inhibition fell away one by one until all that remained was a pulsing, pulplike she, attuned to everything and sundered by it, as the poet had no doubt intended. What had happened to her today had been an act of poetry? Surely not, though it had skinned her alive, bustling her through an initiation raw and curt, so she knew the dialect of the tribe but was unable to use it. A ghoulish meal began, prepared by put-upon-looking private soldiers with filthy hands, torn uniforms and hopeless eyes. Lights were brought in. Pork, duck and fish sat on the floor with wine and tea. It was a vampire's dream, she told herself. It was that old scene in Wu's novel when the meal went wrong: a rat fell from the rafters into the bird's-nest soup; the cook kicked at a dog and one of his shoes flew off and landed on a dish of dumplings. Outrageous. She took no food, of course, though Hayashi offered her some, even volunteering to feed her by hand as if she were an invalid. She could not link outrage with the pleasant suppositions of the meal, steam rising or burp sounding, the smack of chops as younger officers chewed with open mouth, unaware of being uncouth. A meal of mud and feathers would have been appropriate, with sharp vinegar to drink and sand for salt and the galls of the fishes slit to make the repast bitter. After what had happened to her, she thought, eating was out of the question. Too much had intervened, and the blank words that went with it—rape, atrocity, violation, abuse—were not words she had ever needed, although she had heard them. That life went on was grotesque. She expected them all to keel over, writhing, and die within seconds. Truly proper meals, she had heard, went by rules: *wu-huo,* military heat, was fiercer than *wen-huo,* literary or civil heat. If you have just cut scallions, then use a different knife for bamboo shoots. Eat geese by all means, for geese were of no earthly use to humans, and shrimp or fish because they laid so many eggs; but do not eat cow or dog, friends to humankind. She knew all this by heart and found it coming back to her changed. After what had happened, the human race should not go on eating, not even for mere sustenance.

If her parents were here, to succor her after so savage an event, they would know what to do, arranging deep white porcelain dishes around the center to resemble a star. There would be word games and Canton litchis, bear paws and sea slugs, black beans and fried lamb. Somehow thinking of these matters cleansed or eased her, but she quivered with indignity as she realized she had just learned a whole new set of emotions for which there were as yet, for her, no words.

Who am I, she thought? Where do I go?

The unsaid answer was that she would stay where she was while Hayashi and his subordinates turned the well-appointed middle-class villa into a headquarters-cum-brothel, dragging in other girl survivors whom they tried to feed like animals for the slaughter, without however assigning them rooms. The villa degenerated into a miscellaneous Venusberg for officers, a saki and cigarette paradise into which no one higher than colonel ever came. It was Hayashi's world, in which his juniors lolled with their private parts exposed, some of them inundating their organs with warm saki right from the cup, others lying in their own vomit. It was important to behave like victors, but just as important to degrade the Chinese, to befoul their places and spoil their wives, daughters, children of either sex. The country whose male poetry had been full of odes to virgins ("sweet and ripe as a melon for cutting") had now come full circle. Scald Ibis began to discard an old idea of hers, which saw culture as soft loam into which abominable experiences would sink and vanish; so long as she held fast to her culture, nothing would harm her. Now she saw culture falling like snowflakes upon the uproar and mayhem of Shanghai, 1937, and leaving her behind. She felt naked and dismembered, afraid to ask about her mother and brother, and from time to time rudely set upon by one or two Japanese whose lusts had rekindled themselves. Now they stayed in Shanghai, and later they would go, taking her and the other girls with them. She heard herself singing in agony, though not a squeak escaped her. She writhed without moving and wondered what was this terrible urge the men had to open and pummel her, back and front, as if ramming home an inferior argument. Vaguely she recalled that it was for pleasure, but she had no idea how. The objective, she decided, was to lay her waste until she was no good for anything; but the worse she seemed, the more defiled and disheveled, the more they pestered her, inflamed by her very mess. Swarms of bees would alight on her corpse and she would soon become a source of honey, given back to nature far from useless. When you were only a girl, perhaps your finest destiny would be postmortem, not least because you were not given a chance to thrive alive.

No matter how irately Hayashi barked and strutted, he remained for her the pawn of his venereal instinct, a morose and tricky man with a feral cry deep inside him; when he climaxed his tupping, he let it out like one being disemboweled and boiled. That was it, she decided in her amateurish way: he needs it out of him and therefore inflicts upon himself a repetitious pain. One day the pain will fall silent and he will leave me alone forever. I am a hutch and he is trying to take up residence within me. I am a kennel and he is its dog. I am a coffin in which he wants to die. Hayashi, however, thought otherwise: commandant of a circus, with power of life and death over its performers, he did not so much want to purge the lustful part of his being as to build it up until savagery, like some overgrown overtone, shimmered forth from his body without his having moved. He wanted to be incandescent, able to demolish and climax women at a distance by having, a touch at a time, worn away in him the template of goodwill. That was the theory. The fact was that he liked Scald Ibis and tended to favor her, though without quite assuming toward her any consistent kindness. Suffice to say, he allowed spots of consideration through, thus baffling her for days on end with a pat on the cheek, a hearty smack on the butt.

Living as she had with father and brother, Scald Ibis had seen the male organ in all its undeviating monotony, and had shrunk from it with only the faintest desire to know more. It was what made boys boys and men men: a porridgelike appendix, a pipe to do one's peepee through. Now, within the space of hours, she had seen this offending apparatus in all sorts of modes, and it had been applied to her without apology. She was still trying to join the appearance to the sensation, the one's drab redundancy to the other's almost neutral punch. You, silent listener, must be eager to reassure her that most women come to this rudimentary favor sooner or later, with a great deal of hilarity and vainglory, or with trembling and fear. It is Scald Ibis's rude awakening that we have to peer into, lamenting and wishing there were more wholesome matters to write about. Alas, she must be dealt with in prose as in life, crudely thumped from one state of glory into another, of humdrum familiarity. Deflowered. Robbed of the child she was. Cut off from all chance of family as well—when will her father return, if ever, he the calligrapher and professor with the slight stammer, the vast knowledge of literature and art?

So, she tries to make ends meet.

Tells herself that experience in which you have not consented changes you not at all.

Prepares for the worst to happen again and again as Hayashi and his cohorts hold a sheet of paper in one hand, idly reviewing it, and twiddle her labia with the other.

There are other girls in here, she instructs herself, though she has taken such a monstrous interest in herself of late that she notices no other female.

Reassures herself that all of this will end someday, and she will be led back into a garden where all will be healed, and the ravenous future will be denied admission. Hayashi will have been led away to be tried and hanged.

For the moment, however, Hayashi, an expert in geography (sent here lest the Japanese army get lost?), had his men instruct her in what to do with her mouth and hands, acquainting her with appalling services that made of her a sleeve, a groove, a clamp, a bag, as if she had been dragged in from the fields, from sucking on a manure heap, cleaning a horse's teeth with her tongue. It was only a matter of time before she allowed herself to be bathed and scrubbed, actually showing them where the superior soaps were kept. When there was no water, they washed her down with saki and poured perfume on her from her mother's upstairs vials. She was not allowed outside, but they did urge her to read, to calm her down. She still, however, without warning let out cries suggestive (to us readers) of Tourette's syndrome; she barked and yelped even when not being interfered with, and she ate her food sloppily as if all she had to do was get the load near her face somewhere: feeding had become vicarious and sketchy. One lieutenant was so nervous he drank all the time, and when he attempted to use her body he could only hug her tight, having lost his virility; she wished he would hug her unendingly, whereas another officer, more senior, with an unappeasable urge took her several ways, one after another, without even looking at her. Such paperwork as went on was conducted during post-coital sadness, passed from hand to hand and routinely inspected by Hayashi, who sent his officers out at regular intervals to check the streets and get in some shooting practice.

Scald Ibis had seen war in history books, but usually counterpointed by exquisite reproductions of art. Neither was noisy or painful, and she had developed the habit of aligning war and art as compatible pages in the book of life. When she closed her book, both stayed put, shrunken to a page's thinness, humbled into black and white. She wanted to long for something, but longing was too narrow and specific a thing; she felt gigantic heaves of emotion bundle her from one state of mind to another, merely wanting it all to come right, to go backward to where things would be again as they had always been. Yearning was praying. That was it. She would go on being abused until the day she went insane, and then they would lock her up for life, the orphan of Shanghai, not even eligible for spoliation in a subsequent war: used up, unchosen, unimproved. That she was one of millions never occurred to her. Had she known, she would have questioned the purpose of such a world – oh base old world, why did it come into being at all? Would the reader even try, telling her what had come to pass and what, after 1937, was in store? Poised there in broken Shanghai at one of the sundered cornerstones of history, she slowly embarked on the inflammable tragedy that was to be hers merely for having been there at the wrong time, defenseless, and pretty beyond belief. In all this tiny time, she had said one *No*; but otherwise not a sound. What other word would have served her half as well?

One image of her father, wafting and wavering through the remnants of loving memory, helped her a little, not in a sentimental way, but for being a parallel enigma. Well-to-do, and inclined to smoke in a certain robe, read in another, and to wear both when doing both, he nonetheless gardened in his oldest clothes and shoes, even going so far as to rub them against rocks and railings to age them further. It was as if at some point they would crumble away from him and fall as powder into the soil, an offering perfunctory and drab, yet, if timed right, of uncanny symmetrical congruity. One minute he would be hoeing; the next minute he would be naked, without a thread or an inch of shoe leather, an emperor of earth revealed and clean. Her father had never achieved this feat, at least as far as she knew, but his horticultural marcescence egged her on; if she ever got to understand her father, she would be well on the way to understanding the world into which he had brought her. She had especially loved the gaps in the soles of his shoes; a beetle or a worm could have crawled in and made overtures to his sock. With her father gone, however, and still no news of her mother and brother, she saw her entire world in rags; no matter of instructive analogy, but an abrupt deterioration visited upon them all by the jinnis of history.

Being pounced upon and pummeled, she had little chance to note the routine of the Japanese officers, if by her standards they had one at all. Morning, afternoon, evening: she had gone through all three, but now it was night, and the other girls in the downstairs part of the villa had fallen asleep. The Japanese, however, seemed not to need sleep at all. It must have been the saki and smoke that kept them awake. She tried to doze, but even sheer fatigue gave her only the shortest of respites. She saw the most junior of the half dozen officers carrying boxes of papers upstairs, perhaps to get them out of the way, perhaps as the first act in a general reorganization. Who knew what these almost spastic guttural mutterers wanted; spoken Chinese seemed to her so lilting and lyrical by comparison, not so much a language as a twangy hymn. Miracle: she was being left alone. Now by lamplight they nailed to the wall a rising sun battle flag, inscribed with what she did not know were Shinto prayers: a huge crimson disc surrounded by writing. There was a fist-sized rent in the upper left-hand corner, and the center sagged, needing a central nail at the top to hold it. No one bothered. It had been enough to hammer the thing into place. Honor was satisfied. The lights went up again, with no blackout over the windows, a sign of confidence. Shanghai was a Japanese city now, in which the triumphant hordes squatted, devoured balls of rice and compared field postcards by the light of braziers stoked with furniture. Usually, each soldier had two kinds of cards, one the bravado battle scene with appropriate war cries drawn in bubbles or clouds poised above soldiers' heads, planes in the sky and more distant clouds exploding. Anguished surrenderers poured out from earthen bunkers while banzai shouters roared from a hillock. In the other kind of card, birds perched consolably on lovingly tinted branches, mountains loomed through the mist, lanterns bloomed amid chaste chrysanthemums.

Scald Ibis's officers had no such cards, or at any rate did not bring them into the open. What they did expose was more intimate: the *senninbari,* the soldier's belt of a thousand stitches, made for him by his family to wear in battle. Worn about the waist, it brought luck, courage and immunity to enemy fire. She saw one in the shape of a tiger done in red stitches, slid lovingly from beneath a shirt and brought to the mouth for a kiss. It resembled a much-used bandage, and she decided it was the poultice of ferocity, longing to apply it to some naked waist loaded with scalding rice. Astounded to have come up with a thought so violent, so contrary to her parents' teaching, she mentally cooled the rice, but just as fast heated it up again to plant on soft unpublic skin, there to make a blanched scar. She wanted revenge, but shrank from enacting it; most of all she wanted to lie still, unaccosted, unabused, for almost ever, still a girl of precocious poetic response, going to be a painter, perhaps, or a calligrapher like her father, who was also a professor: an amateur soldier at best.

From a pocket in his tunic, Hayashi produced what looked like luggage labels, no doubt for the boxes going upstairs or out the door, as they now were. She was wrong, however. In the faltering lamplight he brandished them at her, and she saw front and back views done in red of a short man, muscular and naked. Now Hayashi took a pencil from his side pocket and shoved it through the card, as if wounding the outline figure in the stomach. Wound tags, he shouted at her, though the double room was quiet. "You thought I had dirty postcards! See, from behind he is alive, from the front he is a dead man. We do this to all shit-eating Chinese." Comprehending little, she took his basic point and made no answer, no gesture, having not so much vowed silence as lost power of reciprocity. Had her parents and brother wandered in at that moment, she would have been just as wordless, just as much without voice. Oddly, with the room cleared of boxes, papers and maps, Hayashi seemed more genial, as if he suffered from a special claustrophobia brought on by printed matter. Walking slowly, he came to where she lay and fastened the wound tag to her finger, smiling ingeniously at the pencil hole. "Now we know what wrong with you. Big hole in you for Japanese officer. You sleep this night."

Oh no she would not. Anything might happen during sleep. Hayashi's nose was too small for his nostrils. He might come for her at any time during the night. Would he be more frightening if she were alone in a bedroom, covered by a blanket, or down here, in the open? Was it better to be cocooned or defenseless? Which gave the greater shock? The groping hand of the stranger in the darkness of a private room or the same hand in the half light of a fire made from the family chairs, lit in the family's grate? She could not tell.

Now, with an importunate sigh, he reached behind and produced another box, smaller than the others, not wood but metal; she could hear his hands making an almost melodic battuta on the sides. It looked like one of those big biscuit tins the British introduced to the Orient: Peak and Frean or—she lost the other names as Hayashi opened up the tin box by wedging it between his arm and chest and tearing at the lid. Surely a gun would appear, or some prized morsel of food now rancid, or a starving pet animal? Instead, he extracted a fat book, clearly the object of chronic admiration, and opened it gently, fishing at the same time in the box for his magnifying glass, which he then held close to his eye, making a sound of husky approbation. She could not see what he was looking at, but the book seemed distended, like some family albums or scrapbooks. What was he picking at with his fingers? No, with sheenless tweezers? He made a lifting motion, almost a surgeon adjusting a flap of skin, and then she knew. Colonel Hayashi, stamp collector, had brought his collection to the rape of Shanghai, to soothe him at night and quell the shiver in his genital-fondling hands. Did she hate him all the more for this little flash of the pacific? Or did it mellow him, giving him a human fascia? It did not humanize him at all, not even when, like some hovering attendant ghoul made over into the family ghost, he beckoned to her, wanting her to stagger bleeding across the room and peer at his unlicked treasures. She did not go, but he lurched toward her, raising the album with almost an outright gasp and tapping a page of triangular and diamond-shaped stamps whose patterns she could not quite make out; it was clear they pleased him, though they were not Japanese. So: the demon had his bookish side.

Now he was shining a flashlight on the two pages in question and she saw the name Tannu Tuva, at last, under his insistent gaze picked out stag, mountain goat, camel caravan, Mongol and tent, bow-and-arrow hunters. She saw the map of Tannu Tuva, horses fording a stream, and then was unable to resist the connection between sublime gardens she doted on and the cherished vignettes of the tiny country whose more or less ornamental stamps this introverted warlord relished: the lamb within his lion. Was she therefore like him? No, all of her was Tuva, really, pensive and dilatory; she had no army, was no rapist, and was astounded to think she had anything in common with this colonel. Soon, tomorrow perhaps, young as she was, she would have to ponder the fact that some philatelists were rapists and plunderers, animated by that adored inward pastoral of theirs yet far from motivated by it. The population of Tuva was less than that of Shanghai, at least until yesterday. How could she use Tuva to save herself from this man and his rampant juniors? She feigned attention, interest, nodding, shaking her head, and some of this appeared to calm him; he withdrew, closing the album with ritual motions, almost seeming to whisper a prayer between the pages before he brought them together.

The way, she told herself, if I am up to it, is to beguile this oaf with culture: gardens, peach blossom in spring, teal-painted pavilions, flags flying above the Canton factories, the emperor Wanli—that do-nothing—seated affably on his royal barge, the refitting of the observatory on Peking's eastern wall with sextant, quadrant and astrolabe. With a quiet rehearsal of Chinese patience unfurling, she would tame him, bring him to heel, if only the Tuva side of him remained within reach, and she would become familiar with him, almost as if he were her father saying "You're very quiet today."

And she to her father calling out, "Yes, but I *am* peepeeing loudly." It was a family joke. Not on quite that level, but on one adjacent, she might be able to get by. On the other hand, he might regard such efforts as venereal overtures, masked but direct, and vent his gratitude on her body all over again, aching to possess her by stamp-lamplight, then urging his men to do likewise before she fell asleep or passed out. It would be safer, maybe, to refer to the stamps only, omitting all that came to her own mind by way of recollected idyll. She would have to fend him off on his own terms, saying Hayashi again and again, miming him to bring the metal box over to her and tap its hollow tune.

From Red the Fiend
Gilbert Sorrentino

Red the Fiend *is an almost-completed episodic novel told in short, essentially self-sufficient chapters. The "Red" of the title is a boy of about twelve, the year is 1940, the environs Bay Ridge, Brooklyn, the seasons various, the ambience mean.*

Red is a character who first appeared in my 1970 novel, Steelwork, *along with his grandmother, some of whose reprehensible attributes are detailed in the chapter entitled "Red's Grandma." She may be thought of as a garden-variety monster.*

What is there to say of Red? Steelwork *shows him to be a brutal if cowardly man and suggests that his childhood was one of lovelessness, emotional turmoil and malaise, and endless cruelties both petty and profound.* Red the Fiend *attempts to invent aspects of that childhood as manifested in a single year. Red may perhaps be pitied, but he cannot be cherished or, for that matter, even liked. Or so I think, but one never knows about readers. I once knew a man who thought that the loathsome Zampano, in Fellini's* La Strada, *was a wonderful guy.*

I have rigorously avoided describing Red or any of the other people except in the most general terms. I have also avoided direct dialogue. These two simple techniques serve to locate the characters, I hope, as the human abstractions that spring to mind when we hear terms like "humanity," "the people," "men" and "women."

Red is, of course, an invention, and an invention, if you will, who belongs in another, less officially compassionate era. Be that as it may, the world of bewildered misery that he inhabits is always present.

RED IS A CONNOISSEUR of odds and ends, and knows that things which seem inexplicable will often be illuminated, if not understood, in due time; that solid, intractable, irrefutable facts are almost always, and without fail, interchangeable with other solid, intractable, irrefutable facts; and that nothing, no matter how clear or obvious or settled, can be taken for granted. Above all, he is convinced that wholly discrete phenomena or elements of information, placed side by side, ultimately explain each other.

Some of the things in the cellar storage bin don't belong to Grandma or to Grandpa or to Mother or to Father but to an "Alice Magrino," a name often brought up when Father is being excoriated.

One of the old, creased photographs in the cellar storage bin is of what seems to be either a dead, bloated cow or a large, shapeless sack of what may be flour. On the back of the photograph is the name ALICE and the date 1921.

Mouse turds dissolve completely in chicken soup, vegetable soup, green split-pea soup and bean soup.

The cunning knife-sharp pleats on the yellow dresses, blue dresses, white dresses and pink dresses that Mother wore as a little girl were laboriously ironed by the orphaned Cousin Katy, whose failure to do so perfectly was the invariable occasion for her to be beaten black and blue, by Grandma, with a wooden yardstick.

A "Theresa McKenna" has something to do with Grandpa's life as a young man. She is occasionally brought up in conversation wherein she is variously described, by Grandma, as cross-eyed, walleyed, knock-kneed, box-ankled, stringy-haired, pimply-faced, lard-assed, potbellied, louse-ridden, sanctimonious, hypocritical, stuck-up, common, needle-nosed, bald, squinty, overdressed, shameless, trashy and man-crazy.

Mother sometimes secretly drinks from Grandpa's bottle of Wilson's "That's All" whiskey.

Whenever Grandma mentions Grandpa's mandolin, Grandpa smiles the same smile that Uncle John had on his face in his casket.

Grandma flirts with Mr. Svensen when he comes to collect the rent, then later bawls Grandpa out for giving him too large a hooker of whiskey.

A few drops of urine are undetectable in the glass of water in which Grandma keeps her teeth.

If Red looks glum when Mother is buying something in Bloom's Drugs, Mr. Bloom gives him three Hershey's Kisses instead of two, and it serves the kike chump right.

Red gives Grandpa two packs of Lucky Strikes for his birthday, and Grandpa, mysteriously, hugs him.

When Mother goes to the Novena on Tuesday nights she comes home smelling like Sen-Sen or peppermint.

Red sees Mother naked one day and is upset to discover that she has what seems to be fur between her legs, just like hooers.

Red immediately goes out of the neighborhood to break the one-dollar bill the old man in the park gave him to let him play with his thing a little.

When Red pretends deafness and lets his mouth hang open and his eyes glaze over, Grandma's purple-faced rage is worth the beating that she invariably gives him. After these beatings, Red often turns his attentions to her false teeth.

When Red begins the Lord's Prayer, "Our Father, Who farts in heaven, how low be Thy name," and the nuns hear him but can't *hear* him, the world of guile opens up for him in all its devious splendor.

To answer Grandma's rhetorical questions infuriates her; to ignore those questions to which she wants answers infuriates her.

One evening, after supper, when Mother is preparing to go to the movies on "dish night"—Grandma's treat, for which Mother will pay and pay—Red is bewildered yet somehow thrilled to see her slip a green glass saucer into her handbag.

Father drunkenly introduces Red to a drunken young woman with an enormous bust and spindly legs, whom he calls Alice, his kid sister. Or cousin. A friend of his. A niece.

Red's essential understanding of life is rooted in the belief that there are few situations that cannot be improved upon, rescued by or utterly destroyed by a blank disingenuousness.

Red knows that people have to live until they have to die, and this fills him with hollow joy, for it means that *all* of them will die. That all of them *have* to die.

* * *

The desserts served at Grandma's table are such that Red dislikes them as much as he dislikes most of what Grandma sometimes calls entries. These desserts include Woolworth's sugar cookies which Grandma has Mother buy at the five-and-ten by what seems to Red to be the bushel; stale macaroons; stale Scotch shortbread; Jell-O, which, after two days, develops a thick, rubbery, rindlike surface; rice pudding and bread pudding, neither of which contains anything but the most negligible amounts of raisins, cinnamon and sugar.

The sugar cookies, macaroons and shortbread are made of sand, gravel, dirt, cement, pebbles, ashes and ground glass. The Jell-O is but sweetened head cheese dressed up in garish colors—red, green, orange and a gruesome pale yellow that is the color of piss. The rice pudding is, quite clearly, massed white cockroaches and the bread pudding some unearthly slime to which no name can be given.

On the rarest of occasions, Red voices what might be construed as negative opinions concerning one or the other of these desserts, especially as they grow older and staler. His remarks, no matter how mild, are always met by Grandma's warnings of destructive poverty and the poorhouse, tales of her destitute girlhood when she ate nothing but fried banana peels for a week, rehearsals of the heroic labors performed by Grandpa in order to earn the money to buy *any food at all,* oblique as well as blunt remarks on running a Goddamned charity for Mother and Red, suggestions as to what Red and Mother *might* be eating did they suddenly find themselves out on the street, God forbid, irrelevant asides on his shiftless Father and the slut of a bimbo he dares to pass off as his wife, may God have mercy on the son of a bitch, and addresses made directly to Jesus, or His Mother, or the Holy Family, imploring them to look down upon and forgive ingratitude as bold as brass.

There is nothing for Red to do but eat dessert forever.

Unless he decides to give up dessert. All of it.

So it happens that one night at supper when Grandma is supervising the servings of lemon Jell-O that his Mother is spooning out from the shallow bowl in which the quivering horror is invariably stored, Red says that he doesn't want any dessert, thank you. Mother asks him if he's feeling well, if he has an upset stomach or a fever, and Red assures her that he's fine. Grandma says that he had better damn well be fine, she's never seen a boy Red's age sick so much of the time. The incident passes, and supper comes to its usual morose end, Grandma drinking tea from her saucer while she farts and reviles the neighbors, Grandpa reading whatever garbage-effluvious newspaper he's rescued from the dumbwaiter, Mother washing dishes and scrubbing the kitchen, and Red struggling with incomprehensible homework.

The next night, Red refuses his ration of four Woolworth's cookies, and this time Mother feels his brow and presses him about his health, but again Red assures her that he's feeling fine. In a sudden dazzle of inspiration, he says that Sister Theodosia told the class that things that kids love—like *dessert*—can be sacrificed and offered up to God as an indulgence for the souls in Purgatory.

Grandma, who is beginning to get annoyed with Red, who feels a frustrated, focusless anger, sucks on a tooth before saying that the nuns are liable to say anything, living as they do like a bunch of hens, and what in the name of God would they know about sacrifice, sitting down beJesus as they do to their roast beef and mashed potatoes and rich gravy and all manner of steaks and chops and whipped cream, and with the pure silk that they all wear, oh yes, next to their pelts? But Mother is smiling at Red, and Grandpa says that a little willpower never hurt any boy. Grandma grumbles and stares so hard at Red that he can feel her eyes scorching the side of his head. He dares not look at her. That night, in bed, Red feels a thrill pass through his entire body. For a terrible moment he is afraid that he will shout with wicked laughter. His penis tingles and twitches erect. All is secret and silent.

Some nights later, Red still rigidly and humbly fasting his false religious fast, there miraculously appears on the table, along with the tea, an angel food cake with chocolate icing! From Ebinger's! Grandma cuts three large pieces and serves herself, Grandpa and Mother, while Red sips his tea, his face as dully beatific as his crude, smudgy features will allow. He is attempting to mimic the semi-moronic look that Mass-card art inflicts on Jesus. Nothing is said of this extraordinary dessert save for Grandma's remark that she just felt like a little treat would do them all good. The stupendous lie floats over the table, offering itself for silent examination before it fades. As Grandma eats, she looks at Red, but he is talking to Grandpa about the Dodgers' pitching staff. Grandma punctuates their conversation with lip-smacking and little grunts, and as she washes down the last bit of cake she notes happily that there is enough for tomorrow! Her gold tooth glows.

Red smiles, crosses himself, and asks to be excused. It is as if he is deaf! Grandma reddens and scolds Grandpa for smoking another cigarette that what with the price nowadays might as well be made of gold. Jesus Mary and Joseph!

The next day Grandma whips Red with her belt for getting a towel too wet. The day after she pinches his arms black and blue for not changing his shoes after school. The next day she boxes his ears until his head sings and buzzes for not washing his hands before supper like some kind of a black nigger. And the day after that she drums on his skull with her knuckles for getting a spot of ink on his white school shirt. There are many more manifestations of her irritability scattered throughout the next ten days or so: Red howls with pain, weeps real tears and brilliantly feigns shedding others, doubles over in agony and frustration, and has unbidden nocturnal visions of Grandma being eaten alive by stray hydrophobia-mad dogs. At supper, he continues to refuse dessert, making known to all that each evening his sacrifice earns three hundred days' indulgence for the poor suffering souls. He is by now adept at gazing modestly at the table as he speaks of his small act.

Grandma plays with her upper plate, yells at Grandpa, criticizes Mother's housework and complains about the tea that they have the nerve to call Irish tea nowadays, she'll Irish tea the kraut nazi of a grocer!

Twice more Grandma serves surprising desserts—once a pineapple upside-down cake, once fresh strawberries with whipped cream. Then she stops, muttering and grumbling icily for several weeks, sporadically whipping Red, smacking him in the face unexpectedly, insulting the unfortunate bullet head that he got from his imbecile of a Father, his flabby arms, his green chalky teeth, the wild shock of red straw that grows on a scalp covered all over with dandruff, his entire life and being, the poor little pimp.

These events begin to form Red's nascent understanding that the things and ideas which people love and covet can be exploited, devalued, wasted and destroyed. In bed, he realizes that he has assumed some of Grandma's wisdom. It glows soft and warm in the dead center of his cold hatred.

* * *

In the dream there is a shape that is a woman at the end of the long hallway, a woman silhouetted against the light streaming in from the door open to the landing.

Red is not permitted to see her face, but he knows, for certain, that the woman is Grandma. She is, suddenly, next to him, the door is closed, yet the hallway is filled with sunlight. Grandma is saying something that Red tries very hard to understand, although he knows that he is not really trying to understand, but that he is creating the words for her, shaping them, attempting to make them come together in a message that will carry Grandma's reasons for standing alone in the hallway, first as a shape, then as a faceless woman, for what Red knows has been a long time.

Grandma says that she's pretty sure that they'll be playing ball today, that they'll be playing ball this afternoon, that she's pretty sure, Grandma says, that she knows that they'll be playing ball in

Ebbets Field, that she's sure that they'll be playing ball today, this afternoon, and probably in Ebbets Field, she's certain. She puts her arm around Red's shoulders and he feels her freezing-cold body. Grandma says that they'll be playing ball today in the afternoon. Red says that it will be in Ebbets Field? She squeezes his shoulder, her hand a grapnel of ice.

Grandma says that Grandpa wants Red to give him the Lucky Strikes, that he needs them to go to Ebbets Field. Her voice is Mother's voice now.

Grandma says in Mother's voice that Grandpa wants his Lucky Strikes in time for the game and that she knows that Red is a good boy except when he talks back like a nigger monkey.

Grandma walks into the kitchen to stare at Red's Father, who sits at the table, reading the paper and drinking from a chipped cup. Grandma looks at Red's Father for a moment, then turns to Red and beckons. She says that Red's Father is a hardworking bum who drinks like a fish. Red walks toward Grandma, who stands in the blinding light streaming into the long hallway from the door open to the landing. Red's Father is now behind her, smoking and smiling, and he holds up his cigarette and describes it to Grandma as a Lucky Strike. He moves it up and down in front of her face. Red knows that his Father is going to take him to Ebbets Field but that he can't go because he has to get Grandpa his Lucky Strikes, the Lucky Strikes that he wants. He says that he thinks his Father has Grandpa's cigarettes. His Father curses and shouts about begrudging a man everything, even his wife. The landing is dark. Grandma says in Mother's voice that the trunk will be here soon for Red's clothes and there will be another one to put Red in, the disobedient ungrateful pimp. Red starts to cry and watches Grandma slide and float down the dark hallway, past pictures of her that frighten Red, for in them, he can clearly see, she is showing her gold tooth in a grimace. She is sliding, she is floating. She is an unearthly white, wrinkled and shapeless and bulky. She has no head. She slides up to Red and he tells his Father that Grandma has no head, but his Father is gone. Grandma laughs coquettishly, and in a harsh voice tells Red that she has no head but that it will be here soon in the trunk. She presses against Red, she is soft and slippery and icy cold. Red looks at her and sees that Grandma is something else, some other thing. Grandma is her corset. She leans against him, she grows a little smaller, she starts to laugh. She calls out to Red's Father at the kitchen table as if he is Grandpa and tells him that she's got the Lucky Strikes he wants. She surrounds Red. He is wearing Grandma.

* * *

Red is on his way home from the Scotch bakery where he has been sent to buy fifteen cents' worth of day-old mince squares. Red loves mince squares and has an idea that he'd love them freshly baked even more. Perhaps one day he'll be able to discover if there is any truth to this notion. Then, too, Red—being Red—considers that by the time he has the chance to eat fresh mince squares he'll probably hate them. Red is beginning to understand that the world is a ruthlessly fair place in that it has no designs on or concern for anyone, and responds, if it responds at all, to threats, cunning and violence.

Red goes out of his way to see if anybody he knows is in the park or the lots, and as he walks beneath the peeling sycamores, he sees a bird fluttering amid the leaves. He stops, picks up a sharp stone, and throws it at the bird. For something to do. To add his little bit to the general cruelty. To be in touch with the spirit of the world. The stone hits the bird, there is a flurry, a choked, constricted sort of whistling chirp, and the bird falls onto the cobbled walk.

Red looks down at the bird and discovers that it is still alive, so he decides to kill it. As a matter of fact, it seems very much alive. One wing is grotesquely twisted, one leg cracked, and its black beady eyes are shining. Its plump gray body twitches irregularly.

Without a moment's hesitation, Red picks the bird up and, underhand, throws it up into the air. Red never hesitates when it comes to attacking animals or insects, for he knows that to kill things successfully they must not be given a chance to consider fleeing. The bird comes down and smacks against the cobbles. Red throws it up again, a little higher, and then again. And again.

The bird's head is broken, both of its wings horribly awry, its beak splintered. Yet its black eyes gleam and the bird lives.

But Red is merciless and throws the bird up overhand, almost to the top of the tree, then hears it crashing through the leaves as it plummets to the path. Blood is leaking from its mouth now, and its breastbone is cracked. Still the bird's eyes shine.

Red thinks that this Goddamned fucking bird is still alive for Jesus Christ's sake! He picks up the dead thing and pitches it against the path with all his strength, then looks at the smashed, pulpy body, the louse-ridden feathers raggedly disheveled. Red sees that the eyes, though still gleaming faintly, have the dullness of death in them.

But Red believes that the bird is still alive and will be alive while it has its actual presence in the actual world. He picks it up and carries it to the gutter, then drops it down a sewer grating, and licks his fingers. He thinks that it's good riddance to the stupid little son of a bitch. He is a little sick to his stomach, but he feels good. Completed. He feels as if he is, just for a moment, one with the vast entropic systems of the earth.

* * *

Red's wound is horrifying. It doesn't matter much how he got it, or where, or when, or what street riffraff he was with.

It's a ripped-open knee, pebbles, dirt, grease and wood embedded in the bloody flesh; a deep puncture beneath the arm caused by a fall on a rusty picket; a purplish-blue knot on the forehead, its center a nucleus of black blood.

It doesn't matter what it is.

Mother says that Red might get lockjaw Mr. Bloom says. Mother says that she forgot to ask Mr. Bloom about blood poisoning but that she thinks blood poisoning and lockjaw are the same thing. Grandma says that Mr. Bloom thinks he knows everything but he's only a Jew druggist, that's all he is.

A long ragged gash from buttock to the back of the knee, from doing something on a roof somewhere with God knows what dumb micks and dago scum of the earth Red calls his friends and where are those wonderful friends now?

Blood poisoning, infection, gangrene. Mother says that Mr. Bloom says Red should see a doctor immediately to get a shot against tetniss and Grandma says that tetniss is not lockjaw but like the mumps and Mother says that Mr. Bloom says that lockjaw and tetniss are the same thing.

It doesn't matter.

What matters is that Red has got Grandpa so upset that he can't enjoy watching a softball game in the park. Grandma says the poor man is going to stay home because he can't enjoy a softball game what with Red and his carelessness and his lockjaw tetniss, the stupid clumsy horse's ass of a boy! Grandma says that she's God-damned if the money she's giving Mother — and she points out that Mother is upset, too, she looks at least ten years older since this morning — she will be good and Goddamned if the money she's handing over to some Jew doctor for a tetniss lockjaw infection is going to be forgotten, not by a long shot!

Mother is sobbing and trying to comb her hair and put on a little lipstick and rouge, clutching some bills in her free hand. Blood is staining Red's shirt or his pants or his socks or his hair.

It doesn't matter.

Grandma says that it's all right for that rich sheeny, Bloom, and his sidekick with the little moustache that he thinks makes him look like Astor's pet horse, Fink, that's his name, it's all right for *them* to say that Mother should take the boy to the doctor, oh certainly, it's not their money that they're throwing away. She says that she wouldn't be a bit surprised if the doctor is Bloom's cousin by Jesus, you know the Jews.

It doesn't matter.

A knocked-out tooth, a split lip, a lacerated ear, a splinter, blood and pus.

Grandma points out Grandpa's inability to enjoy a little ball of whiskey before supper what with the confusion and expense. She says that even if she doesn't show it the way some people do, shaking and crying and running to everyone for advice and begging for money that Grandpa works himself half to death for, even if she doesn't carry on like somebody gone crazy it doesn't mean that she's not upset. A stupid careless unthinking selfish gawm of a boy like Red doesn't care one iota about the hullabaloo he causes for the people who took him and his Mother in off the street when they had nowhere else to turn. That's because he's ungrateful.

Just by being there. Just by being alive.

It doesn't matter.

A crushed foot, a broken arm, a fractured skull, black eyes and abrasions and boils.

Grandma says that as God is her judge she doesn't think that there's anybody on the face of the earth who can cause more trouble than Red, he's so clumsy that he falls over his own feet. He's exactly like his Father that way, God bless us and save us!, the poor pitiful lummox of a rummy.

It doesn't matter.

* * *

The boys are sitting in a circle on the sidewalk outside the rear entrance to Flynn's Bar and Grill. They are talking about pain, and how much of it they can stand, about games and how fast they can run, how well they can hide, about food and how much they can eat, what they like and what they hate.

Red says that even things that are puky and disgusting don't bother him. Blasé, he says that when he's hungry he'll eat anything.

Bubbsy says that he doesn't think that Red would eat a worm sandwich with pus on it, and the other boys agree. Red looks at them, his lumpy, beefy face registering a perfect ennui. He says, bored, that he's not falling for that kind of crap, they know what he means when he says he can eat anything. They know damn well that he means food, normal food, like people eat, no matter how lousy it is. Normal food.

A drunk staggers out of Flynn's, reels over to the gutter, and vomits copiously. All the boys think precisely the same thing, but no one speaks.

Red says that his Grandma makes head cheese that is so terrible the third or fourth time that even Frankenstein would get sick just looking at it, all dried out but still kind of slimy too. And cold. But Red says that he eats all his Grandma gives him and even takes a second and a third helping sometimes. And he eats and eats and eats till he can't move, if she lets him.

The drunk staggers back into Flynn's, his shoes and trouser cuffs spattered with vomit.

Red waits for somebody to ask what head cheese is, since it is precisely here that his prowess as a consumer of the inedible will stand wholly revealed. He leans back and looks appraisingly at a black Nash roadster across the street. Duck asks him, then, exactly what head cheese is, what is it, is it made out of cheese or out of heads, just what is it?

Red says that he's never seen all the things, he's never even been *allowed* to see all the things that his Grandma puts in it. But he knows that she puts in chopped tripe and lamb fat and chicken feet and leftover spuds and flat beer. And probably turkey skin to make the stuff bind together into a big like loaf that looks like brown Jell-O, like shit. With little specks of green stuff sort of floating around in it. Like weeds.

The boys are impressed. Bubbsy seems pained, Duck awed, Little Mickey slightly sickened. Red stretches and gets up and says that it's getting to be suppertime and he's starved. He's really *starved.* He smiles and says that he thinks head cheese is probably for supper.

At this moment, Big Mickey swaggers around the corner, spitting, as he does so, on the low step that leads up and into Flynn's front door. His thin, tough face is shadowed by the peak of his cap, and he sticks a Bull Durham homemade into his hard, sneering mouth. He carries a paper bag and as he sees the boys there is a slight, momentary flash of pleasure in his eyes. The boys are terrified. Big Mickey, whose true name is John McNamee, is a thief, bully and sadist, who is as careless of others' well-being as he is of his own. Red considers, for an instant, bolting for home, knowing that he can outrun Big Mickey. But he knows that the next time he runs into Big Mickey, he will remember. Oh, he will remember all right!

Big Mickey stands in front of the boys, who do their best to seem delighted to see him as they cower and gawk and laugh at his hateful remarks and contemptuous stares. In a terrible seizure of fear, Duck begins to ramble about Red's gastronomic achievements, his gustatory feats. He insists that Red can eat anything. Just anything! So Red himself says, yeah.

There is dreadful silence, broken by the sounds of drunks arguing in Flynn's. In the air is the realization that this remark has put Red in jeopardy: the door has been opened for Big Mickey, who flashes his astonishingly white teeth and takes a last drag on his cigarette. He holds up his paper bag, opens the top, and gestures to Red to sit down. He says that Red should make himself comfortable. He says that Red should *relax.* Then he dumps out the bag.

At the boys' feet are some two dozen tiny crabs, boiled to a pale pink, and recognizable as the crabs that can be caught off the 69th Street pier with a string and a piece of spoiled meat. Nobody ever eats these crabs, whose bodies are each about the size of a fifty-cent piece. No one ever *cooks* these crabs. But Big Mickey has. The boys say nothing and stare at the crabs stupidly. Everybody knows they eat corpses and turds and scumbags.

Big Mickey pulls the peak of his cap lower and says to Red that he's waiting for him, the big eater, to tear into these delicious crabs, these dainties from the sea. God's blessed bounty. He pushes two or three of them toward Red with his heavy reform-school shoe and suggests that since they're so small Red can eat them shells and all. Oh easy. He smiles and says that to waste not is to want not. Red is looking at the crabs which seem to be, horribly, alive, or partly alive. Some of them are still a mostly blue-green in color.

Big Mickey tells Red that he's waiting, that he knows Red is no bullshit artist and that he hates anybody to bullshit him. He says that he really does hate it! It makes him mad. Red remembers Big Mickey stripping a kid in the lots, sticking a branch up his ass, and making him go home naked. He remembers Big Mickey chopping a kid's hair off down to the scalp with his fish knife. He remembers Big Mickey holding a kid off the roof edge of Warren's apartment house by his wrists. He remembers Big Mickey hitting a bohunk super around the corner with a brick right in the mouth. He remembers watching Big Mickey make a kid drink half the whiskey from a pint he'd stolen. He remembers Big Mickey stabbing a stray dog to death. He remembers Big Mickey doing something dirty to a girl and making her little brother watch. He knows that Big Mickey is a scourge, that he is a message.

Big Mickey is rolling another cigarette, his fingers deft, the sack of Bull Durham hanging from his mouth by its red string. He says that he expects Red to be enjoying his seafood, his fucking shore dinner, by the time he lights up. With a remarkably soft laugh, he kicks Red viciously in the shins for emphasis. Red picks up one of the crabs, the boys are goggling at him, Big Mickey snaps a match into flame against his thumbnail and smiles sweetly.

Red suspects, not for the first time, that there can't be a God. Not one who cares about Red. There's a God for Big Mickey, though, Grandma's.

* * *

Grandma never goes to Mass. The cold marble smell of the church and its lingering incense fills her with panic, as does the sight of the celebrant priests and their altar boys. She is, nonetheless, always involved with Red's preparations for church.

Red's blue serge knickers have a tear, not yet mended by Mother, in one of the knees, damage for which Red has already paid with a desultory cuff to the face from Mother and several serious whacks on the buttocks with a wooden hanger from Grandma. He thinks they're made of money. Grandma says that he's not fit to be seen in those pants on a Sunday and Mother agrees. He looks like some ragamuffin on the home relief. So Red is told to wear his blue serge shorts and long white cotton stockings. Red hates this outfit. Only little kids, kindergarten kids, wear long stockings—and *girls*—stockings that are attached to humiliating garters sewn into the legs of the shorts. He says that he can wear short socks, that he *will* wear short socks, he's not a baby and he's not a girl.

Mother swats him across the head a couple of times with the rotogravure section of the *News,* and Grandma sharply pokes a finger into his ribs to convince him of his error. She says that she has a mind to let him catch his death of cold but then who will have to take him to the hospital and pay the bills? Who? Of course!

If Fredo sees Red on the street he'll knock him flat on his ass.

Red says the blue-and-white-striped tie is choking him it's so tight, and can't he just wear the red clip-on tie that Mr. Svensen gave him for Christmas? He begins to loosen the tie, coughing and gasping assiduously.

Mother slaps him rather desperately across the face one way and then, with the back of her hand, the other way, and Grandma nods contentedly as she pinches the skin of Red's forearm just below the crook of his elbow. Her nails draw a little blood, just a little. She says that the red tie is a sure sign if ever one were needed that Mr. Svensen has his brains hid in his ass like the rest of the Swedes. They're always soused anyway, as everyone knows. Mother adds that the red ties are what Communists wear.

If Fredo sees Red on the street he will kick the sweet beJesus out of him.

Red says that he hates to wear that green gooey stuff in his hair, it makes it greasy and stiff, and it smells like perfume. He's decided to just wet his hair with water, that's all, just wet it down with a little water.

Mother grabs a handful of Red's hair and pours the syrupy lime-green liquid on his head, then combs the tangles and knots into a glistening red helmet, while Grandma tightens the knot of his tie a little more and says that she doesn't want to see it loose when he comes home or he'll rue the day.

If Fredo sees Red on the street he'll bang him over the head with a garbage-can lid.

Red leaves the house, walks to the corner, and then quickly heads for the park. As soon as he enters, he veers off the deserted path and walks across the grass to a clump of shrubs. He looks around carefully and steps behind them. He pulls off his tie and puts it, knotted, into his jacket pocket, ungarters his stockings and rolls them to just above his ankles, and pulls off and puts on his knitted nooby five or six times, until the brittle surface of his hair is somewhat softer. Then he returns to the path and trudges down it to the first tunnel. He lifts up a loose cobblestone just inside the tunnel entrance and from a little depression dug in the soil beneath, pulls a half-pack of Wings and a book of matches wrapped in layers of oilcloth, newspaper and brown butcher paper. He reclines on the sere, cold grass and has a smoke. He knows that he is committing a mortal sin by skipping Mass, and he knows that he will commit another mortal sin by not confessing it.

He feels very good.

Sin! Sin!

Red smokes another delicious cigarette, rearranges his cache carefully, places the stone on top, and then walks up a small rise, under a sparse copse of crabapple trees, and onto the street. He walks slowly around the block, strolls over to check the clock in the gas station, and sees that it's five to ten. Perfect. He stands behind a car, puts on his tie and knots it tight, pulls up his stockings and garters them, checks his hair to see that it seems naturally mussed. All right.

He enters the apartment to the smell of roast leg of lamb. Grandma steps out of the kitchen and looks him up and down as he walks toward her down the long hallway. She bars his way to the dining room, her face beginning to darken angrily with blood, as she stares at his face and then at his feet. Shaking her head sadly, she asks him why his shoes, his Sunday shoes that cost a king's ransom at Thom McAn, are caked and by Christ *covered* with mud and grass. She asks him why. She asks him why. She asks him where. She asks him *why*. She wonders what has happened to Our Lady of Angels, what has happened, she wonders, to its floor, she wonders if they say Mass in a barn now, like the Albanians. She asks him.

Red's mind opens, rather peacefully, onto an interior white space that is suddenly filled with a pain that enters through his left ear, ringing and clanging with the solid blow delivered to it by a wooden potato masher.

He says that it must have rained? Last night? He says that Sister Margaret Mary said she liked his tie. All his sad flags are flying.

* * *

The new teacher of the 6A-4 rabble is Miss Crane, a horrifyingly thin woman with hair of a startling tomato red. She has some difficulty in controlling the class, but does as well as might be expected. Red likes the way her dresses hang pathetically from the jagged angles of her bony body and the way she squeezes her eyes shut and clasps her hands together when Big Mickey or one of the

Rongos spits on the floor or suddenly breaks something. At these moments, she seems like a girl a scientist has captured for some experiment. She also has endearing twitches and she coughs and clears her throat obsessively.

Miss Crane has a belief in the practice of writing compositions, and considers it a prescription for educational, ethical, moral and mental ills: she trembles and hacks wildly as she tells the wretched pupils of the joys of writing well. She assigns a composition a week, and so as to allow the class to boost each other up, as she puts it, everyone must write on the same subject at the same time. Miss Crane's subjects are diverse, from Fun in the Summertime to Making Friends With the Grocer, but may be reduced to three major themes: pets, family, friends.

Red likes to write these compositions, even though his organizing abilities are virtually hopeless, and his spelling, grammar and syntax never improve. Yet his unwavering conception of the mean world and his talents for mendacity find a perfect locus in the small sagas that he writes in a kind of distant stupor.

C – . Very interesting. Miss Crane's elbow pokes sharply into her sleeve.

Red writes of his little Scoty that he raised from a pup that jumped out the window and flew a few feet until he dyed a paneful death hiting the closeline man in the court yard and then bounce on a pickett fense, of the wonderful pals he use to have when he lived in the cuntry when his Father was a farmer, of his Mother, the beautyful actress who is now deaf and dumm and a crippel it is a trajady. He tells of Rex and Prince the poliece dogs that a snake ate down in the cellar bins and of the rich kid he met at a party on Park avenue who had leprosey even though his father owns a Bank it gos to show you and how his Grandpa once had a casuel chat with Hubert Hoover the Head of the Depresion. Then there is the milkmans horse who likes to ate his joly Grandmas' delacacy headcheese, his Boy Scout pals that he will soon join who have neckacheifs with frankfooters in camping, and his Father inventing a new mashine for the Defense effort. He speaks about Rollo the dog who could talk in a saloon and once and told a joke about a dog who could talk in saloons, of the neat kid he met in the playground who dyed from tomane ice cream and came back to Life when his mother litt a candle after the Benedicton, and of his Grandma taking him to Steeplechase and Luna park even though of her clubfoot. There was a crab about as big as a water rat that followed a kid all the way home that he knows from the 69 street peer and the kid was running, there was a boy he knew from release-time religion class with a dirty book and he went blind also his hands fell off, and his Father has a little boat in Sheepsead bay christened Margie after his mutt dog.

C – . Very interesting. Miss Crane reaches for her Carstairs and water.

Red tells the astonishing story of a mouse that would not dye though it was cut in half. He recalls the bully that fell in betwen a scow and the peer and his gutts came right out of his mouth after he socked a girl in her private place. He confides that his cousin Katys husband used to be mayer of Union city Jersey till he fell off a trolley whos door that opened by a nigger he is now a crippel.

C – . Very interesting. Miss Crane lights a Herbert Tareyton.

The canarye Red owns that can sing oh my darling Clementine and barnacle Bill the sailer that his Grandpa taught and who likes a puff of ciggarette and some Wilson's from a shotglass. The kid he knew whos mother could not be buryed in Holy ground since she was a Protessunt and he foam at the mouth. His poor Mother whos cheeks are still rosy pink that his dear Grandma takes in a wheel chair with her bum foot every day to look at the Bay in the park. What about the praying Mantiss that it cost 40 dolars fine if you kill it because it eats Japonese beetles and rubish and the secret gang who burn you with a ciggarette on 69 St. if you're not a ginnie and the giant Christmas tree that his Grandpa goes up to the woods to chop down with his Buick? And the animals in the Zoo in Prospec park all remember Red you can allways tell with a wild animals' roar. Red has many many freinds surround him but most of them are chumps and he does not have time to waste for chumps because Life is short. That is what Red's Father like to say as he invents a mashine gun for the U S army of America. And the Champion St. Bernodd dog that they owned for many years that won 20 Blue ribbens ate a poisoned rat with J-O roach paste and drowned himself in the toilet, and a good pal of Reds' tried to do something funny with a girl and fell off the ferriss wheel just an hour later after the Tunnel of love and his Miracleous medal in his hand burned right through his hand, and also just last night Reds' beloved Grandma got knocked off the platform on DeKalb ave and crushed to death by the Sea Beach express and the wake is tonight and it is a real hart braking thing.

C – . Very interesting. Miss Crane says that maybe Jesus Christ in His infinite mercy, maybe Jesus Christ. She starts to laugh in nervous frenzy, twitching, trembling, convulsively jerking back and forth on a chair in the ferocious light of her kitchen.

NOTES ON CONTRIBUTORS

RAE ARMANTROUT's *Necromance* was published by Sun & Moon in 1991. A new collection, *Made To Seem,* is scheduled to appear from the same press. Her poems will be featured in two forthcoming anthologies: *Postmodern American Poetry: A Norton Anthology* and *From the Other Side of the Century: A New American Poetry 1960-1990* (Sun & Moon).

The paperback edition of ROBERT ANTONI's first novel, *Divina Trace,* was published by Overlook Press in March. The excerpt published here from his forthcoming novel is a chapter titled "A Nice White Little Box."

MARTINE BELLEN's *Places People Dare Not Enter* was published by Potes & Poets Press. Her poem in this issue is from a recently completed collection, *Poems from a Height.*

MEI-MEI BERSSENBRUGGE's new book, *Sphericity,* with drawings by Richard Tuttle, is available from Kelsey St. Press.

CULLEY JANE CARSON is the author of *Céline's Imaginative Space.* She has published translations of a series of critical articles on Claude Simon, including an interview with the author and an introduction by Serge Doubrovsky. She lives in Guam.

ROBERT CREELEY's edition of Charles Olson's *Selected Poems* has just been published by the University of California Press, who published his own *Selected Poems* in 1991. His collaboration with Susan Rothenberg, *Parts,* will be published later this year by Hine Editions, San Francisco.

JANICE GALLOWAY's collection of stories, *Blood,* was published last year by Random House.

PAUL GERVAIS's first novel, *Extraordinary People* (Harper Collins), was a finalist for the 1991 PEN/Faulkner Award.

BARBARA GUEST's latest book, *Defensive Rapture,* will be published by Sun & Moon this spring.

JESSICA HAGEDORN is the author of the novel *Dogeaters,* which was nominated for the National Book Award in fiction. Her collection of poetry and prose, *Danger and Beauty,* was recently published by Penguin.

ANN LAUTERBACH's latest book, *Clamor,* was published in 1991 by Viking.

JIM LEWIS is an art critic and the author of a first novel, *Sister,* published by Graywolf Press. He currently lives in New York.

BEN MARCUS's *Reports from the God Fossil* will be published by Knopf. His fiction will appear in the anthology *Writing from the New Coast.*

CAROLE MASO is the author of *Ghost Dance, The Art Lover* and *AVA* (Dalkey Archive), from which the excerpt in this issue, titled "Morning," is taken. A fourth novel, *The American Woman in the Chinese Hat,* will be published in 1994.

YANNICK MURPHY is the author of *Stories in Another Language* (Knopf). Her second collection of short stories is due out next year from the same publisher.

DAVID MUS's most recent volume of bilingual poetry is *D'un accord / Double Stopping* (Ulysse fin de siècle, 1991); and of poetry in English, *Wall to Wall Speaks* (Princeton University Press, 1988). He lives in France.

JAMES NARES's most recent exhibition of paintings, "Prescripts," was on view this spring at Paul Kasmin Gallery, New York.

JAMES PURDY's most recent novel is *Out With the Stars,* published by Peter Owen, London, in 1992. Other recent works include his *Collected Poems* (1990) and *In the Night of Time and Four Other Plays* (1992), both published in English by Polak and Van Gennep, Amsterdam. At the present time he is working on a novel about Chicago in the 1950s titled *Gertrude of Stony Island Avenue.*

DAVID RATTRAY completed assembling the manuscript of his collected works, *The Curve,* shortly before his death on March 22. A recent story of his, "Max," can be found in the Spring issue of *Bomb.* His most recent book, *How I Became One of the Invisible,* is available from Semiotext(e).

SUSAN ROTHENBERG, whose series of mezzotints inspired Robert Creeley's poems in this issue, shows at Sperone Westwater Gallery in New York. *Parts,* whose visual images are from Buffalo, New Mexico, Maine and San Francisco, will be published in a deluxe edition by Hine Editions later this year. Rothenberg lives in New Mexico.

LESLIE SCALAPINO's *Defoe* will be published by Sun & Moon Press in the fall of 1993. *The Return of Painting, The Pearl, and Orion / A Trilogy* was published by North Point Press. *Crowd and not evening or light* was published by O Books and Sun & Moon Press.

CATHERINE SCHERER lives in Chicago. Her recent work has appeared in *American Fiction 3, Washington Review, Black Ice* and *Exquisite Corpse.*

AARON SHURIN's new book is *Into Distances,* from Sun & Moon. He teaches at San Francisco State University, where he is Associate Director of The Poetry Center.

CLAUDE SIMON won the Nobel Prize in 1985. *Coma Berenices* was first published under the title *Femmes* in a limited edition in 1966 by Editions Maeght to accompany a series of prints by Joan Miró. It was republished in 1983 with the title *La Chevelure de Bérénice.* This is its first appearance in print in English.

GILBERT SORRENTINO's most recent novel is *Under the Shadow* (Dalkey Archive). He is the recipient of the 1992 Lannan Literary Award for Fiction.

JOHN TAGGART's translation of *Aeschylus/Fragments* has recently been published by Parallel Editions. His latest collection of poems, *Standing Wave,* will be out soon from Lost Roads. A book on Edward Hopper and the nature of reading (SUNY) and his collected essays (Alabama) should be out in the fall.

NATHANIEL TARN's latest books are *Seeing America First* (Coffee House Press) and *Views from the Weaving Mountain: Selected Essays in Poetics and Anthropology* (University of New Mexico Press). His sequence, *Architextures,* is reaching completion.

FIONA TEMPLETON wrote and directed *You—The City,* an intimate Manhattan-wide play for an audience of one, published by Roof Books. Her contribution to this issue is a section from *Realities,* a performance work. #8 contains lines from a letter from Robert Kocik, and George Perec's *Espèces d'Espaces.*

ALEXANDER THEROUX is the author of *The Lollipop Trollops,* a book of poems published by the Dalkey Archive in 1992. His novel, *An Adultery,* was published in 1987 by Simon & Schuster.

KEITH WALDROP's most recent books are *The Opposite of Letting the Mind Wander: Selected Poems* (Lost Roads), *Potential Random* (Paradigm Press) and *Shipwreck in Haven* (Awede).

ROSMARIE WALDROP's new book of poems, *Lawn of Excluded Middle,* is just out from Tender Buttons Press.

DAVID FOSTER WALLACE is the author of *The Broom of the System, Girl With Curious Hair* and, with Mark Costello, *Signifying Rappers.* He lives in New York State.

PAUL WEST's *The Women of Whitechapel and Jack the Ripper* won the Grand Prix Halpèrine-Kaminsky for the best foreign book published in French in 1992. His most recent novel is *Love's Mansion,* and his next book will be *Duets,* a collaboration with Diane Ackerman (Random House, 1993).

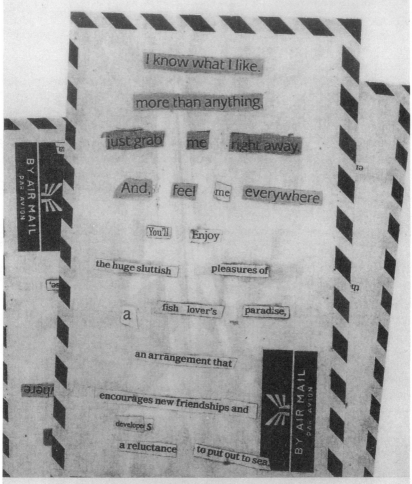

burning • deck books

ELIZABETH MACKIERNAN: **Ancestors Maybe**
A comic fantasy about the Pagano-Christian tradition as experienced in Connecticut. Three sisters, all named Marie, and their companion Hugo, probably a dwarf, entertain dead family members in a burlesque of the family novel and Irish-American traditions. 160 pages, offset, smyth-sewn, paper $8, signed paper $15

BRITA BERGLAND: **The Rebirth of the Older Child**
These poems fuse a sophisticated sense of language with a predilection for the "rural voice," the "whacky grandeur" of everyday life on a farm. 64 pages, offset, smyth-sewn, paper $8, signed paper $15

CLAIRE NEEDELL: **Not A Balancing Act**
In this first collection, language is delivered up with a sense of failure: a name that cannot reach its object. Images are replaced so rapidly that even the most concrete tremble as the physical is drawn into the abstract, and the abstract into a rich immediacy. 64 pages, offset, smyth-sewn, paper $8, signed paper $15

RAY RAGOSTA: **Varieties of Religious Experience**
Poems that explore the "margin" of our field of consciousness, the border toward the residual. "Ragosta is more participant than onlooker... He succeeds in penetrating to the unpredictable center of all experience."—*Northeast Journal.* 80 pages, offset, smyth-sewn, paper $8, signed paper $15

PAM REHM: **The Garment In Which No One Had Slept**
"Hesitation has been used 'to have something to give back,' shyness has been used as 'a nerve into all circumstances.' What Pam Rehm has given in these poems is worthy of our intense and serious attention."—John Taggart 64 pages, offset, smyth-sewn, paper $8, signed paper $15

Serie d'Ecriture No.6: JEAN DAIVE, **A Lesson in Music** (trans. Julie Kalendek). 64 pages, offset, paper $6
Serie d'Ecriture No.7: Dominique Fourcade, Isabelle Hovald, Jacques Roubaud, Esther Tellerman etc. translated by Norma Cole, Tom Mandel, Cole Swensen and others. 96 pages, offset, paper $6

71 Elmgrove Ave. #1 C
Providence, RI 02906

Burning Deck has received grants from the National Endowment for the Arts, the Rhode Island State Council on the Arts, and the Fund for Poetry.

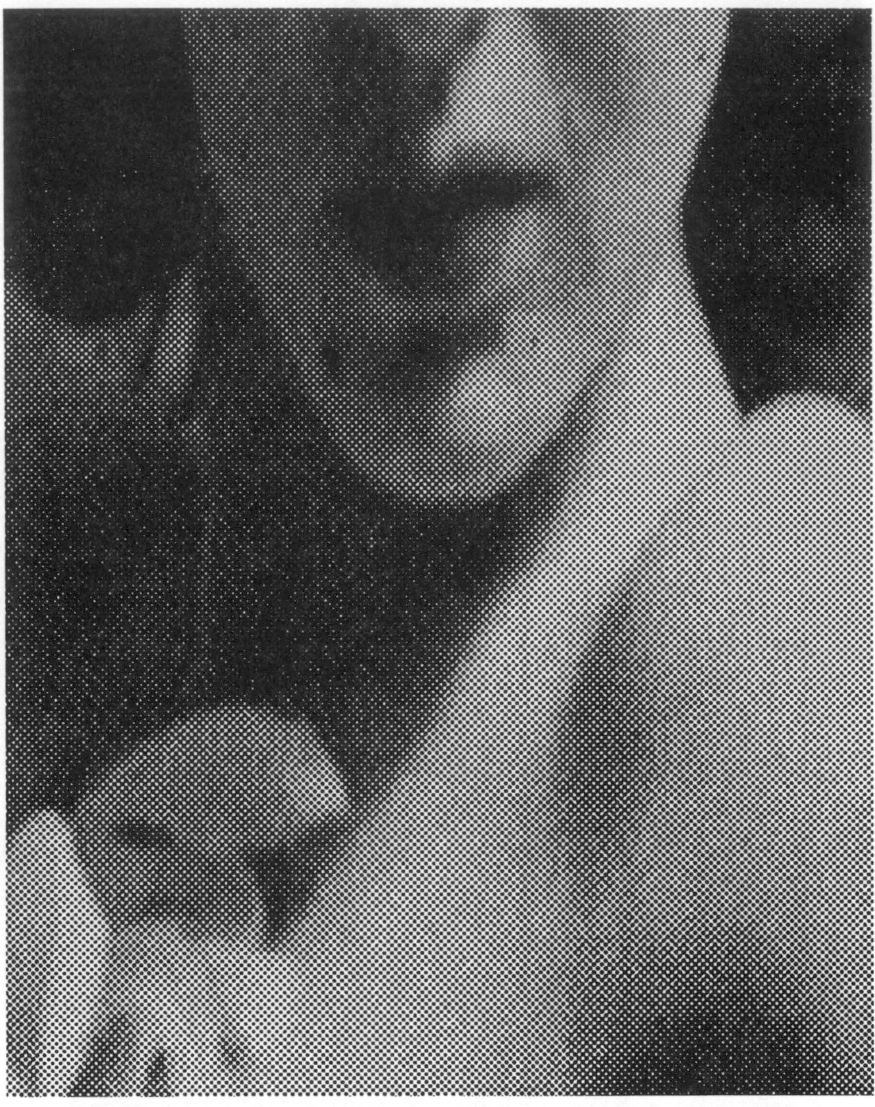